DARK ARTS

MIKE ROSS

« AN AUTOBIOGRAPHY »

HEROBOOKS

DARK ARTS

MIKE ROSS

《 AN AUTOBIOGRAPHY 》

with Liam Hayes

HERO BOOKS

HERO BOOKS

PUBLISHED BY HERO BOOKS
1 WOODVILLE GREEN
LUCAN
CO. DUBLIN
IRELAND
www.herobooks.ie
Hero Books is an imprint of Umbrella Publishing

First Published 2018

A CIP record for this book is available from the British Library

ISBN 9781910827055

Printed in Ireland with Print Procedure Ltd
Cover design and typesetting: Jessica Maile
Cover and inside photographs: Inpho and the Ross family collection

DEDICATION

For Kimberlee,
Kevin & Chloe

★ CONTENTS ★

ACKNOWLEDGEMENTS

WHEN LIAM HAYES first approached me about writing a book, I must admit my first reaction wasn't positive. It wasn't a route that I'd thought about going down. I'd read lots of other players' books of course, but for me to do one? I didn't see myself there.

Liam is fairly convincing though, and as he put it, 'It's not an opportunity very many people get!' There's been a lot of work involved, mostly on Liam's part, and I must admit now looking back that I found the whole process strangely cathartic. My path to a professional career was not the usual one. My first pro game was at the age of 26, and I finally hung up the boots at the age of 37. In the intervening years I managed to cram a huge amount, with the bulk of my international caps coming after I turned 31.

I loved every day of it, and it's strange to me even now, a year out from my last game, that I'll never be in those dressing rooms again.

Part of what compelled me to write this book is the fact that there might be people out there who will read this and think, 'If he can get there then so can I.' I never came through any academy or underage teams, but still managed to have the tremendous honour of pulling on that green jersey. There's always a way if there's a will.

Of course, no man is an island and I owe a massive debt of thanks to the people in my life who helped and supported me through that journey. Without them, things would have turned out a lot differently.

First of all, my family. My father Frank, my mother Patricia, my brothers Matthew and Alistair and my sister Kathryn. You've been with me the whole way, turning up to games no matter what the weather or opposition, and helping to keep me going when things were tough. In return, I've missed a lot of your big days, whether I was playing away that weekend or on tour. I promise I'm going to make up for lost time.

I also want to acknowledge my other brothers; the teammates I shared a dressing room with for years, and who had to deal with the delightful sight of me getting changed every week. Thanks for making me look better than I was. Rugby is such a team game that everyone depends on everyone else. I look forward to the slagging that this book will no doubt generate. In fact I'll be disappointed if there isn't any. I had some of the best days of my life with you all, and it's something that I'll always have and cherish. Enjoy it while it lasts, because it'll be over before you know it. But treasure the good days, linger on them, because it's all too easy to look ahead to the following week and let that feeling go too soon. The bad days hang around long enough!

I remain indebted to the coaches I've had throughout the years; from my first coach, Jerry O'Donoghue (sadly no longer with us), to my last ones, Joe Schmidt and Leo Cullen. I learned so much from you along the way, and a lot of you had patience beyond that of a saint! Now I'm on the other side of the fence, I can see what a difficult job it is and the long hours that are required. It's hard to see the amount of work that goes into preparing a team to take the field until you experience it.

To all the medical and physio staff at Leinster and Ireland, especially the late, great, "Prof", Dr Arthur Tanner – thanks for keeping my body together near the end, even though I tried to avoid you as much as possible! I hope never to darken the front door of Santry again, despite the excellence of the service provided to me there.

My lifelong friends – Conor, John and Shane – thanks for keeping me grounded lads, and for reminding me at all times, 'It's only a game you're playing, it's not like it's serious!.' I look forward to finally being able to make it to your birthdays, children's christenings and other family events.

Finally, and most particularly, to my wife Kimberlee. You've made all this possible. Without your love and steadfast support, I would never have achieved a tenth of what I have done. You've been the glue that holds everything together, and the rock upon which I depend on when times are tough. You have given me the greatest gift of our two children, Kevin and Chloe, and I'll be eternally grateful and a little baffled that you've stuck with me until now!

Here's to the next phase, it's going to be great.

Mike Ross, September 2018

FOREWORD

by Joe Schmidt

VERY EARLY IN my professional coaching career an ex-hooker and coaching colleague advised me that the most important person in a rugby squad was the tighthead prop... and the second most important person in the squad was the reserve tighthead prop!

I've certainly not forgotten the advice and would acknowledge that there's probably a degree of merit in it.

After moving from Clermont in France to take up the position of Leinster Head Coach for the 2010-11 season I got together with the coaching staff and we put together a schedule for player preview meetings in the early weeks of the pre-season. The big South African tighthead prop, CJ van der Linde had moved on and we were going to need someone to step up and take the lead in the scrum, so I was aware that my meeting with Mike Ross might be significant.

I must admit that, at the time, I didn't know too much about Mike because he'd played a fairly limited amount of game time the previous season. Jono Gibbes, our forwards coach was in the meeting, along with Greg Feek, the scrum coach and Richie Murphy, the skills coach.

Mike walked in, and was asked to sit down – my first thought was that he certainly took up some space, which was a promising start.

It did not take him long to tell us that he would lock our scrum out better than anyone else we could get our hands on. I have to admit that I was a little taken aback. He was forthright, and very convinced of his scrummaging prowess but, instinctively, I asked him... 'That's great, and what else are you going to do?' He seemed surprised that I asked him that question so quickly.

'I'll hit rucks!' he told me.

'I don't just want you hitting rucks,' I replied.

'I want you making good decisions.'

I also let him know that we did not want him or anyone else hiding when we needed people on their feet. I thought it was better to be candid as I'd had some feedback that he had a tendency to 'anchor' himself at times, when he should have been working to get into positions where he was needed.

That also seemed to surprise Mike. But I should call him Rossy... that's what we all called him.

Rossy did not appear too comfortable with what had just been demanded of him.

It seemed to me that he had been given a brief in his early years as a professional player that if he just ticked the traditional boxes of being solid in the scrum, hitting rucks and defending close to the ruck, then that would be sufficient.

For me, Rossy was almost limiting himself to these key parts of his game but we felt he could do more and, to be honest, we needed more from him than just the standard prop fare... without undermining the importance of his crucial role in the scrum.

We suspected that Rossy was comfort-based around the collision areas, and that he felt a little bit threatened when he was asked to make a decision or to take his place in the wider channels.

He had every reason to be fearful.

On a rugby field, when players like Cedric Heymans, Doug Howlett or Stuart Hogg are ready to take off most opposition players tend to be a little bit uneasy. Hogg seemed to find Rossy every time we played, whether it was when Rossy was playing for Leinster against Glasgow or for Ireland against Scotland. Hogg's acceleration was beyond Rossy, as it was for many international players. But there was also more than one occasion when Rossy was in the wider channels and he ended up doing a great job. I remember one superb drag-down tackle on Tevita Kuridrani of Australia.

Kuridrani looked likely to get away after breaking the first line of defence, only to be man-handled by Rossy.

When Rossy was asked to do more, he committed to getting it done and his confidence to contribute, even when uncomfortable, grew. It wasn't an overnight metamorphosis but Rossy added to his game during the years I knew him, without losing his focus on being the 'rock' that we needed at scrum time.

HE WAS LATE coming to the professional game. Ten years ago, that wasn't too unusual, particularly for players in the 'tight five.' It's a bit different for us now with our current tighthead prop being just 25 years old, and our back up tighthead during the recent Six Nations only 21 years old.

Rossy went in at the deep end by becoming a full time professional player at 26 years of age with Harlequins. In the Premiership at the time, the really big teams like Leicester would bully their opponents into submission so when Rossy turned up at Harlequins he literally went head-to-head with some pretty strong characters in the English game.

In this book, for instance, Rossy talks about Andrew Sheridan being his most difficult scrummaging opponent. Sheridan worked to get an angle and then would use his immense power to drive up and through the floundering tighthead. Rossy was no different from so many other tightheads at the time who had to contend with the massive challenge that Sheridan presented.

However, opponents like Sheridan were a big part of what helped to make Rossy. It meant that when he did come back to play in Ireland, he had endured and learned some very tough lessons in the 'dark arts' of scrummaging.

He'd had a tough first season with Leinster, and to be brutally honest when I came in it was a matter of me being obliged to have faith in Rossy. We didn't really have anyone else. As mentioned, CJ van der Linde had gone home to South Africa. Stan Wright, the other imported prop, had ruptured his Achilles tendon. To cover Rossy on the tighthead side of the scrum we got Simon Shawe down from Ballymena, where he was playing in Division Two of the All-Ireland League. It was a big challenge for Simon but he did a good job for us, backing Rossy up during the first half of the season.

Through the early part of the season, after overcoming a calf strain, our faith in Rossy grew. The 'acid test' came in the first of our European matches against a powerful Racing Metro side. It was a huge game for the squad but particularly for Rossy and for me, I guess, as the pressure to win at home in the first round of Europe was stifling.

Rossy stepped up and locked down the scrum but also contributed around the pitch. The season that followed hinged on Rossy and, to a degree, on Richardt Strauss in the front row. Cian Healy was established at loosehead, but Straussy was like Rossy, he had not played a lot the previous season and was an unknown quantity, but he became the pocket dynamo and combative scrummager that we needed.

We had back up for Cian with a young Jack McGrath coming through, and Heinke van der Merwe was a powerful man and a very good loosehead scrummager. But at tighthead it was down to Rossy, and we were going to be hugely reliant on his durability.

Maybe, if you don't move too quickly then you are less likely to break! The thing is, Rossy didn't move at all when it mattered most.

He anchored the scrum for us.

He did an incredible job that season as we went the whole way in Europe to win Leinster's second Heineken Cup.

I KNEW WE needed a cornerstone that season.

If Rossy had done nothing else other than anchor our scrum, we still would have selected him. But lucky for us, I think Rossy was ambitious enough to get more out of himself.

The other players also knew he had more and that they needed more. It was common enough to hear:

'ROSSY... ROSSSYYYYYYYYY!'

'ROSSY... MOVE YOUR ASS... ROSSSSSYYYYYYYY!'

But he had a good engine for a big man. He worked away on the field. He enjoyed it, almost, and that is what you need. You want players to get excited about the work they're doing and what they're contributing to the team. You want everyone fully involved because if a player is prepared to leave what is potentially his work to the other 14 players then, at some stage, the other team are going to find some space. Conversely, at some stage, we are going to be short at the breakdown or we will miss an opportunity that we should have capitalised upon.

Rossy got involved. He had the ability to carry the ball, he just lacked the confidence to do it regularly and the acceleration to make the most of any space but on the relatively rare occasions that he carried or passed, he showed his competence.

Rossy developed into one of the most capped tighthead props in the history of Irish rugby. In the short time available to him, after coming back to Ireland at 30 years of age, he still represented his country 61 times, and played over 150 times for Leinster. That is an impressive achievement.

When I joined Leinster I was told that Rossy was the man who liked to do his research and had plenty of data on the other teams and what they would be up to in the front row. He liked to have as much knowledge as possible about the opposing front row, and to share it amongst his fellow front row colleagues. But we brought Greg Feek in, when I joined Leinster, and Rossy was too busy doing his job on the pitch to be worried too much about accumulating data off it.

Feeky's job was to filter and deliver the information, and he did a great job. As front row fanatics, he and Rossy spoke the same language.

It was important to keep Rossy ticking over. He played best when he was in a weekly rhythm. If he ever got a little time off, even a short amount of time, he could be a little bit scratchy after it.

To our mutual benefit, Rossy preferred to play, partly because it meant that he avoided the exhausting conditioning sessions that the non-selected players would have to suffer through, but also because he just loved playing the game.

IN THE FINAL of the 2011 Heineken Cup against Northampton we got a first half pummelling in the scrum. Northampton had Brian Mujati angling across the scrum at tighthead, with the hooker Dylan Hartley, and giant loosehead Soane Tong'uiha driving upwards, popping Rossy up and forcing us backwards. In that first 40 minutes, the Northampton scrum dominated and we floundered.

In the second half we responded by adopting Northampton's tactics.

At half time, Rossy and the guys knew what they had to do in the second half, and after Feeky got them together, they went out and turned the game for us, giving us a base to build our way back into the game and to achieve the incredible comeback, from 6-22 down at half time, to win 33-22.

The following year, when we retained the trophy, we scored our first two tries from Ulster scrum feeds. That was a major achievement against an Ulster pack filled with Internationals.

That game showed Cian, Straussy and Rossy at their very best.

Sean O'Brien scored the first of the tries, and he was brilliant that day, but when you track back to where it all started, it was from an Ulster scrum feed just inside their 22. We got a turnover when they were forced to carry it off the base. Rossy even carried and gained a couple of metres in the lead up to that first try.

The second try came from the scrum where a decisive shunt allowed us to get the ball to Brian O'Driscoll, whose off-load to Sean O'Brien was as good as you'd see, but again, looking back to where it started, the scrum was pivotal.

The front row did a remarkable job for Leinster in those two European finals.

THE SCRUM HAS its dark arts alright and I would never claim to know the intricacies that go on in that dark corner of the game.

It's a fickle place, where the smallest things can go wrong. You want to stay low, but if you drop your hips and your shoulders come up you're vulnerable? Or if their loosehead angles or stands up, can you attack their hooker and go straight through him or will that have a destabilising effect on your pack mates?

One of the things about Leinster, I felt, until Feeky came along, was that the players could be quite individual in their scrummaging. I knew the previous year, in the semi-final against Toulouse, the scrum had suffered.

Leinster didn't seem to be as collective as the Toulouse scrum.

One thing that made a difference was that everyone bought into what Feeky said and, as a result, if one person got into some trouble, there was less of a consequence. They didn't get completely destroyed when one little thing went wrong.

ONE OF THE things with Rossy is that his wife, Kimberlee is a dangerously good cook. It's probably not ideal for Rossy as an international rugby player but Kimberlee is a fantastic match-up for Rossy in every other way.

Rossy liked his little treats.

We were coming back from Munster once, and Rossy was getting onto the team bus when he was caught red-handed with a packet of crisps under his jacket. He claimed that they were 'Kevin's favourite.'

I'm not sure what age his son, Kevin was at that time, but I'm fairly sure he was not yet eating packets of crisps.

But, we'd won that day and while Rossy got a bit of a ribbing, it was all good humoured. He also got away with some of the worst jokes we ever heard in Leinster and Ireland – they were so bad, they were always funny. That was Rossy, well liked and much needed.

He was also our tech guru!

Again, I can hear the yell... 'ROSSSSSYYYYYY!'

If something, some piece of equipment or other was not working in the team room and we were in some strange hotel where we did not have help at hand, that shout could be heard running down the corridor.

Any problem

Any breakdown.

'ROSSSYYYYYY!'

He was our best chance to solve the problem whenever we had a technical issue. That was important because we wanted to get the thing fixed, but we were also a very integrated team, and he was a crucial part of that integration. Not just on the pitch, but off the pitch as well.

REPRESENTING IRELAND WAS Rossy's great ambition.

He wanted to make a career for himself here, in Ireland. He dreamed of representing his country and, along with some help and some hard work, he made that a reality.

He built himself into what we needed him to be - the cornerstone for back-to-back Heineken Cups and back-to-back Six Nations Championships.

He was crucial.

I suppose it offers some credence to the advice I received over 15 years ago... to be a competitive rugby team having the right tighthead prop is fundamental.

Unassuming, understated and indispensable, Rossy was the tighthead we needed!

PROLOGUE

'DAD... I NEED TO PEE.'

MY SEVEN YEAR old son was not kidding.

One look at his face told me so.

We needed to go, even though I did not want to move from our seats in Twickers.

Kevin's face was sort of contorted. His face issued a warning that only a kid's face can unleash. Disaster was not far off. Anything from a nuclear attack to a zombie apocalypse, and back again.

We needed to move.

Or he was going to wet himself. Therefore, Ireland bidding for a Grand Slam would have to be put on pause. Joe and the boys, all of my old teammates, they'd just have to wait for us until we got back for the start of the second half. I knew we'd be hitting a queue.

But I'd no idea that the queue would be out the door, and would continue down along one wall. Kevin was still looking up at me.

'DAD...'

OUR THIRD GRAND Slam was in the making.

Our third Championship title in five years. We were winning 21-5. After Rob Kearney had done enough against Anthony Watson in the air, Garry Ringrose had grounded the ball for our first try. Jacob Stockdale grabbed the third try of the half, taking Conor Murray's lightning pass, kicking it into England's 22, overtaking Mike Brown, kneeing the ball over the line and touching it down just before it went dead. That was seven tries in the Six Nations for Jason, a record, and I was there with my son to witness it.

Lucky us.

But the second try, after 23 minutes, was the try that tickled me even more. I'd find out about the genesis of it afterwards, from Tadhg Furlong, who told me they'd tried the move a thousand times in training all that week and it had never quite worked. But they still had the balls to call it when the stakes were highest.

Tadhg showed magical hands and freed Bundee Aki.

Bundee feinted the pass outside.

CJ Stander finished it off. In the first half he must have carried the ball for the same distance as the whole English pack combined, and he ate up some of those yards despite two Englishmen hanging out of him before touching the ball down.

I know that was the try that had Joe happiest too.

Joe Schmidt. The man is a genius. But the man is also the hardest worker I have ever observed in my life in rugby. Joe prides himself on the inches and the fractions of seconds that make all the difference between a team being very good, and a team being simply outstanding.

'I'M GOING TO wet myself…

'DAD!'

I am watching Ireland about to win the Slam.

I am an Ireland supporter. I am a former Ireland rugby player. I am sitting in decent seats, but I'd love to be out there. I realise that. It impacts on me. But who am I to complain? What is Sean O'Brien thinking? Or Simon Zebo? The two of them have a more legitimate reason than me to believe that they should be out there.

It's tough, in some ways sitting here.

I'm sitting with my son, and it will be a golden memory but, nevertheless, a day like this only comes along now…and in another 20 or 40 years? The boys with Joe have the ability to win two or three Slams, of course they do but, in the past, once every half a century was considered good timing.

Out seats are bloody cold. I know Kevin is feeling the chill, but I do not expect him to demand a race to the toilets at half-time.

We move.

We get out of our seats and retreat, but there are queues.

Unbelievable queues. And Kevin is now hopping around, bursting to go…

THE NIGHT BEFORE was my first Legends game

Ireland Vs England.

I stayed with the team the night after the game, because I guessed my wife would prefer not to have me crashing through our bedroom door at 3.0 in the morning. I slept in the Lensbury, in Teddington. It was 'old school' so I was rooming with Tony Buckley, like when I was in my playing days, though Tony and I at one point in time were on a collision course, seeing who would be fit to take on the role vacated by John Hayes in the Irish front row.

Tony or me?

Who would be up to taking over from The Bull?

For a long time Tony had looked the man who would be chosen. Tony was always a monster, a massive man, a man multiplied by two. There was no way I could match him in raw physical strength, or in his running around the pitch, but there was one place I could prove myself better than him.

The scrum.

If you looked at Tony's highlights reel you would throw your eyes up to the heavens. The man had an unlawful strength. Like when he played Perpignan, and some unlucky buck was picked up by Tony and tossed to one side. Like a small, tidy sack of potatoes. He had played one of the best games I had ever viewed an Irish prop playing, against New Zealand – the game in which Jamie Heaslip was sent off for kneeing Richie McCaw in the head, which some people would argue was exactly what the All Black legend needed in order to put some manners on him.

You ever see McCaw? He's always, forever, just... and you are always asking yourself how on earth is he getting away with this? It's like he has one of those invisibility cloaks, like the one Harry Potter and his pals wear and, I have to admit, Leo Cullen, my former Leinster captain... Leo also owned such a coat.

Maybe referees never saw them do it. Or maybe they did it just barely within the laws of the game. Either way, Leo was in exalted company. Half of us never understood how Leo got away with some of the plays he pulled on the field. A lot of the time, I guess, he and McCaw were technically correct and they might leave their hand on the ball a second long enough to slow it down but not long enough for the referee to think that either of them had a material effect on possession, but it will always have an effect on possession because... there was a hole there, but now there is no hole there any longer!

The margins were always so fine, and Leo needed to be so scientifically exact. It is why he was a special player who never fully got the credit he deserved from an adoring Irish rugby public who were served up Paulie O'Connell and Donncha O'Callaghan as Ireland's premier second row pairing.

So, Tony and I were looking at Bull's empty boots.

But Tony ended up going over to Sale and once you are over there, in England or France, and out of the system, that's pretty much it.

I should know.

I'd been over in England for three years.

THE QUEUE HAD mercy on Kevin.

There is a 'bro code' I guess... let the young lad through. That sort of thing. The second half was about five minutes in when the pair of us got back to our seats.

The rest of the game sped by.

24-15.

Less thrills, but we'd taken England and the Slam in one fell swoop, and we'd done it in the home of English rugby.

I felt okay. I felt better than okay, I felt really happy, even though Ireland's two modern day Grand Slams had now book-ended my career. I came home to join up with Leinster a couple of months after the Slam in 2009. And I'd retired the season before the Slam in 2018. When all the heroes of those two Slams are remembered 10 and 20 years down the road, my name will not be amongst them.

When whoever is left, alive and gingerly moving around the place in the Aviva Stadium or whatever it will be called in 50 years time, I might still be in the stand looking down on them on the field and applauding them.

And Kevin will be by my side, asking his doddery old man if he's alright? 'How's the bladder holding up… Dad?

'You need to go to the loo?'

But all I can think is… *lucky me, if that is the case!*

I HAD NO doubt in the world as I waited with Kevin in the toilets at Twickers that Ireland would get the job done.

There is one thing I know about a Joe Schmidt team and it is this… give them a 10 or 14 point lead and… that's it. They'll strangle you after that. They are never going to give up that lead.

It usually does not happen.

Whereas, if you make a Joe team chase the game, then that is a lot more difficult and players can then start making mistakes. Once Joe's team gets its nose decently in front, game over. A lot of the time Joe's rugby is not overly high risk. He keeps the penalty rate below five or six most days. We've got one of the lowest penalty rates in the world. And Ireland's breakdown times are the lowest out there most of the time too. Our average ruck speed, I think, is about 1.8 seconds.

And that is no accident.

It happens because of the relentless focus that is placed on it during the week, every single week. Therefore, where is the other team's possession going to come from? If you look at the tackle counts of teams that play against us, they're stratospheric. Of the five highest tackle counts in world rugby, I believe Joe's opposition are responsible for two of them.

It's about changes in the point of the attack.

You've got a bundle of players on the ground, and suddenly the ball is gone and everyone has to readjust to a new attack. It's exhausting for other teams. If your ruck is slow the defensive line can get ready in their own time for the next attack, but if the ruck is quick... if the ruck is doubly quick? There's no time to adjust. We ruck the ball in a second and a split of a second.

New phase of attack, new point of attack.

Joe's processes in training always resulted in quick ball.

He'd have you taking a step for correction, and going in straight, and not from a line less direct. You are going to be more powerful and more forceful if you are moving in a straight line and clearing out a ruck.

Joe had us all adjusting our running angles all of the time.

The man has a clearer focus on how he wants the game to be played than anyone else I have ever met in rugby. He knows exactly what he requires from each individual component for the whole thing to work. That's why Joe is all about speed and accuracy. Without that pairing, it does not work.

I've been lucky to work under a great number of coaches, here and in England. Deccie Kidney, for instance, as amazing as he was as a winning leader, was not someone who was a hands-on coach. Joe is the polar opposite. When I first met Joe, he challenged me, personally and professionally. At the start of his first season in Leinster he asked each of us to visit him in his office and, there, once we sat down in front of him, he asked each one of us what exactly we were going to bring to his team?

Me?

I told Joe... 'I'm the best scrummager you have!'

'I can lock down your scrum better than anyone else.'

I added that, in case he was not listening. But Joe listens to everything, and he asked me what else I was going to bring to his team?

I was not expecting that.

Joe also needed X, Y and Z from me.

I had thought about our first meeting for so long because I had endured pretty much a whole season in 'Siberia' in Michael Cheika's final season in Leinster, and I had worked myself up to hit Joe with the big statement... 'I can lock down your scrum better… than…'

I had just told him I was the best he had, that there was no other tighthead in the country who could do for him what I could do for him. And he seemed dissatisfied. He was plainly not one hundred per cent impressed by what I had said.

A few months down the road, although I knew I was impressing him, he was still asking me questions that no other coach had ever chucked in my direction. We were sitting in the video room and looking at some tape. We'd conceded a try. And I was quite relaxed.

The try had sweet damn all to do with me, I felt. Someone had made a break and a winger had got on his shoulder, and we were cut open.

Joe swings around to me.

'Rossy…that's your fault!'

What!

WHATTTT DID HE JUST SAY?

'Rossy….'

'You hear me, mate?'

I did not respond, initially. I had looked at the video like everyone else and a winger had flown onto possession and… how am I going to catch that winger?

WHAT THE FUCK?

HE'S A BIT QUICKER THAN I AM… JOE!

Luckily, I had kept my mouth shut because Joe was replaying the try, and he's suddenly showing me where I am ahead of the same winger just before he gets the ball.

'You're jogging… and he's sprinting past you,' Joe tells me.

'Why weren't you moving faster?

'If you moved a fraction of a second earlier,' Joe continues, showing me my position in the offending play, '… you would have been in position to make the tackle, Rossy!'

Joe is looking at me hard.

Seriously, and hard.

He is waiting for my response, but I have no response initially, and Joe starts talking again.

'It's not a question of you being as quick as him,' he explains to me, and the whole room, '… it's a question of thinking Rossy… smarter, harder, earlier!'

That, I would quickly discover alongside everyone else in the room, was Joe Schmidt's personal homemade mantra.

SMARTER.

HARDER

EARLIER.

'Look around you!' Joe would tell us.

'Anticipate… see what is going to happen before it happens!'

'And make sure you are there earlier… BEFORE IT HAPPENS!'

As I write this now, I know Joe will not be happy with me. I know what he is going to tell me, next time he sees me.

He's going to tell me…

'Rossy… you giving away the secrets on me?'

IN TERMS OF career disappointments, missing out on that first Grand Slam in 2009 would not be right up there at all.

I was playing for Harlequins at the time. I was also in the Irish training squad, but Declan Kidney did not see me. He wasn't looking at me. I was nowhere near the match 22. Not at all. I had agreed to move to Leinster in the spring of 2009. I was way too late coming home.

I came home, instead, to stake my claim for the future. To take my place in the Irish team, and aim for 2011, and the World Cup. I did that. I came back, I won a green shirt and held onto it, and played in the World Cup in New Zealand and got to be part of the team that rocked Australia off its feet, but then agonisingly fell to Wales in the quarter-final.

Neither 2009 nor 2018 and the pair of glorious Slams are true regrets for me.

The biggest blow for me was missing out on Lions selection in 2013. That, and not being in Chicago in the autumn of 2016 when Ireland at last summoned up the courage to bring down the mighty All Blacks.

Most other years, I believe I could have made the Lions.

But, the 2013 season was one in which Ireland had a horror Six Nations. The whole thing imploded. Injuries did not help, but there were other factors. Ireland needed a sweeping change. Ireland needed Joe Schmidt.

In April, before the final Lions selection by Warren Gatland and his coaching team, packs went out to about 50 players who were in the wider squad. I received mine. I signed the contract. I sent it back double quick.

I could smell it.

I was holding Lions-headed paper in my hands and it felt so close. The famous jersey. The opportunity and the memories that would follow for years. But, where the hell did Matt Stevens come from? I knew that it was going to be a tight call. In the middle of March, even the Irish media did not have me as a sure thing. Many did not see me going.

Which I felt was a bit harsh.

Gatland's Welsh side had been the strongest performing home nation in the World Cup admittedly, and they had just won back-to-back Championships. If Gatland chose six props, then *The Irish Times* had Gethin Jenkins and Adam Jones from Wales, Cian Healy, the English pair of Dan Cole and Andrew Sheridan, and Geoff Cross from Scotland as their fairly sure things.

'Even if there's a third tighthead Mike Ross will be under pressure from Cross,' I read in the paper, 'while Andrew Sheridan, given his track record against Australian scrums since he almost single-handedly beat them in the 2007 World Cup quarter-final in Marseilles, could be a dark horse. If the decision is to bring five props, then the versatility of Paul James will become even more valuable.'

So… Matt Stevens?

He had retired from international rugby so it hadn't even crossed my mind that I was in competition with him. He'd been on the 2005 tour, but he'd retired from Test rugby 12 months before Gatland announced his squad for down under. He'd also been out of the game for two years after failing a drugs test after Bath had played Glasgow in the Heineken Cup in 2009, and he was tested positive for cocaine. Stevens was not anywhere in my head. But our poor Six Nations was there! I knew it was an abhorrence of a performance that would be difficult to overlook by very many neutrals.

At the same time, I had European Cup wins in 2011 and '12 in the bank.

That was serious credit. I knew that Jones and Cole were sure things. And I thought I might be in trouble if Euan Murray had some people speaking up on his behalf.

I was certain that I had a 60:40 shot at the last position. But Gatland said that Stevens offered him possibilities on both sides of the scrum, whereas myself and Murray were 'one dimensional tight heads.'

The morning came and I was sitting down in my home in Goatstown that I was renting from Bob Casey, with my wife and my Mom, Patty when the squad was announced on Sky Sports.

Position by position.

Alphabetically.

And Matt Stevens' name was called out.

I stood up and left the room. I also left my wife behind me in tears, and I walked upstairs and sat down on our bed, and stayed there. I was numb. The anger was still some way off.

COLE... JONES... STEVENS...

As the names repeatedly swung through my head in that sequence, over and over again, the anger was not slow in mounting. The disappointment was massive. I felt blind-sided. It took me about six weeks to get over it, and that included Ireland's tour of the United States when I couldn't watch the Lions in any of their matches but sincerely hoped – and would have got down on my knees if I was praying man – for tightheads to start falling in Australia.

Instead, one loosehead after another began disappearing like flies during that Lions tour. *Come on… just one tighthead… COME ON!*

Tom Court got called out to Australia.

He got his jersey.

I wanted just one jersey… *COME ONNNNNN!!!!*

Any other year!

That's what I was thinking, and still believe. In 2012 after coming off the Heineken Cup win over Ulster I would have been there most probably. Or in 2014 after winning the Six Nations with Joe Schmidt in his first year! It would have been bloody hard to overlook me that year as well.

The Lions tour concluded, and I couldn't watch one single game.

IF I COULD have played both sides?

Not many men are able to make it happen at both loose and tight. Peter Clohessy did it successfully in a different era. But I always told myself that I should aim to be one of the best tightheads in the professional game, and nothing less than that. And that meant sacrificing any notion of being able to cross over to loose.

I believe that I became one of the best tightheads, in Europe at least.

Why should I try to put myself in any other position, and find that I was not the same player, or that I was considered a much lesser player? I'd waited so long to get my chance as a professional. I was 26 when I became a professional rugby player and joined Harlequins, and I was 30 when I came home to fight for the Leinster and Irish jerseys.

I knew what I wanted, and I knew what I could do better than anyone else.

And I didn't want to look back at the long, tough journey I had taken to get to where I was, and regret taking any wrong turns.

TIGHTHEAD AND LOOSEHEAD?

Moving across from the right to the left hand side of the front row is a bit like trying to write with your left hand.

When you are playing tighthead most of the weight goes through your left leg. Loosehead, most of the weight goes through your right leg.

Loosehead, you're pushing up.

You are looking to pop the tighthead up into the air.

Tighthead, you're pushing down.

You are looking to drive the loosehead down into the ground.

It's like a suspension bridge, and what keeps the scrum intact is this up and down pressure. But, there's more.

The tighthead is the most vulnerable point in the whole scrum in terms of weight and leverage. Therefore, the tighthead potentially also represents the weakest point. It's where the opposing scrum want to attack.

On his own feed the tighthead seeks to stabilise his scrum. That's what I told Joe... you want your scrum 'locked down' then I'm your man Mr. Schmidt! But on opposition ball the tighthead works like mad with everyone else on his side of the ball to fracture the opposing scrum. It's not complicated. Though it can get so damned complicated.

In the good old days a tighthead was permitted to lower the height of the scrum any way he liked, and if his shoulders were dipped below hip height, then, well and good. But the laws changed. Looseheads were given the opportunity of getting under tightheads. More than that, if a good loosehead gets his head, neck and shoulders under the tighthead, there's a long day ahead. Unless…

Unless the tighthead can change his angles. Unless the tighthead can reduce the exact surface area available to the loosehead to work with. The less room a loosehead has to work with, the less damage he can do. Even great looseheads need surface area to work their particular brand of magic.

It was my job to rob them of their magic.

Change the angles.

Alter the weight distribution.

Minimise the magic…and, as I've just written, ultimately deny my opponent any of his Harry Potter tricks of the trade.

When the scrum engages, the tighthead must apply downward pressure. If he only looks to drive forward then, sure as eggs, he is going to be forced upwards. The tighthead drives forward and downward.

And us tightheads aim for a point between the hooker and the loosehead. Downward pressure and an inward angle is just about perfect. Our right arm is there to control the loosehead, to pull him out and find more room and separate him from his hooker. In attacking the centre of the scrum we've got to keep our left shoulder on top of the hooker, and our right shoulder on top of the loosehead.

Then, we get to work our own brand of magic.

Simple.

Extra simple, if all the referees in the world had even the foggiest idea of what is happening in the scrum.

Some of them are clueless

Half of them depend on guesswork. And even the best referees I had for company during my career regularly defaulted to sharing penalty counts between teams.

I'll introduce you to them shortly.

AS EVERYONE WITHIN the Leinster and Ireland camps knows, I liked my data. I wanted to know everything about the loosehead I was facing. I wanted to know everything about the hooker. After all, I'm competing against the pair of them, and not just one man. But I also wanted to know who the opposing tighthead was - and what he liked, and disliked, and what made him tick, or not.

Being good at tight or loose comes down to a combination of factors. I figured out early in my professional career that I could never have enough information at hand.

So, I had my sheets

Sheets and more sheets. Sheets for myself, and sheets to be shared. I watched hundreds and hundreds of hours of scrummaging. I guess I must have watched every decent prop in the world until my eyelids became too heavy. I had all the information in my head.

But it made sense to have it down on paper too.

Some of the lads thought I was a scrum nerd. Damn sure I was, but when I produced my sheets before big games not too many people said... 'No thanks, Rossy!' I was able to tell my hooker and loosehead, and also the replacements, extra things.

This is who we are playing against.

This is what they like.

This is what they don't like.

This is the shit they will try to pull.

BUT THE RULES around the scrum changed so much since I started out in the professional game. It switched from massive impact... to more of a wrestling match.

CROUCH, HOLD, ENGAGE!

All fine with me, and we would all be positioned further back. As I will shortly explain, I was reared as a professional on a whole different engagement.

When I went to England in 2006 and found myself in Harlequins' famous jersey, I also found myself in games that were essentially 'Willy Waving' contests. It was all about the hit. It was almost all about the bigger, stronger man.

But…

With greater stability, the more the scrum became a wrestling match. The big hitters were either redundant, or else they had to change, and adapt fast. Most of the impact went out of the scrum contest.

The impact on engagement fell by twenty-five per cent at elite level. A lot of the scrum specialists suffered when the brute force was dramatically reduced. I did too, but as time went on I believe I became an ever better scrummager under the new laws. If someone beat you to the hit under the old laws you were in trouble straight away. You might never recover. You had to accept that impact, but with the new rules you had a far greater opportunity to get yourself back.

Of course, I still had my sheets of data, and I always had far more information at hand than all of the other props. Of course, I needed to be a little bit selfish with my sheets of information. I wasn't going to give everything away to my teammates.

My teammates in the front row were also my primary opponents – before I actually got to scrum down against our actual opponents. I wanted Harlequins and Leinster to do well every weekend, and I did everything in my power to help us to that win. In rugby, as in any professional game, you must be selfless to a degree. It's impossible to separate the self from the team.

Say you get injured? And your understudy comes in, and he is not as well prepared as you had been? If he's not, and the team loses, then you are also going to lose out in some shape or form in the longer run.

The team has to win.

At the end of the day that is the bottom line. Every day.

In Leinster, however, we did not have a dedicated scrum coach until Greg Feek arrived in and joined up with Joe Schmidt. I had come back home and left the extremely forward-orientated game in Harlequins where the scrum, every weekend, was a repeated test of your manhood.

You dominated.

Or you were dominated.

Back home, I was surprised to find that the scrum was viewed more as a means to restart the game.

You were not being challenged as much in Ireland in the scrum.

In England, you were asked, you were being questioned, you were bloody well being examined from head to toe every single day you put on that Harlequins jersey. And days when you were in your training gear were no different. Every day could turn into a 'Man Up-athon.'

One of my earliest days in London I had John Kingston sitting on a scrummaging machine and asking me... 'Shall I take some of this weight off... ROSSY?'

I was dying. It was about the 20th scrum in-a-row that we'd had that session. JK had a false look of concern on his face.

'ROSSY... YOU OKAY THERE, MATE?'

I felt ready to collapse.

'NO...!' I shouted back at him... 'More weight!" I could hardly get the words out, so I repeated myself...

'MORE... WEIGHT!'

HOW COULD I have any serious regrets?

I turned professional at 26. And I came home from London as I turned 30 years of age, and before I finished up here I had earned 61 caps for Ireland, and made 151 appearances for Leinster. We won two Heineken Cups, and two Six Nations Championships.

But I have them. Regrets.

They live under my skin still.

I regret how it all finally ended, and I especially regret not getting a chance to pull on a Lions jersey, and then not getting the opportunity of a lifetime to be part of an Ireland team that finally beat the All Blacks and brought 111 years of trying to a screeching halt. A huge regret.

Of course I knew it was ending.

When I saw Tadhg Furlong exit the Leinster academy and make one of his first starts for Leinster I knew the writing was on the wall. I was in one of Joe's camps, with Ireland for the November internationals, as Tadhg got his start for Leinster. I went to the game.

There was no denying what I saw that evening. None.

'FUCK'

Yeah, that's all I needed to say.

'AH FUCK!'

The kid had it all, or almost all of it. He was not quite as good a scrummager as he is now but I knew. One more year, two more… max… and he was going to be something else.

Tadhg came through fairly quickly in the end. In the Six Nations in 2016 they discovered that he was not quite ready, but in the summer when we got out to South Africa he had already grown from the experience. He was excellent in the second Test against the 'Boks and announced himself on the world stage. Coming into the 2017 season I was still slightly ahead of him. That lasted until the first European game where he got the nod. I still had the idea I could push him even then.

But I tore up my hamstring, and Tadhg came bursting through. That was that. It was a sudden turnaround, but I was still happy enough at the thought of acting as his back-up. There could be no complaints from me.

Every single day Tadhg was brilliant.

I PLAYED MY final game for Ireland, my 61st cap, on June 25, 2016, in the Nelson Mandela Bay Stadium in Port Elizabeth. It was the third Test of our South African tour and Joe wanted the old boys to start the game, and the young boys to bring it home. We were sitting on one Test victory each.

I was facing The Beast.

Or Tendai Mtawarira, to serve up the full name that his mother and father gave to him. I have to admit that I did not get a lot of joy out of him in the scrum that day. Or any other day. I always found him difficult. Not just because of his size and strength. I'd faced bigger men, and it's not all about absolute power in the scrum. There are always multiple factors at play, but The Beast had a particular power that was explosive. It had a hydraulic quality to it. Tadhg came in for me after 50 minutes. But The Beast was gone after 56 minutes, so I'd like to think that I'd also done my part in bringing him to a standstill.

Generally, Tadhg has since done better against him than I ever did. Looking back, I realise that I went into 'survival mode' any time I played against him. Tadhg, instead, took The Beast on every time since, and that tells you everything you need to know about Tadhg Furlong.

We lost the game 19-13, and the series.

But an even bigger scalp was right around the corner, in Soldier Field, Chicago. To be honest I don't know if Joe actually targeted that November Test, or whether it was a happy circumstance.

I had the impression that a famous victory over the All Blacks was something Joe Schmidt envisaged for the Aviva Stadium when New Zealand came visiting.

'MAKE THE MOST of this… Rossy!'

Joe gave me the news in the matter of fact way Joe Schmidt does business. He always fronts up with the good news, and the bad news.

Before the first Test against South Africa, which we had won 26-20 in Cape Town, he had taken me to one side. 'Play well Rossy…' he continued.

'Because there are not many more of these for you!'

That's Joe.

Brutally honest.

'Make it count!' he added.

Not many, in Joe speak, may have been four or five more appearances for Ireland. Or, not many may have been a big fat zero. You just don't know. But I'm thinking… Shit!

I'm also thinking… *He might give me a few more games!*

I'm 36 years of age.

I'm finally thinking… *I've got two or three more!*

But, there was only one more. And after coming off the pitch after 58 minutes that day in Cape Town I would only get one more Irish jersey… and a total of 50 minutes that day in Port Elizabeth.

I had a suspicion after the game. My nephew was born that same day, June 25 - my brother Matthew's boy, Caleb. I got the jersey I wore in the game, got it signed and framed and it now hangs in Caleb's bedroom. There's a nice synchronicity to it.

Eoin Reddan also played his last game for Ireland that same day. I got my photo taken with him in the dressing room after. My suspicion was strong but, hell, I was not giving up hope. Maybe I would get one more game?

Maybe... *Chicago?*

The All Blacks?

JOE NEVER ACTUALLY told me it was over.

He wanted to have a look at different lads in Chicago against the All Blacks. Tadhg was going to be starting, and Joe wanted to check out Finlay Bealham. Joe didn't tell me this himself. He asked Greg Feek to give me the news. It was four, maybe five weeks before the game.

Feeky texted me.

He wanted to know if he could drop into my place?

I asked him if he was thinking of taking me behind my own wood shed?

He dropped in at five o'clock.

He didn't wait to bring me out of sight. In the front garden, he told me straight. Though Feeky did not tell me that it was all over either. 'Barring injuries,' he said, '... we're going to be going with these young guys for the next few months!

'Tadhg... and Finlay.'

I nodded, told him I understood.

I always liked Feeky. I enjoyed his company, I loved working with him. I learned so much more from him, and I was also happy that he went to the trouble of calling into me to tell me what was happening. I was about to turn 37 a few months down the road. The time had come for Joe and Feeky to look to the future.

Still, I thought... *Maybe?*

Joe is not the sort of coach who is going to take a player and put him in a box, and place him on a top shelf and forget about him. Joe is never going to deny himself access to any tool.

Joe will always do what's best for the team in the very next game.

I phoned him straight after Feeky left. I was still walking around my front garden. I thanked him. I told him that every medal I had in my arse pocket was down to him. Bar one! I told him I would be there for him if he needed me. I told him that I hoped he would need me. And I wished him the best in Chicago.

The week before the team left for Chicago, Leinster played Connacht and we milled them out of it in the scrum. We horsed them up and down the field. Finlay Bealham, who'd come on as a sub, had to leave the field. Feeky called me again that evening.

He said that it looked like Finlay was out. Concussion.

'Can you come in?' he asked.

It looked like Finlay was gone.

It looked like I was packing my bags for Chicago.

But Finlay passed the concussion test, and instead of the happy long-haul flight to O'Hare Airport in Chicago I was on my way to Zebre.

I found myself in Parma, and I was sitting on the bench as the game against Zebre kicked off. I'd gone into the Ireland camp, as asked by Feeky. I'd been in the camp on the Monday and Tuesday, so Michael Bent was named by Leinster.

It was pissing down in northern Italy.

Miserable, shitty weather, and I was feeling well pissed too by kick off time. I was still thinking about Chicago. *The All Blacks.* Had I just missed out on making one final appearance for Ireland? The game was into the second half. It was still wet and horrible. I was sent in for Benty. I saw the ball and pushed Peter Dooley to hell out of my way to get to the ball. I ran into two lads.

SNAP!

One busted up hamstring.

ON THE FLIGHT back home I could barely remain seated.

The pain was excruciating. I could not find a comfortable position no matter how I shifted around on the seat. I shouldn't have been in Italy. I should have been in Chicago. I was so close to Chicago.

The lads were pestering the cabin crew to make radio contact with traffic control, and tell us what was happening in Chicago.

They told us that we had put 40 points on the All Blacks.

They're kidding... right?

Who puts 40 points on the All Blacks?

They then told us with absolutely serious faces that Ireland had just beaten the All Blacks. Not beaten them...

Whipped them.

IT TOOK THAT hamstring forever to mend.

Month after month after month I was waiting. Working away on it on my bike and waiting, and then I had to get match fit. I was 37 years old when I came back. And then I had Stuart Lancaster to look forward to.

Stuart's favourite day of the week seemed to be Tuesday.

We called them STUESDAYS! Games always seemed slow when compared to STUESDAYS.

On Tuesday he liked to run us harder and further than we were ever likely to run in a match. His drills had us over and back between the 22s. Defensive sets, and defensive sets, and defensive sets.

I was back. Thirty seven years old alright, but fitter than I had been at any time in my whole career.

I'm thinking... *Games.*

I'm thinking... *One more year!*

I wanted games. I wanted a contract for one more year.

One more year... just one more!

I knew that if I got games then I could get my last contract with Leinster, and I knew that year would also give me the time I needed in order to find out what I was going to do with myself the rest of my working life.

I got about 20 minutes against Treviso.

I was back... and I'm thinking... *a contract... any contract*!

I felt that I was destroying the lads in scrummaging in the middle of the week. I was training better than I could ever remember training. I was going well. Better than well... *I'm flying.*

I was in against the Dragons and I made a big break up the middle of the pitch, something that not many people had ever remembered me doing before. I'm thinking… *I'm definitely back.*

I knew they were going to chop my contract. I knew that for sure, and I was making the arrangements I needed to make, like changing the repayment terms on my mortgage.

I'm thinking… *one more year… one more contract.* But I knew it would not be a contract with terms that I liked very much.

I'm still thinking… *contract.*

I'm thinking… *mortgage… extend it from 13 years… out to 25 years?*

'WE SHOULD BE in my office with a bottle of whiskey!'

Leo Cullen had taken me into the little meeting room that is just next to where we eat our post-match meals in the RDS. It's more like a broom cupboard. But it's quiet, and it was good to have a private word.

Yeah, Leo tells me that the two of us should be sitting down in his office, and not standing up with our arms folded. He has said that there should be a bottle of whiskey on his desk between us. Two glasses.

'I'm sorry Rossy, but there's nothing for you next year,' he tells me.

He's blunt. He's fast and hard with the bad news because he knows that I've been waiting around to hear this decision, and that I deserve to hear it straight up. I feel crushed. But I know Leo is feeling not much better than me right this moment. I know this is one meeting he has not been looking forward to since he got out of bed this morning.

It's March. We had just played Edinburgh. 'I can not believe I am saying this to you… here,' Leo continued. 'Not here… in this little place!'

I'm listening to him… thinking… *three months.*

I've got three months' wages left.

My mortgage is not going to stop. Our household bills are not going to stop. The cost that underpins my family's life is going to remain just as high as ever.

Only my wages are going to stop. There'll be a tax rebate, which helps all professional rugby players at the end. But I know it will take several months to come through. I know that money will come, and quickly go. I still need another year to prepare for the end of my rugby life.

I DIDN'T THANK Leo, and just turn on my heels. I stood my ground, in the little space we were sharing in the cupboard.

Instead, I told him that he still needed me.

I told him that he would not have Tadhg for very much of the following season, given his commitments with Ireland and his definite chance of hitting the Lions tour to New Zealand. I reminded him that he would be left with Benty and Andrew Porter. I warned him that he was leaving himself and the team very exposed without me and Tadhg.

'Very exposed!' I repeated.

If Benty or Porter get injured, I asked him, what's going to happen? Tadhg is going to be wrapped up in cotton wool for four or five months of the season, I emphasised a second time. Porter was extremely raw, having just made the switch from loosehead. I had it in my head that I could mentor him the following season. 'If Benty or Porter get a bang… what're you going to do then?'

I think Leo was listening to me but he did not engage with me in the numbers game I was playing out in front of him.

'There's no budget, Rossy!'

I COULD UNDERSTAND.

They were soon going to have to pay Tadhg a hell of a lot more. They were going to have to up Benty's pay. Behind Benty, they had a young tighthead with massive potential and the day would come fast when they might also have to pay him an awful lot more.

I know tightheads are not cheap.

Better than anyone else, I've always known that. After the out-half we're one of the more expensive items on the team list. Good, reliable tightheads are never cheap. So I understand they looked at me.

And at 37 years of age, all they could see was a significant amount of money that they knew they would need to divide up between Tadgh and Benty. Andrew Porter, if he maintained his steady progress, would get his share of my old wage too.

It's maths. It's business.

I WAS HOME in 15 minutes from the RDS.

I walked into the house and my wife was waiting for me. I told her straight. It had turned into an evening when bad news was moving fast... from A to B to C. No stops on the way. Kimberlee was making dinner.

We sat down, ate, and opened a bottle of a nice wine, and then a second bottle. My wife was pragmatic. Kim is always pragmatic. She told me we should not be surprised. She reminded me of my own words... *once you get into your 30s... mid-30s... they'll come at you!*

My contract was always destined to be chopped. Or removed entirely. I knew she was right and that her brain was working in a matter of fact order as we talked it through. But my brain was not.

My brain was darting here and there. My brain was revving up, shooting forward at 70 miles per hour. Then reversing up, and changing direction.

I was lucky with the last contract I received from Leinster. Marty Moore had suddenly left, for Wasps, and instead of getting chopped by thirty per cent or something of that order, I held solid.

I still wasn't earning as much as I had earned two seasons before, my highest earning season, when I hit every target, pocketed the bonuses and ended the season with thirty per cent extra on my base salary. In my professional career I had climbed the pay ladder the more and more teams needed me.

I started with 25 grand sterling for four months' work with Harlequins. They moved me up to 40 grand, then 70 grand in season two, which was a great wage for me back then. My final season with Harlequins I was on 130 grand. Still sterling and a solid wage, but one that would double as I continued to climb the ladder with Leinster.

Three months' wages.

My last... three months'... wages!

KIMBERLEE WAS SUPPORTIVE.

She was strong and supportive, and at the same time as being a practical woman, she is a loving wife and she was offended on my behalf.

I decided to pick up the phone to Ryan Constable, my agent, and find out what was available out there?

I needed data.

My brain was shouting at me for data. Like never before, my brain was demanding as much data as possible, and fast. The scientist in me was replacing the rugby professional. I needed to find out what opportunities were out there?

Out there?

And out there, outside of Ireland, what was my worth?

I could still scrummage. I always told myself that as long as I could scrum I would never be short of work. Now... *I'M HERE!*

I'M HERE... WHERE CAN I SCRUMMAGE?

I talked to Ryan and I talked to David McHugh, and I asked David to have as much information for me as humanly possible the next morning.

THE NEXT MORNING.

It was a Sunday morning. David had all the information. All the data. This club, and that club. One English club were looking for a replacement tighthead. The budget was around 120 grand sterling.

I was still thinking one more year, maybe two years, and prepare for my retirement and prepare for the rest of my life. But the figures, they needed to add up.

I would have to move out of Ireland. I would have to move my family out of our home. I was thinking... *somewhere... south of France... Montpellier?*

Twenty grand a month?

A two years deal?

Yes.

I would say yes to that, in a second. But there was no Montpellier, no life in the South of France on offer. There was no offer on the table in front of myself and David that I could possibly accept. And David was telling me not to go.

He was telling me that 12 months, anywhere, was no help. I'd be back before I knew it, back sitting at the same table deciding what on earth I should do with the rest of my life.

AT THE END of April I had finished making all of the phone calls I needed to make. I had recorded all of the data and churned through it in my brain. There was only a finite period of time available to me to think, to decide, to know what I needed to do. I had phoned friends and acquaintances, in England, in France.

My wages were going to be guillotined in June.

At the end of April I stopped the firefighting.

I STARTED LOOKING.

Looking for a job out there... *not just out there... but out there in the real world!*

I have a brain.

I had been a scientist in a white coat once upon a time, before I became a professional rugby player.

I have a mentor, Michael Ryan, former CEO of Kleerex, and the man I shook hands with when the IRFU and Ernst and Young decided it would be a good idea to pair every player with someone in the business community. Michael became an invaluable sounding board for me, and a very good friend.

I had met up with Michael every couple of months during the final years of my career. He seemed to know everybody in the business community in Dublin.

I had asked Alistair, my brother in Los Angeles who works with a recruitment company, to help me build a CV. I was suited and booted. I had my snazzy looking CV in my hand. I had my high profile rugby career in my back pocket – and, in view, poking its head out of my front breast pocket if needed.

I met with Donal O'Donoghue of Sanderson Recruitment.

I was ready to go to work.

Back in the real world, I was ready to work as Commercial Director of Wizuda. I was very happy with that decision. I was going to get a chance to work with good people in a really interesting company.

But I was not back just yet.

I was still a rugby professional. In my final month in a job which had been the greatest, the most enjoyable and satisfying job. The job that had been the job of my dreams. A job that I never thought as really being a job at all, in truth.

One month.

Then days.

DAYS WHEN I wanted to do my job for Leinster.

But the decision to remove me had been made. I was still about the place, but my name was axed from the consciousness of the team management.

I wanted to make my exit. I wanted to go out in a big game, if possible, but I also knew that nobody ever gets to choose the day, the place, the opposition… the hour. Only Brian O'Driscoll got that, and as the greatest player in the history of the Irish game he could not be denied that.

But there was no perfectly timed exit for Ronan O'Gara, or many of the other legendary names that filled the Irish team sheet during the O'Driscoll era. I wanted a shot at one more game in Europe.

I wanted to play against Clermont.

Instead, I got to lead the team out onto the field against Glasgow in the Pro12. Actually, the folks in Leinster made a big song and dance about my last game, which I really appreciated. Everyone likes a fuss made of themselves at times. We're all human. A send off is something we all like, but it also helps us to draw a line under a long period in our lives. A really important line.

I got clapped.

My family was there to shed a tear with me. My son and daughter were in my arms out on the field. Kimberlee was waiting for me on the side of the pitch, with my Dad and my Mom.

All I felt was thankfulness as I wore the Leinster shirt for the last time.

THERE WAS STILL a couple of weeks training to be done, however. I was contracted to the end of June. Joe had put a phone call in for me and I was getting one last game with the Barbarians, a dream come true. Some of the lads in Leinster were travelling to Japan on tour with Ireland. There were fitness levels to be maintained. Additional bodies needed out on the field.

We raced out to the 22 metre line and back.

Three sets of ten.

I was gasping for breath. I raced back to the line the final time and it dawned on me that I had completed my final day as a rugby professional. My final run.

I spread my arms out wide on the end line.

I let out a great big roar.

The lads around me clapped and cheered. I shook each one of their hands, and I walked back to the dressing room. And I sat down.

If I was Superman I would have just been able to walk into a nearby telephone box and magically replace my business suit with my super hero costume.

Instead, I was taking off my costume.

And I had a new business suit to fit into.

PART ONE

ANDREW

CHAPTER 1

I NEVER KNEW that Andrew had left a letter.

Andrew was my kid brother, less than two years younger than me. I was born in 1979, Andrew in '81, but he wasn't my kid brother for long because Alistair came along in '83 and then Matthew in '85. My Mom, Patty had five kids under seven years of age. Kate was the last, my kid sister, born another two years later in 1987. There was just 18 months between Andrew and me, and we had always shared a bedroom, the same bed, because we didn't live in a house with a lot of bedrooms.

It was only in the last year or so that I learned of Andrew's letter.

It was a long time ago, 21 years, an October morning.

1997. A lifetime ago.

Andrew was 16. I was 17. His sudden, unexplained death came close to destroying the family we were. Or maybe it did destroy us, and we had to start again, building a new family. I believe it was the latter.

Andrew used my Dad's shotgun. He shot himself in the chest, on the landing, upstairs, after making up an excuse and not going to school that morning, to St Colman's in Fermoy. Andrew and myself were in the same classroom. I had done Transition Year, he hadn't. Myself, Matthew and Alistair were in school that morning and we were taken out of our classes, and driven home. The priests wouldn't tell us what had happened.

I told them I wanted to know.

They kept saying that there had been an accident on the farm.

I knew that something terrible had happened, and I needed to know. I kept pressing for an answer. Before we arrived at the house, they finally told us. There were two Garda cars outside the house.

MY MOTHER FOUND Andrew, and she was there on the landing, still holding him, when I walked up the stairs. She was absolutely distraught.

But she told me to come over to him.

Andrew's body was still warm, that I remember very clearly. And his lips were blue. So, so, blue.

There was blood everywhere, all around him, soaked into the carpet. My Mom was on her knees, holding him, cradling Andrew's head tightly against her. She had found him. It was in the middle of the morning, ten or eleven o'clock, and she had come in after driving us to Colman's and Kate to national school. We had missed the bus trying to persuade Andrew to go to school that Monday morning.

My Dad heard her screams.

My Mom was always a strong woman. She's American, from Illinois, a farming community in LaSalle County scattered around a little town called Tonica; less than a thousand people in the place, maybe 300 or 400 houses. We all got over there when we were kids, though usually it was one of us at a time. I went over with my Mom when I was four, and travelled on my own when I was 13 and got picked up in the airport in Chicago, O'Hare Airport, a giant metropolis in itself, by my grandmother. It was a cool trip. Six weeks with a big bunch of cousins I hardly knew before that summer. I'd run down to their houses and play Nintendo round the clock, or we'd head off on our bikes, but it was safe. It was real small town America, like a place we usually get to see in the movies. Everyone knew everyone and their kids, and they knew what everyone was doing, and if you wandered too far and hit the stream at the edge of town you'd be warned by someone not to venture any further, not beyond shouting distance.

We never took a family holiday together; we didn't have the money. We didn't go on a family holiday, the whole gang of us, not until I was 19 I think. We were too busy. It wasn't just about the money. My Dad farmed about 100 acres. There was always so much work to be done.

My Mom, Patricia, or just Patty, was 19 years old when she married my Dad and, like him, she came from a farming family. But, as I've already said, my Mom is strong, she's a real frontierswoman. She was on an agricultural exchange programme spending the summer in Cork when she met my Dad. They got engaged in October of 1978 and were married before they knew it, in the spring of 1979. I came along the end of the year.

Patricia Ryan was my Mom's name. The family were originally from Bruff in Limerick, but they moved to New York in 1843, just before the Famine cut through Ireland. They eventually settled in Illinois, and my Mom's father would serve in the US Navy during World War Two. She's a hard worker, my Mom, and she's also a fantastic cook. Ireland in the 1980s was a culture shock for her, of course, but in the kitchen she never lost the sense of who she was and where she had come from, and her cookies or her chocolate cake were the real things. They were the best treats I ever tasted, and whenever I went to a friend's house and ate anything with chocolate in it, I knew something had turned out all wrong.

My Mom never stooped to using baking or cooking chocolate, and she made sure to haul her own bags of milk chocolate from the States any chance she got.

She was introduced to my Dad by a mutual friend of theirs, John Kearney, who then orchestrated their first date by saying my Dad wanted to talk to her but he was too shy. Mom started the date by sitting into Dad's car. Conversation was sparse at first, but then she asked him, 'What's this I hear about you being shy?'

She thought he was a nervous Irish boy.

But anyone who knows Frank Ross knows that he has never been nervous one day in his life.

BUT ANDREW'S DEATH rocked my Dad, and as a father myself now I find it difficult to imagine how he got on with his life.

Andrew's passing, and how he died, had a profound effect on all of us. It was completely out of the blue. We suspected nothing. There were no signs, and I was closest to him. I spent more time with him than anyone else, day and night, and there was nothing wrong that I could see.

Why did he do it? Was it a spur of the moment decision? Madness? Did we fail him in some way? I will never know. None of us will ever know, but Andrew's death weighed down on my Dad heavily, and for a long time. Parents have to ask so many questions of themselves, I guess; questions that siblings eventually stop asking because we all leave our younger lives behind us.

We grow, and we move on to new chapters in our lives. And in my life, my brother Andrew was not in any of those chapters. As I remember Andrew's short life now I have to confess that I do not feel a deep sadness any longer.

Instead, his death is like a scar. It hurts now and then, but it's something I've come to accept. It's something I have got used to, I suppose. Years later, I would read a comment on a website from an elderly man about dealing with grief, and it has stuck with me ever since. It said:

'I wish I could say you get used to people dying. I never did. I don't want to. It tears a hole through me whenever somebody I love dies, no matter the circumstances. But I don't want it to "not matter." I don't want it to be something that just passes. My scars are a testament to the love and the relationship that I had for and with that person. And if the scar is deep, so was the love. So be it. Scars are a testament to life. Scars are a testament that I can love deeply and live deeply and be cut, or even gouged, and that I can heal and continue to live and continue to love. And the scar tissue is stronger than the original flesh ever was. Scars are a testament to life. Scars are only ugly to people who can't see.

'As for grief, you'll find it comes in waves. When the ship is first wrecked, you're drowning, with wreckage all around you. Everything floating around you reminds you of the beauty and the magnificence of the ship that was, and is no more. And all you can do is float. You find some piece of the wreckage and you hang on for a while. Maybe it's some physical thing. Maybe it's a happy memory or a photograph. Maybe it's a person who is also floating. For a while, all you can do is float. Stay alive.

'In the beginning, the waves are 100 feet tall and crash over you without mercy. They come 10 seconds apart and don't even give you time to catch your breath. All you can do is hang on and float. After a while, maybe weeks, maybe months, you'll find *the waves are still 100 feet tall, but they come further apart. When they come, they still crash all over you and wipe you out. But in between, you can breathe, you can function. You never know what's going to trigger the grief. It might be a song, a picture, a street intersection, the smell of a cup of coffee. It can be just about anything... and the wave comes crashing. But in between waves, there is life.*

'Somewhere down the line, and it's different for everybody, you find that the waves are only 80 feet tall. Or 50 feet tall. And while they still come, they come further apart. You can see them coming. An anniversary, a birthday, or Christmas, or landing at O'Hare. You can see it coming, for the most part, and prepare yourself. And when it washes over you, you know that somehow you will, again, come out the other side. Soaking wet, sputtering, still hanging on to some tiny piece of the wreckage, but you'll come out.

'Take it from an old guy. The waves never stop coming, and somehow you don't really want them to. But you learn that you'll survive them. And other waves will come. And you'll survive them too. If you're lucky, you'll have lots of scars from lots of loves. And lots of shipwrecks.'

That was what it was like at the start, endless waves that kept coming. As children we also needed to escape the pain, and the horror, of what had happened. That's natural. Children need to survive. And at that time there was so much pain. As a family, as a unit, we dealt with Andrew's death poorly.

It's different for parents. For my Dad, same as the rest of us, there was no counselling, no question of therapy being readily available. There was never any help for families struggling with a death by suicide in Ireland back in those days. Nowadays we have organisations doing fantastic work but in the 1980s and 90s, families were all alone. But I do remember that my Dad went to see a psychologist on one occasion, and the man advised my Dad that he should take up running.

I know exercise is good for the brain, and as a former professional athlete I would never dismiss the multiple benefits of working out, but my Dad was a farmer. He was out working hard and taking in fresh air every single day.

He did not need to buy himself a pair of running shoes to help him cope with Andrew's death.

WHY HAD I never been told about Andrew's letter?

I was talking to Mom about him one day, and I casually made mention of the fact that he had left us no note, no explanation, no goodbye.

And she said… 'That's not true!'

I was stunned, to be honest.

But, once I discovered that there was a letter I also knew that I needed to read it. My Mom gave it to me one day when I visited. She knew he would leave one, and took the house apart, mentally retracing the steps he would have taken and searching, searching… searching. She had found it a year later, balled up and thrown behind a wardrobe.

I sat down and read it.

It was tough going, both because of the content and the writing, clearly done while he was in an emotional state.

Andrew thought he was ugly. He thought he was stupid, even as the quality of the writing and the vocabulary he demonstrated in the note belied his words.

Andrew believed that life was not going to be good to him. Reading it made me want to go back in time, grab his misguided 16 year old self, and shake him for his foolishness. He had everything going for him. He was unbelievably smart, and strong, and quick-witted. How could he not see it? I asked my mother why didn't she ever tell me?

Mom said that she couldn't have at that time.

'When I saw that you all had begun to breathe again, adjust to the silence that rushed into the vacuum that Andrew had left, was I going to rip off the protective fragile cover and bring everyone back to live it all over?

'It wasn't time.

'I wouldn't. I tucked it into my wedding ring box… there would be a time but not now. It wasn't the content or the note, Michael.'

She knew that time is the greatest healer, and I guess she also instinctively felt that there would be a day when I would be equipped to deal with whatever Andrew had written.

ANDREW AND I had spent the summer before he died in France.

My Dad liked us to experience different working environments, and I had worked for a portion of one summer on a farm outside Belfast that was owned by a friend of his. But France was a whole bigger deal.

Andrew and I thought it would be one big adventure, the two of us, for the guts of two months, away from our folks and able to do what young men wish to do in a country far from home. I quickly discovered that there was a young French girl in the neighbouring village, close to the farm where I was staying, who was deserving of my attention, if only my handle of the language could improve fast enough.

I was in France, 17 years of age, and of course the moment I caught sight of her she looked the most beautiful girl I had ever seen.

We were working in the Champagne-Ardenne region, in the north-east of the country, where farms played a less distinguished role than the fancy vineyards that produced sparkling white wine and the prestigious houses dedicated to the finest of champagne.

Andrew and I were excited.

We were brothers and best friends, but we also constantly fought great testing battles with one another. When those battles were at their most furious we were also fully prepared to wipe one another off the face of the earth. Well, that's what brothers do, and that's how they think 10 times every day.

The thing about Andrew was, he was so damn clever.

Smarter than me, and he was also a better rugby player than me. It has crossed my mind if we might ever have played for Ireland together? Definitely, of the four boys in the family, Andrew had the most promise and I am not just saying that because he ended his life so tragically. He played in the centre in Fermoy, and he had speed, and his feet were a whole different pairing than mine. Andrew could turn on a sixpence. Plus, he was clever on the field.

I always thought that he was smarter than me, and that is not always a good thing for a younger brother. We fought like cats and dogs and, too often, I lost. Because I was bigger he knew that good planning was imperative on his side, and so when he locked me into the bathroom one evening he knew that I was at his mercy. The door opened in. So he knew I could not kick it down, no matter how fuelled my temper might become after an hour or so. I was not going to be responsible for taking the whole frame off the door, even if I could have managed that. Neither could I get out the upstairs window.

Andrew, all the time, remained on the other side of the door.

I can still hear him laughing.

He was always thinking of ways to get one up on me, and he knew full well that the drop down from the window was too far.

That was one occasion when, definitely, I was of the opinion that my brother deserved whatever was coming to him. Most nights, however, by the time we ended up in the same bed that we shared until we were 14 or 15 years old, there was nothing left between us that badly needed to be settled.

Andrew and I always had one another's backs.

If someone messed with either one of us, then they could expect to have the two elder Ross boys powering into them. Though I had more power on my side as we grew up, and he was never able for me if we got into a fight at close quarters. Since he was smarter, he usually avoided those quarters, though by the time we ended up in France together I noticed he was starting to fill out. Andrew Ross was not going to be a pushover, physically, when we got home.

That was a note written in my head that summer.

Shit… he's really getting some muscle on him.

That's what I was thinking.

But I'm still taller… for now!

However, I knew that my days of being able to physically dominate him were fast coming to an end. Though Andrew didn't know that, so he remained mischievous, fun loving, and of course really annoying to a 17 years old me, but like a lot of teenagers he was waiting to find his own voice, his own place in our family and in life. He would have had such a great life.

Who you are as a teenager and who you are as an adult are entirely different persons most often. I know that I am one hundred per cent different to the boy I was when I was 17 years old. There are physiological reasons for that. Teenagers, in most cases, are poor decision makers as parts of their brains are not fully developed, and that, folks, is why they end up doing so much stupid shit!

I should know.

But in France, Andrew and I got on with our lives, and handled things as best we could, and we also consulted with one another when we met up in a local town or some village and found a bar that had no hang-ups whatsoever about serving two Irish boys whatever choice of alcohol took their fancy.

Our Dad has done a lot of sales work for a French company, on a part-time basis, and he knew many French people. He felt that France would only be good for the pair of us, and when we drank together Andrew and I were not in disagreement. The two of us were in two different farms.

I had landed with a farmer, Joel Baty and his family who looked after me well. They were decent. Andrew did not have the same luck.

The family Andrew ended up living with treated him as farmhand and not as part of the family. They didn't put him up in the main house, but in an outbuilding. The farmer was also a bit of a bollocks according to Andrew. But we were in the country to learn something new about farming, and hard work, and also work on our French, and therefore our Dad believed that the upsides far outweighed the downsides.

I thoroughly enjoyed the two months, and still retain some of the French that I picked up. It was unnerving, of course, the first few days trying to talk to the family and the lads working on the farm, but quickly, very quickly indeed, I stopped asking myself... *Ahhhhhh Jesus... what have I done here?*

The following week things were better. And the week after that, I was not fluent, but I could actually have a chat with some of the locals without feeling a total idiot.

But Andrew was not happy from day one.

The farmer he was with was grumpy. Andrew did not want to stay with him. When we met up at the weekends he would pour out to me his unhappiness, but I felt helpless. We were living on farms that were 20 miles apart, but Andrew's French was twice as good as mine. He was upset, but I thought he'd be okay. Our parents also believed that he'd get through it, and in that first week when he asked them to bring him home they had no reason to believe that he would not grow and benefit from the whole experience.

We received room and board, and it never crossed our minds to ask for any money. It appeared to the pair of us that we were only doing the same work that we did around our own farm back at home in Ballyhooly. All the same, at the end of the week the family I was staying with gave me a few bob.

In the villages the locals quickly knew who we were, and Andrew and I enjoyed our Kronenbourg that was served in plastic cups. We also had our fair share of yellowy coloured glasses of Pastis, which appeared to be the local favourite, and went down well with two boys from north Cork, even if the anise and liquorice can be questionable after an hour or two. Luckily, the pair of us did not have all that much money in our pockets.

Andrew also stayed with me, with my French family, some weekends. He reminded me he was not having a good time. The farmer he was staying with had a strange accent and Andrew struggled to understand what he was telling him. My memory of everything Andrew told me is foggy, I have to confess, but I felt bad for him. I knew at the same time that his French was vastly superior to mine and that if I landed in the grumpy man's farmhouse I would have no chance of finding out what he was on about. I did not fancy swapping places.

He'd asked to come home. For the first couple of weeks he wanted to get back home to Ballyhooly. Eventually, after a month, Dad had him moved to another farm where he was treated better. The desire to come home disappeared. After that, things got better and we got back home in flying form.

I CRIED OFTEN in the days after Andrew died, but I have never cried since. I have never cried, full stop!

For a while, as a young man, you grow numb, and then faster than you ever expected your life speeds ahead. Now, I can't remember many of the conversations we had in the house, though I will never forget the devastation that wrapped itself around my parents, and remained in place, for so long.

Ten years?

A good 10 years, I think. My Mom remains teary, as all mothers are, on the birthday and anniversary of her son's death. My Dad would bring up Andrew for a long time to me, but it wasn't a subject I was eager to discuss.

My family struggled, and fought to remain alive.

We did not do well in that fight.

ME? I FOUND it hard too, but as a young man I did not realise why? I was playing rugby with Fermoy at the time, but it was not serious rugby. I was also sitting my Leaving Certificate the summer after Andrew died and it was then, and in the months leading up to the exams, that I struggled.

I found it incredibly hard to focus.

Before Andrew's death I was able to get lost in my books for hours and hours, but after, my concentration was completely floored. I did okay in my Leaving, but not as well as I knew I could have. In all honesty, I could not give a damn about it. I got 440 points in the end, but I should have done better,

I never looked back very often, but I guess the past kept creeping up on me. When I was 21, I went over to the United States for the summer, to Boston, and I ate myself to oblivion. It was 2001. I was a student, working, having fun, earning money, and eating and eating and eating. In college, in UCC where I did a general science entry to begin with, I had found it tough still to put my head into the books, but I got by because I do have some degree of natural smarts. I got second class honours in college.

It should have been first class.

I knew I should have got first class, no doubt about it, but it was easier to have the craic, leave the books till tomorrow evening. I came back from the States 20 kilos heavier than I had been on the plane on the way out. The suit I had brought out with me was no longer operable.

At the end of that summer, back training in UCC I could see lads looking at me and I did not know what they were thinking, but I could have guessed.

What the hell happened to him?

I always loved drinking Coca-Cola, but that love affair in the summer of 2001 in Boston went right through the stratosphere. I was getting refills and refills, and I was probably drinking two litres of Coke every day and that is 2,000 calories, right there, straight away. Before you count up what I was eating.

I was staying with a cousin of mine in the city and I was working in the furniture moving business, and that seemed to fuel my appetite for junk food and fizzy drinks even more. Pizzas, burgers of all descriptions, and Coke and more Coke, thank you, and goodnight!

I came back to Ireland weighting 144 kilos and that is 23 stones, in case you're wondering. And it took me a couple of years to get back down to a size that was correct for someone who wanted to make a serious rugby career for himself.

THERE REMAINED A circular pellet shaped outline in the wood panelling on the wall on the landing.

It was the shape of the gun blast that had poured through Andrew's body. I have no idea why that wall was not repaired. Perhaps my parents saw it as a reminder of Andrew's last act in this life. It could have been filled in, or else sanded down, but it remained, there, like a testament.

Not that any of us could ever forget.

The blood was cleaned up, and the carpet was lifted and changed, but why did my Mom never want that wall removed from her sight. Every time I walked by it I was brought back to that same morning.

And, the strangest thing about that morning was that after I spent a little while with my Mom and Andrew, as she held him tightly, I went to the room which Andrew and I shared and I changed into my working clothes. There was milking that had to be done, and there was a lad working for us who needed my help.

There was no way around that.

I changed, and I passed by Mom and Andrew as I walked towards the stairs, and I went outside and I worked for the next couple of hours, even though there were people gathering, even though the Garda cars remained parked outside.

THE PANELLING WAS eventually painted over, but the holes were never filled in. On the landing, therefore, Andrew remained with us.

But he also lived on in my dreams for so many years as I grew out of my teens and into adulthood. I would meet him there many times. And I'd spend a great deal of time yelling at him, though more recently when we meet in my dreams we are back at home, in Ballyhooly, and we end up having good chats together. I know they are good solid conversations even though I can never remember much about them the following morning.

Initially, when we met up in those dreams, I was filled with anger. And questions. *What the fuck were you thinking?*

The family through those years, when the rest of us were still living at home, had cosied up to formal religion. My Dad would be fairly religious, and in that I would not be like him at all. Every Sunday, however, the family went to service in Ballyhooly Church of Ireland. It's a small little church but beautifully fashioned out of cut stone, perched on a cliff over the River Blackwater.

It was what you did in the country. You went to church and you made charitable donations, and you met and greeted neighbours. If there was a manual for living a good, straight life then going to church every Sunday was one of the main tenets of that manual. Once I stepped outside of that life and that same community, I could see that attending Service was also a form of meditation. You know all of the words, and you sit there in the morning, in a quiet place and you're calm, and then you step outside and you talk to people you know, and everything seems quite good with the world. There is nothing wrong with that, even if I am not a religious man.

The village was packed for Andrew's funeral.

People were lined up on both sides of the street, and it was sort of crazy when I think back on it now because we had buried my grandmother, Caroline 11 days earlier. She was a teacher in the community, and well known and hugely respected and she also received a huge goodbye from our friends and neighbours.

Andrew and I had been together saying goodbye to our Gran.

THERE WAS NO question of my parents ever leaving that house. It was where they worked, and lived. It was a place of business, and also a home full of amazingly warm memories, and one horrific act.

My Mom and Dad still live there.

The pellet holes in the wall are still there too. I now understand, more than ever before, that my Mom and Dad can never leave the place where Andrew made his last act in his young life.

CHAPTER 2

MY GREAT GRANDFATHER, GEORGE left Carrigaline in 1926 where the Ross family had lived for generations, and he travelled the 40 miles north to buy a farm in the townland of Convamore, in Ballyhooly. He took ill and died when my grandfather, Michael Edward was just 16. He was the eldest, left to mind his early widowed mother and his seven siblings.

My father is Michael Francis, though everybody calls him Frank.

I'm Michael Robert.

My Dad was just 23 years old when I came along and although he was hard on me at times as his eldest son we've now got a relationship that is more like two brothers really. Mom and Dad are like two of my best friends. It's been like that for a long time, and we talk about everything.

Of course, all through my professional rugby career Dad was still telling me that I should be doing this and that I should be doing that. But that is just what he does. There was a time when I felt that he needed to calm down a little bit; maybe when he was trying to be too helpful and actually was proving no help at all, and in my early years he was always talking to coaches or alickadoos, or talking to team management. Usually about me.

I'd tell him that I wanted to fight my own battles.

He didn't listen.

On the flip side, I probably would not have become a professional rugby player if it was not for his persistence. He pushed me hard down that road, and there were days and whole seasons when I know that he had more belief in me than I had in myself.

Yes, he was a pushy father.

HIS OWN PLAYING career was one pitted with frustration. And, therefore, he felt that total, unwashed honesty, an honesty never varnished, was the best way to appraise my game.

I would go to him to hear the good, the bad, and the unpalatable, and as I began any conversation with him I always knew that he was prepared to tell me things that I might not wish to have told to me.

Frank Ross had attended Midleton College, where like me he was a front rower. He went for a Munster schools trial and won 10 or 11 against the head but did not hear anything more from the provincial selectors. Two guys he destroyed that day got in instead, because they were schooled at Christians. I can totally believe that; because that was how it was in Irish rugby for so long. This was in the 1960s, but over 20 years later when I was playing for UCC I managed to make the Irish under-20s squad. That made no difference to the Munster under-20 selectors, however, who did not give me a second look three months later.

Things are better in the game today.

That bullshit does not fly anymore. The politics and scratching of backs are over, and it's because of that that Irish teams are so good at every level.

Nobody stops the best making their way to the top anymore.

My Dad was a provider. He never changed a nappy in his life. However, I write that knowing it to be untrue – he changed a nappy on me once I am informed, but my Mom was looking over his shoulder and she saw him prick me with the pin because of his big old sausage fingers.

I yelled and yelled, and Frank Ross was off nappy duty for the rest of his life, though he never cared to thank me for helping him out.

He worked hard to provide for us. And he made us work hard when it was our turn on the farm, but he would also hug us, and he'd kiss us goodnight, but it was not like he would do that every night. It was very hard to get praise out of him, so when you got it, it was worth an awful lot more.

The four of us were always fighting, though that was before Andrew's death. It seemed like it was fight after fight after fight before that, but I believe there has not been one fight since, not a tiny quarrel even. Andrew leaving us brought an end to all that stupidity and to this day if I ever have a disagreement with my brothers, we talk.

Before Andrew's death, my Dad spent a great deal of his time with us on peacekeeping duties, though we would not care to wait for him to arrive. We'd run when we heard him coming. He had an old fashioned sense of discipline and luckily for us four boys, Kate came along at just about the right time.

Our kid sister softened him up.

THE FAMILY FARM was originally split down the middle between my grandfather and his brother, with a road running straight down the middle of it. My grandfather's half was then also split in half between my Dad and his brother, George. My uncle concentrated on tillage and agricultural contracting. My Dad did dairying.

We all did dairying.

As soon as any of us could walk we were outside, doing jobs. To begin with, that is a pain in the backside for young boys but, on the plus side, if you are carrying buckets of meal weighing 20 kilos around the place you are going to get big very quickly. I also think my Dad was the last man in Cork to graduate to those large round bales. We had the smaller square ones to get to grips with and, every summer, we must have carried a couple of thousand of those from here to there.

We had out-houses that needed to be mucked out every summer. After a long winter, the dung would be up to my knees.

It was hard work, and it was grim work. But, then again, the 1980s in Ireland were grim for most people. My Mom tells us that she would feed the whole lot of us off a fiver some weeks.

She had just five pounds for her shopping. She would get to supplement her groceries with whatever we were growing or whatever ducks or chickens she killed herself. Any heifer that found herself not in calf would disappear into the chest freezer too. Of course, as children, we didn't know the difference between a tight house and a house flush with money. We had everything we wanted. We were loved and we were fed well. We were worked hard, and we were allowed to run and chase and try our hands at every single sport that took our fancy.

Soccer and Gaelic football came first.

I was of the opinion that I was a better footballer, but most of my time down in Ballyhooly GAA club was spent in goals. I was a heavy kid. I took up a lot of space between the two goalposts.

When I was 11 years old, Dad took me to Fermoy rugby club, his old club, where he had propped and a fella named Dick Heaslip was his No.8. Jamie's Dad was in the army and had been stationed in Fermoy for a period of time. It's a funny little country of ours, when you think that their two sons would end up propping and wearing No.8 for Leinster and Ireland.

But, to begin with, the showers in Fermoy favoured cold more than hot. Usually they were freezing, but I loved it there from the start. All of a sudden I was not standing in one spot for an hour. I was running up the pitch with a ball under my arm and other kids were bouncing off me.

I was a big kid, and this was something I was good at.

I was a big kid, and this was something I was valued at.

Big was good.

Who would have thought?

CHAPTER 3

MY DAD DECIDED that it was time I turned pro.

Who else?

I was 26 years old, and I had no job.

I had no job and I was ready to get married. And I was more than ready to emigrate to the United States, because that's where Kimberlee was living. And she had a good job. Kim was a medical scientist, and she enjoyed her work at Hartford Hospital in Connecticut.

Emigration looked to be on the cards. Kim's Mom and Dad worked in hospitals all of their lives, and Kim grew up in hospitals. I wasn't working, but I had my American passport as well as my Irish passport thanks to my Mom.

It looked an easy choice to make.

It was 2006.

I left my job at the very beginning of the year. I got my chance of turning professional with Harlequins in the middle of the year. And we were married by the end of the year.

That's why I'll always love 2006.

WE WERE IN the Lough Field at home, myself and Dad, working on fences when the phone call came through from Dean Richards.

It was May of 2006.

He told me that the two trial games had gone well but that it didn't look like they'd be able to offer me anything.

Fuck,

And fuck, and fuck.

My Dad was looking at me.

It was he who had decided I needed to give it a shot, and it was he who got talking to Frank Cullen, and asked Leo's father what he should do about getting me an agent? Frank told Dad to give Justin Paige a call.

Neither of us knew that Justin Paige was Dean Richards' agent. Neither of us knew that Richards, who was taking Harlequins back up to the top flight in England, needed players and needed cheap players.

I was ready to be one of Richards' new men at any price.

I went over for my two trial games.

But Quins didn't see it happening for me and I think I started to beg Richards for a chance as we talked on the phone. Yeah, I'm pretty sure I begged him. For anything... three months... one month... ANYTHING!

'Just give me a chance!' I pleaded.

'Give me a shot!'

And that's what it boiled down to.

My Dad's stubborn streak.

Two trial games.

One call to my mobile in the Lough Field.

Dean Richards' decency.

Twenty-six years of age and I was about to become a professional rugby player. For three months.

What was the worst that could happen? I'd come home, I'd get married to Kim, and I'd emigrate to the States. What was there to worry about?

I KNEW I could scrummage.

I just didn't know what would happen once I was being paid to scrummage.

But, yes, I could scrummage, right from the very beginning when I first wore the green and yellow of Fermoy at 11 years of age.

I put on a stone for every year after that. I was getting the ball and I was bowling lads over. I was gassed after it, but at the same time I was good at it. All of it made sense to me from the very beginning.

In football and soccer, goals were not coming for me thick and fast.

But tries were, lots of them. My size was only a good thing. Coaches took an interest in me and they valued me, and Jerry O'Donoghue, who sadly passed away in 2012, was the first person who went out of his way to seriously give of his valuable time to me when I played on his under-12s and under-14s. Jerry wanted all of us to love the game. Winning and losing came after that, but we did pretty well for Jerry.

We wanted to win for him as much as ourselves.

We won the North Cork league and we were in the running for the county title. We lost. But Jerry cheered us up and told us we were great. I was so lucky with Jerry and all of the underage coaches I had. They gave of their time and their knowledge, and they could not give us enough, and there are still people like that working in every club in the land, helping kids, coaching kids, picking them up when they're crying. They are the real heroes of our game.

I wanted to play in every position.

And Jerry and the coaches in Fermoy let me play in the front row and the back row, and when I told them I had no interest in trying out being a hooker, they didn't ask me to think about it a little longer. There was no specialist coaching. It was all about the basics, and the purest enjoyment of the game.

Though I did find myself watching TV a lot more, watching the tighthead and the loosehead approach the scrum, watching where they planted their feet, watching their shoulders, watching and imitating… and watching and imitating. I see it in my own young fella today, in Kevin.

He can do Johnny Sexton's kicking style, and Jimmy Gopperth's and Ian Madigan's, he's watching as well all these years later. It's what kids do. Every kid who watches rugby in Ireland wants to be Johnny Sexton.

Except, when I was that kid, I wanted to be one of the fat guys in the front row.

THOUGH, THAT CHANGED for the smallest amount of time when I first walked into UCC. I thought to myself... *No.8?*

Why not?

I'm fast enough... faster than people think!

And... I'd like to see more of the ball... definitely.

Daylight would be nice!

For a change...

The summer before, when I was 18, I worked on a building site and a large amount of my time, amongst other things, was spent carrying fire doors up seven and eight flights of stairs, and then nine and ten flights of stairs.

Whoever thought fire doors would be so popular? But I finished the summer with a pair of really strong legs. I could take off down the pitch, and I knew I would be really explosive off the back of the scrum. Especially at junior level in Fermoy, I could move.

I was getting my fair share of tries, and some more.

I liked scoring tries.

I was playing junior two and junior three with Fermoy, and then I started in UCC in October. Next step was to reverse out of the front row.

Tell everyone I was all ready to start No.8.

I was in the dressing room, prepared for a swift reinvention and then John Madigan walks in. He was six feet and six inches tall, and he looked taller from where I was sitting.

What's more, he just happened to be wearing a jersey with No.8 on it... in case anyone was mistaken about the physical requirements of such an animal? And a question popped into my head... *Who's going to believe me?*

Who's going to say... 'Sure Mike, you're a little on the short side but... here's the jersey you want!'

I chose to delay my big announcement.

But in a matter of weeks as a prop I moved from minor B to minor A, to junior, and there was no stopping me. I was on the senior college team.

That was okay because we were busy winning, and in my first season in UCC we won the European Students Cup which was as good as you could get at the time. We beat Grenoble in Donnybrook, 14-10, and that same day at Lansdowne Road we got to walk onto the pitch at half-time as Ulster were also busy with French opposition and about to take the scalp of Colomiers in the Heineken Cup final. There were 49,000 people in the old stadium.

It was the last weekend in January, 1999, and I was in good company. Peter Stringer was out there on the pitch with me, and he'd been majestic in seeing to it that the whole team pulled itself together when it really mattered. We'd been 10-0 down and that looked like becoming 15-0 but they spilled the ball in a maul. Our coach, Peter Melia then saw all of his expert work present itself in glorious technicolour.

We ran at them like a French team. We passed like a French team. We bamboozled them with risky, adventurous moves, and our locks, John Fitzgerald and Mick O'Driscoll got to work like two seasoned veterans. Jerry Flannery shifted up the gears too like only he could. Colin Healy kicked a penalty to make it 3-10. We won a lineout in the right corner and bulldozed over their line. Niall Kenneally emerged with the ball and a try to his name. Our captain, Aidan O'Shea who had been on the bench at the start of the year because of a broken nose, dropped a goal to give us a 11-10 lead on the hour. Four minutes from the end Brian O'Mahony nailed down our win with a penalty from 30 metres out.

The college had lost in the semi-final to Toulouse the previous season, in the inaugural staging of the competition. Now we were top dogs. It felt great to be part of a winning pack. I had never won anything of real significance before. Life was good. The complaints department was seeing no business.

I was living in Cork too.

My own man. And part of a winning team! Life was definitely very good, and it was to be enjoyed. We did that on away trips especially, partying on buses and trains. Cans, sing-songs, shaving our heads, colouring our hair when it returned, and in between all of that learning in the scrum. Brian Hyland taught me so much. He was a former front rower and my first specialist coach.

Every year, I was getting better.

Bring it on.

ALLEN CLARKE WAS part of that Ulster team that conquered Europe in 1999. He was hooker, and the loosehead in that 21-6 victory was Justin

Fitzpatrick, who had made his debut for Ireland the year before and would win a further 25 caps. They both played for Dungannon in Division Two of the All-Ireland League.

We met them in The Mardyke.

They absolutely hosed us.

It was an afternoon of education.

I was totally taken apart.

And left an untidy mound on the field.

There was nothing I could do with Fitzpatrick, and nothing I could do about him. I tried, I really did. I remember collapsing a five metre scrum, and having a purple-faced Clarke screaming at me that I was going to get myself killed. Together, Clarke and Fitzpatrick helped me to fully understand that every single day I would have to learn something about being a tighthead.

Hero and zero were not all that far apart.

That I understood, and whether I was playing with UCC or not, I resolved that afternoon to never stop being a student of the scrum.

If that labelled me a nerd for life, fine.

I never stopped.

If people looked at me funny, or listened to me and threw their eyes up to the heavens, that was fine too, but I never stopped doing my homework on opponents, building up my data, sharing it around with my front row teammates. There was always something extra to discover and impart.

Down the road of my professional career, I was still at it, and a very young Cian Healy felt he had enough of me one afternoon, and finally interrupted me.

'MAN...' he exclaimed.

'Just push... HARDER!'

CHAPTER 4

SO, I WAS in my mid-twenties, and I was wearing a white coat, working in a laboratory in Clonmel, in Tipperary.

That was my life.

Unless I moved to United States for good with Kim, that was indeed destined to be me. Five days a week in a lab. Evenings and weekends on the pitch with Cork Constitution.

I had graduated from college with my degree in Plant and Microbial Biotechnology. It was something I reckoned would be interesting, possibly thrilling on the edges, but certainly worthwhile, especially Plant Biotechnology, which is a science that offers itself more to the developing world than those of us in western Europe.

I'll make this quick!

Over 800 million people do not have enough to eat, and 100 million children are deficient in vitamin A. Also, a total of 600 million people suffer from iodine deficiency. Biotechnology is aimed at helping to increase food production and alleviate hunger, and the technology uses genetic knowledge and scientific techniques to add specific traits to crops, like an ability to fend off pests, survive droughts, delay ripening or require less herbicide or pesticide. All, as I say, to aid farmers in developing countries especially, who need all the help they can get.

Microbial Biotechnology, on the other hand, is about the processing of products, by microorganisms associated with the food and dairy industry. Its chief aim is the prevention of the deterioration of processed foods. Technologists work in areas of research and development, implementation of processes and quality of the resulting products.

There!

Possibly, I was on a mission as a young man to go and save the world. Or maybe not, but the stuff interested me.

I was working for Enfer.

To begin with I spent nine months in Newbridge, in Kildare, at their BSE testing facility but when they opened a microbiology food testing lab in Clonmel I was shifted down there and closer to home. It meant I could live at home in Ballyhooly and drive the 45 minutes to work every day.

At the same time, that brought on its own challenges as I was now playing with Cork Con. In Newbridge I had debated switching to Carlow rugby club. The driving had been killing me. Newbridge to Cork, twice a week, for training. Staying overnight in Ballyhooly, and up early the next morning for work in Newbridge. It was exhausting.

Leaving work at 4.0 pm.

Getting to Cork for 6.30 pm.

Late into Ballyhooly.

Up again at 5.0 am to drive to work.

AND THEN I was jobless.

There were four of us in the lab. The work was repetitive and tedious, but the pay was okay. The money in my pocket balanced out the tedium to begin with. And then, it didn't.

I wasn't enjoying it.

I was thinking two words.

Career

And path!

I was soon asking myself if this was what I wanted to do for the rest of my life? The whole area still interested me, but being interested in something and actually working 40 hours per week in that area can be two different things entirely.

Lab work by its very nature is repetitive. You have the same processes. You need the same processes so that the results you get are accurate. There is never going to be a whole lot of variety mornings and afternoons. In the mornings we would get our samples in from abattoirs. Maybe 50 different samples.

Twenty five grams of each sample, and get to work on it.

Mince and steak and chicken.

And other foods for bacterial analysis, to see if the hygiene systems in the abattoirs were working satisfactorily.

Salmonella.

Listeria.

E Coli 0157, which is an E Coli that is highly dangerous and that can cause your kidneys to shut down. If you suspected something bad, then you headed to the Level Three lab with its extractor fans, and got suited up and hooded.

On the face of it, quite exciting. If you only had to work in the place for a day, or even one week. But I had to work weekends too, and I would get into work at 5.0 am those mornings so that I could also get myself back down to Cork for an AIL game in the afternoon.

I WAS BUSY with my amateur rugby career.

And I was soon to get married. Kim was texting me from the States quite regularly. She was planning everything. She had a lot to check with me.

Meanwhile, I felt I was running around in circles. Career and path… CAREER… AND PATH?

Before I knew it I was back on the farm in Ballyhooly.

Full-time.

THE GOOD THING was that I was left with more time for rugby.

More time to think about my life.

Listen to Dad

Talk with Kim.

Time on my hands also meant that I was able to train with Munster, whenever they gave me a shout and wanted me to make up the numbers when the International crew was away and they were short of bodies. I answered all their calls. There was no money in it for me, but the experience and the opportunity of visiting a professional environment was something I lapped up.

There was nothing else for me in Munster. Deccie Kidney chatted with me, and told me that he had nothing for me.

However, my short time with Munster gave me an insight to the pro game and it was invaluable, because when Harlequins brought me over I had some idea at least of what to expect. I also lined out with Munster in a couple of A games. I remember, precisely, getting the full kit, shorts and socks included, and putting the shorts and socks at the very bottom of my kit bag as soon as I got back into the dressing room.

Those shorts and socks were not coming back out of that bag.

IN THE FIRST week in April, I played in the inaugural AIB Cup final at Lansdowne Road. Con beat St Mary's 37-12. Cronan Healy scored four tries to stuff it to them. Their out-half was a young lad called Jonathan Sexton. He didn't get his name on the score-sheet.

That was on the Saturday.

On the Tuesday I had my first trial with Quins.

I did well. I carried the ball a few times, and I made bits of my man in the scrum. He was an underage international who had played for Gloucester in the Premiership. His name was Nick Wood. I'd meet up with him again on the pitch as he was a lifer with the West Country club and would play for them over 250 times. He'd also come within a nose of being capped by England the year after that first game, but after getting the nod for a tour game in Bloemfontein he had to pull out through illness.

I had flown over to London knowing nothing.

Nothing about Wood or anyone else playing for Gloucester, and nothing about my teammates that evening. All I knew was that the game was at Imber

Court, a ground out Wimbledon direction. I spent the afternoon at one of the houses they rented for their players. I spent the afternoon shitting myself.

Ignorance equals strength?

Whoever decided that simple equation had never met me, someone who needs all the information he can possibly cram between his ears, who eats his data, who does not at all mind being classified as a scrum nerd.

I was playing against strangers.

I was with strangers

But I survived. I also found out a lot about myself by facing up to the pressure, and I destroyed Wood. So of course they wanted a second look at me.

They had to make sure that it had not been a once-off.

CHAPTER 5

I'M NOT GOING to be shy about saying this, but there was absolutely no doubt that I was one of the very best scrummagers in the All-Ireland League.

But the professional game is a whole different place to be.

It's post-amateur, post-apocalypse if you like.

It's a place where you can feel amazingly well loved. It's a place where you can feel utter desolation and find yourself totally alone.

It's every man for himself. Every single man is suited up and prepared. Nobody comes unprepared. Everyone wants to survive, and everyone is armed. Physically, mentally, there's nothing left to chance.

There's nothing easy.

Ever.

I UNDERSTOOD THAT my rugby education was brief. Maybe even primitive. It's something that dogged me throughout my career. When I landed in UCC lads were calling moves and I had absolutely had no idea what they were shouting out. When I got to Harlequins my teammates had gym ages of eight and nine and 10, whereas my gym age was more like... one or two?

At the start of the serious business in college I barely knew what a 'SWITCH' was, and when they shouted 'UNDERS' or 'OVERS' I was completely lost to begin with.

I'd hear a roar.

And I'd think… *What… the fuck!*

I'd played with Fermoy and it was a good grounding in the game, but the finer arts of the game were beyond me. When I left Fermoy I was bumping into and playing against lads who had been through the rugby school system. I felt behind the curve. I knew I was an outsider. A lot of my teammates at UCC would have gone to Christians or Pres, and they would have been through Munster Schools, and some of them had graduated to Irish Schools.

I'd missed out on all of that more serious education.

It's hard to break into a tight knit group who have a bond, or who share a certain knowledge. You have to earn your stripes in front of them.

At first it seemed I was forever catching up on the finer arts, but I got there eventually.

As for the dark arts?

I got there faster.

I had no choice.

There were far too many grizzly bears in the wood.

THE FOUR YEARS with Con were amazing.

I had joined up with them even though I had another year left at UCC. The level of coaching was superb in Con. Christy Cantillon backed me from my first week with the club and he led the way for me. He was a legend. He could play either side of the scrum in his time, but was blindside in Munster's epic victory over the All Blacks and scored the try that might just be the most famous try ever scored in this country. David Corkery came along later, and I learned a huge amount from him. Corks took an interest and I remember him flogging me after training with extra fitness sessions, for my own good of course.

There were so many good people in the club.

Ian Murray, so strong, had first given me my pilot's wings during my college days when we bumped into another, when he picked me up and tossed me out of his way just as quickly.

There was Ian and his brother, Des.

Ultan O'Callaghan, Donnacha's brother, at No.8.

The incomparable Frankie Sheahan.

We had professionals amongst us on a regular basis. Ronan O'Gara would be with us now and again, if he was coming back from an injury.

Constitution became my home.

But it was also time to move on, even though I've repeatedly discovered that I always find it hard to leave a team. I was happy at UCC. I was even happier at Con. I loved Harlequins, and leaving London and coming to Leinster was heartbreaking.

Sounds sort of soft putting it like that, but it's true, it's entirely accurate. It was the toughest decision I ever had to make in my rugby career. I loved London. But if I stayed in London I had no chance of making it onto the Irish team.

I had to come back home and enter the unknown at Leinster.

HARLEQUINS WANTED THAT second look.

Two weeks after the Gloucester game I was back in the same grounds, in south-west London and it went just as well for a second time. We played London-Irish. Any feedback I got in the dressing room was positive, but I wasn't sure. They said I did well. At the same time I knew that nobody was going to walk up to me and tell me I'd been shit.

I got the plane home that evening.

And I waited.

And Deano called.

It was after 2.0 pm, getting onto 2.30 pm.

He gave me the bad news

Then he stalled and I pleaded, and he said… 'Three months!' There would be no full-time contract. A three-months trial was on the table.

I did not know very much about him at that time. He was old school, that was obvious enough in how he carried himself and how he conducted his business, but I had no trouble becoming one of his biggest fans. I knew he'd played for England back in his day, and that he'd been a policeman at the height of his career. That experience remained a significant portion of his character because he was always prepared to work with people, give us a chance; rough diamonds, forgotten diamonds, overweight diamonds. If he saw something in somebody, he was prepared to work on it.

He was willing to work with me.

I wasn't alone. Harlequins had bounced back into the Premiership after the embarrassment of relegation. The club was not flush. Deano had to bring value for money, and he felt I would bring that to Quins if I made it through the next three months.

He took in Olly Kohn.

Olly came in the same year as me. He'd spent the first seven years of his senior rugby career between Bristol and Plymouth, and it wasn't quite happening for him because of a knee injury in particular. Olly and I would become the best of friends, along with Jim Evans who also lived nearby. Every day, we'd drive to training together – we dubbed ourselves the Twickenham Tripod. I loved that drive, there was a lot of slagging, and also arguments over whose turn it was to pay for the coffees. Olly usually ended up getting his wallet out.

Twenty stone Kohn.

That's what we called him, and he earned that full title because he was simply massive. Deano loved big men. He loved Olly, who would spend another seven years with Harlequins and make 140 appearances for the club. Olly, although born in England, also managed to get one international cap before it ended thanks to a grandfather who was reared in the Rhymney Valley, coming on as a replacement for Wales against Ireland in the opening game in the Six Nations at the Millennium Stadium in 2013.

Olly came onto the field in the 73rd minute as Wales were on their way to a 30-22 defeat. I'd left the field five minutes earlier.

However, neither of us might have been anywhere near Cardiff that day if it was not for the belief, faith and charity of Dean Richards.

PART TWO

BLOODGATE

CHAPTER 6

I WAS AT the end of my third season with Harlequins.

That famous jersey had made me.

Sky blue.

Brown.

Red.

And grey.

The Quins' jersey, quartered with those four colours, and around the place for over 150 years, was one of the most famous jerseys in the world; more defining than any other jersey in the game, with the possible exception of the All Blacks. It was on my back.

And it was my second skin.

London was my home. Harlequins my club. Dean Richards my taciturn mentor, whom I would go through a brick wall for.

It was 2009.

April 12, a Sunday, and we had come a long way as a team in three fast years. We were playing Leinster in the quarter-final of the Heineken Cup at The Stoop. Our ground… my ground. We expected to win.

When I had joined in 2006 we were coming back into the Premiership. Harlequins had dropped out of the top flight but immediately returned and we finished the 2006-07 season in seventh place in the Premiership, winning 12 out of our 22 games. The next season, we finished sixth; again 12 wins from 22. In 2008-09 we ended up in second place behind Leicester. We were three points behind the Tigers after winning 14 games to their total of 15.

In my first season in London we had played in the Challenge Cup and failed to make the knockout stages. In my second season we were bottom of our pool in the Heineken Cup, winning one of our six games, but in 2008-09 we had topped our pool, winning five out of six games in the company of Stade Francais, Ulster and Saracens. We did not believe Leinster could come to The Stoop and stop us.

I did not think it could happen. We were sitting in second place on the Premiership table for a bloody good reason, having lost just one of our last 10 matches.

I knew us, and I thought I knew Leinster.

I knew more about Leinster than anyone else in the club. I was joining Leinster the following season. Michael Cheika had come over to London to meet me.

The Leinster scrum needed me.

CHEIKA WAS WAITING for me in an All Bar One pub in the centre of London, about six or seven weeks before the Heineken Cup quarter-final.

Before the game that would be christened 'Bloodgate.'

The most infamous game in the history of the tournament.

I found Cheika very sound. Convincing. We chatted for over an hour over coffees. He liked his coffees. He said Leinster needed me. They needed more 'quality'... that was the word I remember him using. He was saying everything I wanted to hear from a rival coach.

But, in truth, the conversation was a year too early for me.

I loved London, and after season two with Harlequins I thought that I would stay with the club until the end of my professional career. I absolutely loved everything about the club and the city.

It was so different to back in Ireland.

What people do not fully realise is that when you are playing with Leinster you have your family and all of your old mates around you all of the time. In London it was different. Most of the Harlequins players had come to the city from different parts of Britain. I had come over from Cork. And, very quickly, what happens is that all of your best friends, and the people you live with and socialise with, are your teammates. It is completely different to Leinster or Munster.

If you went out to get something to eat, you usually met up with someone from the club. If you decided to go to the cinema, it was with one of the guys from Quins. If you are in Leinster you'll often meet up with a family member or an old school friend. In Quins, your teammates were all you had.

I loved the lifestyle in London.

I was a professional rugby player, finally! I was living in a nice part of the city. I had disposable income. I was newly married. Kim and I had no kids, so life was easy. It was all fun and the minimum of responsibility. For me especially, having worked in a laboratory just 12 months earlier, in a white coat, I was living a wild and impossible dream.

I was no longer working. I was doing something I loved doing, and I was being paid good money *not to work!* Honestly, every now and then in training I would stop... and look around the place.

And I would take those few seconds... to appreciate the change in my life.

I felt lucky.

Being a professional rugby player is not working.

It was never work for me.

I had, unlike nearly all of the lads in Harlequins and Leinster, a taste of the real world. I knew what it was like to have to work for 40 hours every week.

The alternative was something I had experienced. But, now, I was on a rugby pitch in the middle of the 'working week' for the rest of the whole damned world. It was sunny, and even if it wasn't sunny I was a grown man and I was spending my day throwing a ball around with my friends. That understanding was something that never left me, not when I returned to Ireland and started playing with Leinster, and not when I made it through to the Ireland team and became a first choice for Declan Kidney and Joe Schmidt.

I always understood one thing... *this is not going to last forever!*

But, to begin with, Harlequins seemed the life.

I was never happier.

THE IRFU, UNOFFICIALLY, did not need the trouble of selecting players who were playing abroad. If you were Johnny Sexton, the trouble was well worth it. If you were not Johnny, then you had no chance of winning a green shirt once you remained out of the country.

The English Union pays its clubs to release players. In Ireland it is different, and the IRFU have it nailed down that players will be automatically released for national duty.

So, why would English clubs want to play ball with Ireland?

The IRFU did not need the angst or the cost.

I had done a few Churchill Cups with Ireland while I was playing in London. I had my Ireland A caps. And I wanted to make the next step up. And I knew that I was running out of time, as my 30th birthday was right around the corner. And Michael Cheika had his happy, cordial, understanding Michael Cheika mask on.

But I did not want to come home

Though I was curious.

Why, for starters, would Leinster want me?

I asked him straight up.

Where is the room for me in this equation? You have CJ and Stan, they're great props… CJ van der Linde was one of the strongest men I had ever met in my life and Stan Wright, when he was fit, offered the team a bigger package than I did at that stage. Stan was a Cook Islander. He had hands, feet, and he could move around the park. I was a better scrummager than Stan, but CJ?

Nah!

That was the truth of it in the spring of 2009, and no matter how polite and convincing Cheika was, there was no getting away from that fact.

Why?

Do… you… want…

Me?

CJ's big toe was damaged, and that toe is critical to any prop. Stan too was susceptible to injuries.

I still had to repeat the question... *why do you want me?*

WHEN CJ WAS coming back from injury, which was quite often in the latter stages of his career, Chris Dennis, the Leinster conditioning coach at that time spent more time with him than anyone else.

Chris was Dr Frankenstein.

CJ was the monster.

It looked to me that Chris was doing things with CJ that he did not do with anyone else. He'd have him doing these massive circuits, none of which made any sense to me, but CJ would say absolutely nothing. CJ would just do it, and do another, and never open his mouth.

We were all looking.

Thinking... *what the hell is he doing with CJ now?* The man was a freak by nature. A nice, happy-go-lucky, grand lad but a man with power that was inhuman. He could explode, but normally he chose to soak up punishment. He would be calm and placid, and taking it all, and then some absolute fool would piss him off. I would be watching this and thinking as I looked at the opposing prop... *don't do it... don't waken him you fucking idiot!*

The fool would be launched into Row Z before I could complete that thought in my head. That was CJ van der Linde. He was a bear that you should never poke. When I played against him in games against South Africa, believe me, I never... ever, ever, ever poked the bear.

He was scrummaging on one leg in some games in which Cheika picked him, and he was able to get the job done.

Stan?

He was a man who could perform on the pitch, and was loved by everybody off it. I enjoyed his company too. He was a joker. Nobody would ever try to compete against Stan in the dressing room, because he had that room in the palm of his hand.

I've no idea whether the story told before, that Stan barbecued and ate Toby, his own dog, rather than have the animal taken from him by the authorities back home is true, but Stan did not need such a story in order to be the centre of attention every single day.

CJ and Stan?

Where would you even start in thinking of competing with the pair of them? Besides, my job with Harlequins was very different to what Leinster expected from either CJ or Stan.

I was not a liability in open field, but with Quins there were ball carriers, and I was not one of them. We worked a pod system with two or three carriers, and I was never one of them. I was not supposed to carry the ball at all. I cleaned out the rucks. If a ball did come to me and landed in my arms, then that meant that something had gone completely wrong in the great plan.

My role was locking the scrum, getting my lineout lifts just right, cleaning out the rucks and cleaning them out properly, and if I did all of that then Dean Richards and everyone else was happy with me.

CHEIKA HAD SAT down with me in February of 2009. Kim and I had bought our first house in London three months before.

I told Kim that I was not going to accept the Leinster offer. We were staying in London for one more year and then, hopefully, we would return home and I would do everything in my power to get on the Irish team. The offer from Leinster was good. And I did not even ask Harlequins to match it.

I tried to make it easy for Quins. I asked for just a little bit more. Just a smidge of an increase and I'll stay, I assured them. But Deano said no. I was on 130 grand sterling with Quins.

'Just give me 150 grand!' I said.

Deano was having none of it.

It was like he wanted me to go back to Ireland. I could not understand it. He liked me. He started me in every single game practically, and he wanted to get the full 80 minutes out of me most days. I had never let him down.

'Let's do this, ok?'

The big man was not for moving.

Dean Richards was a big, strong, stubborn, giant of a man, and he was no city slicker. When he said no, he meant it. He was straight, and true to his word. And Harlequins knew that he was just the man to harden the club up and make them one of the powerhouses, once again, in the English game.

Quins was a very established, very British club.

And the club had a bit of a hoity-toity reputation. Other teams in Britain thought they could sniff that about Quins, but they were wrong. Of course, being in London, there were many occasions when the club would merge and indulge itself with the posh city experience. One of my first experiences as a Cork lad in London was spending a day on a rugby pitch with a gang of insurance lawyers from Norton Rose.

They were swapping their suits for jerseys, for one day, and seeking to bond with one another. And we were there to coach and encourage them. All of us spending our afternoon drinking beer and the occasional glass of champagne in the seven acres of private gardens owned by the Honourable Artillery Company, a few minutes walk from Moorgate and Old Street tube stations, the HAC's magnificent Georgian home staring down on us all.

But that was only one day in the life of Harlequins rugby club. Most days were raw and hard. There were a few posh accents around the place, but the owners of those voices were hard as nails. Deano was from the north-east. The stereotype of 'city slickers' was as misleading as the label of 'lady boys' that Leinster were in the business of shedding.

Quins had turned a corner and toughened up long before I came along. The club had been shaped in the 70s by the likes of the lorry-driving Claxton brothers, all three of them, and a Cornish farmer by the name of Stack Stevens. In the 80s and 90s the club's glory days were built around Dick Best, a chef. They had a London chippie in Jason Leonard and a Geordie in Mike Skinner. They also had the amazing Yorkshire combination of Peter Winterbottom and Brian Moore.

Quins, therefore, had no trouble whatsoever opening their arms to a young fella from Ballyhooly in Cork, and I felt at home there from day one. There was no settling in period, no awkwardness whatsoever. I was called 'PADDY' and I was called 'SPUD', occasionally, but never when I messed up. Only for banter, and in return I was always encouraged to trade any insult I could find in my bag.

I always made sure that my bag was full to the brim.

Every single day.

Have I told you how much I loved Harlequins, and how much I felt totally at home there?

And how we expected to smash Leinster at The Stoop?

AND I EXPECTED to remain a Harlequins player.

Win or lose in the quarter-final against Leinster.

I had told Deano that I was good value for 150 grand. I told him I was only looking for another fifteen per cent on my present salary. It pissed me off, to be honest, that he would not move.

I felt that I was good value for that money, considering the number of minutes I had given him over the past three seasons. Admittedly, he had taken a chance on me to begin with, and he had developed me, but I had given three full years to Quins and during that period of time they had paid a fraction of the amount other clubs had paid for a player of my ability.

How much was Castrogiovanni getting with Leicester?

I was not sure, but I knew it was probably twice as much as I was getting from Quins. The bottom line in all negotiations is that you are only worth however much you are needed. I've seen lads hung up on negotiations all the time... *I'm worth more... I'M WORTH MORE THAN THAT!* ... but I always remind them that you are only worth whatever someone is offering you at a given moment in time.

If the market says you are worth X and only X, then that's your worth.

X.

CHAPTER 7

BLOODGATE?

THINKING BACK on it all these years later, I understand better than ever that it never needed to happen.

The only reason Bloodgate happened was that Quins felt a desperate need in the final minutes against Leinster in that quarter-final to get their favoured kicker back onto the field. We were losing 6-5.

It was all about one kick, possibly.

Nick Evans, our out-half, got injured and there was a panic to get him back onto the field before the very end of the game. Nick was new to the club, having joined that season, and he was a very stylish, accomplished player. He had come up through the ranks in New Zealand and had scored over 100 points in 16 appearances for the All Blacks. He was 28 years old when he came to Quins.

Chris Malone had replaced Evans.

Chris came on in the 47th minute, but he was gone in the 69th minute after pulling his hamstring. Tom Williams, our third choice out-half, came onto the field.

Chris was a Sydney boy. He had come over to England in his early twenties, and had been with Exeter Chiefs and Bath before briefly playing for us. He made 11 appearances and then moved onto London-Irish at the end of the 2008-09 season.

The thing is, we had options!

We could have brought in Andy Gomarsall late in the game, and moved Andy Care to No.10. Care was starting into his England career that would result in over 80 caps and he was a decent little drop-goal slotter.

What I'm saying is that we had choices.

Quins did not need to trigger hell upon earth, and suffer consequences that rattled on for years.

We should have done that – brought in Gomarsall, and moved Care – rather than go to all the trouble and mischief of bringing Nick Evans back into the game.

Nick missed the kick anyway.

He had the chance of winning us the game, but the leg was falling off him. Maybe Dean Richards thought that we needed Nick to make absolutely sure, and it is true Nick was a better bet to slot over a precious kick. Nick Evans was a great kicker. On his day he was irrepressible, and he could slot them over from anywhere on the park, and in his decade with Quins he would end up kicking 2,249 points in over 200 appearances.

One of his greatest kicks for Quins – and certainly one of his ugliest, in his own words – had come four months earlier when we had seen off Stade Francais in the most dramatic of circumstances, after 83 minutes and 57 seconds had been played at The Stoop in the middle of December. We were one-try each and losing 16-17, and had one last possession.

Looking back now, this memory had a death-hold on everybody in the club, Deano included, when the opportunity arrived to snatch victory from Leinster.

'Wondrous... WONDROUS!' Our chief executive, Mark Evans was shouting in the minutes after the game against Stade. The kick had only been from 25 yards, and Nick had the wind at his back, and the ball still wobbled over the bar. It was so awful looking that even Nigel Owens had his doubts and asked for a television replay before he could award us the points.

Twenty-nine phases of play, spanning nearly five minutes, had preceded the kick. Twice, Nick pulled out of taking his shot from further out. The conditions were truly shocking. The Stoop's car parks were flooded, and the pitch had needed a long inspection from Owens.

In that closing sequence of play we'd gone backwards a few times but, as a pack, we knew we needed to give Nick every chance and we kept plugging away. At last Nick gave Danny Care the signal and Danny whipped the ball back to him.

It was an epic ending.

But, also, as I've just said, it was a memory that became a death-hold and was directly responsible for Bloodgate.

NICK EVANS WAS visibly limping, his right knee clearly troubling him, when he pulled his drop-goal a few metres wide.

At the time, Michael Cheika had come charging down the steps from where he was sitting and started into officials on the sideline. He was shouting.

'I didn't see any blood... I DIDN'T SEE ANY BLOOD!'

After the game Cheika would complain that Leinster's doc, Arthur Tanner had not been allowed to check on the state of fitness of Tom Williams.

It was Tom who had gone off the field in order to allow Nick Evans back on. And it was Tom who, later on camera, would be caught winking at the Quins' dugout as he made his exit.

It was Tom who had bitten down on the blood capsule offered to him by our physio, Steph Brennan. It was Steph who had bought the capsule in a joke shop in Clapham. Steph was a good, decent guy, and he had just been given the head job with England before the whole debacle.

I liked Steph.

I also liked out team doctor, Wendy Chapman.

She was a lovely woman, but she was placed in an impossible position. When Tom Williams had bitten down on the blood capsule given to him by Steph Brennan, and understood that trouble was brewing, he told Wendy to cut him.

She was put in a position that should never have arisen.

None of us know how we will react in a pressurised situation, not until we find ourselves in the centre of the whole pile of shit. Wendy was a good doc. She looked after us. Same as Steph looked after us on the physio table. Doctors and physios are always there for us, and they make sure to pull out all the stops to get us into the next game. They are people whom every rugby player feels he owes, and would willingly run across hot coals for at any time.

They look after us.

They listen to us, talk us down when we foolishly want to play, and help us to move earth when we tell them we HAVE TO play in the next game.

They are also there to save us from ourselves often enough.

People like Steph and Wendy are heroes in every rugby club.

TOM WILLIAMS WAS the fall guy in Bloodgate.

Tom was a good player. Quick, agile, he could do things with the ball. Some people have never spoken to Tom since, because of the whole fall-out of Bloodgate.

In the end, Tom said what he had to say about the whole thing.

Four months after the game, I was a Leinster player in pre-season as I picked up my paper and read Williams' testimony to a General Medical Council hearing in Manchester. He explained that he became 'very panicky' when he heard Leinster guys shouting at him and at Nigel Owens, the referee.

'IT'S FAKE…

'IT'S NOT REAL!'

Williams then admitted that he asked Wendy, at least twice, to cut his lip. She finally did so with a stitch cutter. But Williams also told the hearing that Wendy had nothing to do with the little plot.

'As I was being brought on, Dean Richards was saying… "You're coming off for blood!" Later on I was given a blood capsule and instructed to bite down on it.'

That's what Williams admitted.

And it was a good thing that enough people spoke up and explained what happened that day in The Stoop. Because cheating in that manner had become normalised in the English game. It was all quite common.

Not in every game. But gamesmanship, any loophole to be exploited, was feasted upon if necessary. Professional sports people will always push the rules as far as they can push them in order to get things done.

In order to win!

A week or so after the game, all of us in the Quins' dressing room were hearing more about what had occurred. We knew there was a problem, but we were thinking... what is this shit?

We had lost our biggest game of the season.

Leinster had won, and they were through to a semi-final against Munster, and they had not been cheated out of anything in the end. They won.

Why on earth are they so angry... still?

We could not understand that.

But, I guess, when wrong behaviour becomes normalised that is how it is, and that is a natural reaction. Quins had cheated and failed to win the game, but so many in the club were asking... *what's biting Leinster?*

Why aren't they letting it go?

Weeks passed, and months and, finally, I believe everyone in Harlequins came to fully understand the absolute importance of what had played out. Everyone in Quins understood that what had happened was wrong.

It was cheating.

It should not be tolerated, and should not happen again.

I STILL BELIEVE it was a game we should have won.

It was a game of inches. Felipe Contepomi kicked a penalty for Leinster after 13 minutes, and a second in first half injury time. It was well into the second half when we struck back. Mike Brown crossed on the right. But he missed with his conversion which would have been priceless. A little later, a 51-yard penalty was also outside his range. Evans had failed with a kick closer in before leaving the field. Care also failed with a drop-goal. The clock was down to its last 37 seconds when Nick Evans took his kick at goal.

Deano tried his best to spin it immediately after the game, and quieten down Leinster's noise. 'You have to know the rules,' he emphasised.

'If you don't know them, that is not my problem. Nick came off, it was a tactical substitution and the rules are clear that, in the event of a blood injury, the player who had come off for tactical reasons can go back on.'

But his words did not wash.

Less than a week after the game the ERC officially launched their investigation and began gathering statements from match officials and players on both sides. Three months later Williams was handed a 12-month ban at an ERC hearing, and it looked as though Deano had got away with it. The hearing also cleared Steph and Wendy of any wrongdoing. But Bloodgate was far from over, and the truth had still to come out. Nobody was entirely happy.

At the beginning of August, Deano quit Harlequins, and the club made an unreserved apology to Quins' supporters for the shame that was brought down upon everyone. Within a week, Deano was banned for three years from the game.

Steph was banned for two years, and Williams' ban was reduced from 12 months to four for his help in disclosing the entire deception. Harlequins were fined £258,000. Wendy was reprimanded by the General Medical Council.

Deano, of course, came clean on his entire role and was greatly apologetic. He admitted to being 'mortified' by his own actions at the time, but in an interview with *The Guardian* newspaper some years later he also tried to put the whole sorry charade into a suitable context. 'I remember my kids looking at the newspaper coverage around me, and it wasn't easy,' he admitted in the interview.

But then he explained that a friend brought his attention to newspaper coverage in general at that time, and the fact that Bloodgate reached its end point in the same week that the Lockerbie bomber (Abdelbaset al-Megrahi) was released from jail. Pan Am flight 103 – which has been labelled the Lockerbie bombing – exploded over the village of Lockerbie in Scotland a few days before Christmas Day in 1988. Everyone on board was killed, 259 people, and 11 people on the ground.

'I was able to get through it from the moment someone said to me, "Do you realise that you've had more front page coverage than this guy (al-Megrahi) despite the fact that he killed all those people? What a strange world we live in?"'

Deano said that this conversation finally allowed him some perspective on what had happened on that fated day against Leinster.

And I think that is fair.

He should be allowed that. He made a stupid mistake, and he paid a seriously big price for it. But nobody died.

CHAPTER 8

THAT QUARTER-FINAL against Leinster was only my fifth time to play a team from home in my three years at Quins. It was an especially important game to me. I wasn't in the shop window, because I had been to Dublin by now and completed my medical, and I knew that I would be in Leinster's blue the following season.

I met with Doc Tanner for a few hours, in his clinic in Charlemont. It was my day off, and I flew over and back the same day. Word was trickling back into the Quins' dressing room that I was off to Leinster but everyone knew that my loyalty remained with Quins to the very end of the season.

I wanted to walk into the Leinster dressing room with a Heineken Cup medal in my back pocket. Nobody in Quins doubted me for one second.

It was no good to me Leinster winning the Heineken Cup in 2009.

As Doc Tanner discovered, I was in good shape for Leinster.

Although I had fronted up for Quins for three full seasons, I'd been lucky with injuries. Deano liked to play me for as long as possible in most games, in my second year playing me for the full 80 for 18 consecutive matches. Only in my first season in England did I end up crocked for a full month.

We were playing Leicester down there in their place, in Welford Road, and I seemed to jar my neck. It was painful, and in the next scrum I felt massive bursts of pins and needles down my right shoulder. I hung in there… and hung in.

By half time I was in agony but I did not want to come off the pitch. I held on for 73 minutes. But, I could not even think anymore. We only had a loosehead on the bench and we were playing the Tigers who had a fantastic pack. I went in for one more scrum and Shane Jennings, who was playing for Leicester at the time, saw that I was in trouble.

'HE'S… FUCKED!

'LADS… HE'S FUCKED!'

True, I was in bits by then.

I could only look at Jennings. Speech was out of the question entirely. After, they took me down to the medical room and put me on the laughing gas. They also gave me drugs for the weekend, and told me that my shoulder would settle down.

It never did.

By Saturday evening, I had gone through the whole bottle of tablets. I'd munched through them like a man who had not eaten in days. I'd taken a chunk of ibuprofen to try and get some rest. Tramadol was a complete waste of time… lasting from four hours, to two hours… to half an hour. I joked afterwards with the lads that I was nearly in the car to Kingston to pick up some alternative relief, but it was only half a joke! I never experienced pain like it since.

I was early into my career with Harlequins, and I had no idea that I could get a club doctor to see me on a Saturday evening. It was like someone had a knife, and that person had slowly pushed it deep between the bones in my forearm. And… every 10 minutes the same person was turning the knife… clockwise… anti-clockwise! I could not eat anything. Sleep was totally out of the question.

I was weak with the pain. Within a week I had lost five kilos, but when I had told people in the club about my predicament on the Monday they looked at me and asked why I hadn't phoned for their doctor? As it turned out, I'd inflamed the brachial plexus, and it eventually settled down after a visit to an acupuncturist of all things. I'm usually highly sceptical of such matters, but I was desperate, and he came recommended by a friend back home. He stuck a needle in here and another there and, suddenly, it was like turning off a tap. I've never forgotten it, even if it baffled the scientist in me massively.

MY FUTURE WITH Leinster was secured before the game, but I still wanted to prove a point.

In my first season in England we'd been in the same group as Connacht in the Challenge Cup. We'd beaten them by a point in The Sportsground and had a 16 points win when they came over to The Stoop, but we were just inched out of the knockout stages of the tournament.

We didn't win a game in the Heineken Cup the following season, but we topped our group to qualify for the quarter-final against Leinster. We had five tries and a penalty try against Ulster at home, and then went to Ravenhill where, as soon as we arrived at the ground Ugo Monye looked up at the sky and announced that he had a spasm in his back. Ugo had a sixth sense about certain things.

We all nearly froze to death on the field. They won 21-10. We hardly cared by the very end. There was torrential rain, and a howling gale which hit 75-miles per hour – they had to evacuate the Yellow Tom Stand because it threatened to blow away. Will Skinner won the toss for us, and we decided to play into the whole shooting gallery of natural elements while we were still fresh.

We ran crash balls up the middle the whole game. We had Epi Taione playing for us, an absolutely massive man who could play in the backrow or the centre. We put Epi at first receiver and had him run straight and hard. There was no point trying to do anything else. We also stomped all over their scrum from start to finish, which I enjoyed of course, but the rest of the game was miserable and completely forgettable.

When Romain Poite sounded his whistle at the very end we all belted for the dressing room, and most of us didn't even take our kits off before hitting the warmth of the showers. The only man we left behind was our captain.

I can still see Will Skinner sitting there, wrapped in one of those foil survival blankets, shrieking with the pain of the coldness.

AGAINST LEINSTER, I had a rare opportunity to show Irish rugby people, and hopefully Deccie Kidney, what they were all missing.

Leinster were not playing all that well. They were up and down. In their group they had walloped Castres in the RDS by 30 points but, six days later, they were turned over by the same team and Cheika had one of his growling evenings. In comparison, we had true form.

Plus, and it may appear foolish to state this now, but we looked down our noses at the Celtic League. Everyone in England thought the Premiership was the be-all and end-all, and the Irish, and the Welsh and the Scots, could have their fun playing one another, but the Celtic League was second rate.

That was the belief in the heads of all our guys in Quins.

I knew some of the Leinster guys. I had roomed with Johnny Sexton and a few of them during Churchill Cup camps. I'd been to a couple of Irish camps, but I didn't know Brian O'Driscoll or the bigger-named Leinster players. I didn't know the lads in their front row, though we believed that Cian Healy would be a good opportunity for us.

He was great around the park, but we believed Cian was still learning his trade in the scrum and we aimed to give him a lesson he would never forget. He was a kid. A strong kid admittedly, but I felt I would take him to school. Scrummaging was probably incidental to him at that stage too. He just wanted the ball. He knew he was spectacular with the ball in hand. Unstoppable. A runaway train.

When I first got to know him and we started to build up a serious friendship, he told me he started lifting weights in sixth class in primary school, which meant that he was 10 years ahead of me in that department.

It wasn't just Cian. We felt that we could get properly stuck into their pack, because they had not been tested like we had been tested, week in and week out, up and down the length of England. Cian and Bernard Jackman and Stan Wright? Tailor-made for us, in our humble opinion.

The first scrum told me that Healy was a strong little bull.

But I knew he would be strong. I expected that, and I also knew how to deal with him. He was leaving space for me to go into. He was trying to go around me and he was letting me bury myself into Jackman.

We had them in trouble from that first scrum.

I knew we would.

I had Gary Botha beside me, and Ceri Jones on the opposite side. Ceri had joined Quins on loan from Newport in 2003 and stayed eight seasons.

He was one of my best friends. He won two caps for Wales in 2009, but he should have won far more. They brought him in as tighthead on their tour of Australia and, while he could play both sides, it was unfair to judge him only on the tight side. It was not his best position. Gethin Jenkins was in his way, but I always believed Ceri should have got more caps than he did. He was a fantastic scrummager, and I knew he would be a handful for Stan Wright. He was also decent around the park.

Gary Botha had been in the South African squad for the 2007 World Cup win and he was a brutally tough man. He never took a prisoner in his life. If he wanted to punch someone, he would tap me on the shoulder.

I'd let go of my bind and Gary would unleash one.

He had a hair-trigger on him. I'd get the tap... and he'd let another one go. Big things and little things might lead to that tap. The tighthead might have dived into Gary's ribs one time too many. Or the other hooker may have given him some lip at the end of the previous scrum.

Tap, tap... tap.

I was in the best of company that day against Leinster. Behind me, I had Percy... James Percival. He was one of Deano's projects, just like me. In the front row, we were always fighting over Percy or Olly Kohn. I always wanted one or the other behind me. Olly, of course, was a mountain of a man, nearly 140 kilos, and he called himself ... believe it or not... The Armchair.

'Come and sit in the armchair, my friend!' he'd tell me, '... and have no worries! Just sit there... nice and comfortable.

'You okay there... Rossy?'

I had no worries facing anybody in the world with Olly behind me. Percy was not quite the same, he wasn't as powerful a scrummager as Olly, but at the same time I was always confident when he was behind me too. Jim Evans was there too of course, a hugely athletic man who was very comfortable in the wide open spaces. In the back row we had Chris Robshaw, Skinner and Nick Easter, and Easter had a rugby brain that was almost a match for Leo Cullen's.

Easter was one of the most intelligent players I ever played with, and he always took the right option. He always knew when to carry, when to pass, and he was always in the right place at the right time.

We had an outstanding pack, and we were ready to fight.

It was a fight we lost.

THE SCRUM WAS the only facet of the game where we got a handle on Leinster that whole afternoon. In the lineout, for instance, they absolutely cleaned us out of it and we resorted to throwing into George Robson at the front of the line. They had done their homework. Leo Cullen had carved us up long before the game had ever begun, as only Leo can, but Mal O'Kelly and Rocky Elsom were unbeatable aswell.

We could do nothing about it.

And then, the one little move we had up our sleeve for three-quarters of the game blew up in our faces. We had no doubt the move would work. More than that, it would turn the game around and make them think.

We were going to make it work.

Get a score, and leave Leinster on their arses after all of their hard grafting. It was simple. We were going to draw them back and make just a sufficient amount of room for a break in the middle of the lineout. Danny Care was going to breeze through.

Easy.

Candy from a baby!

And, next thing, Rocky Elsom had the ball.

It was like Elsom had been with us in our team meetings all week, and through the morning of the game, hearing every single thing we had to say. Instead of us being under their sticks, Rocky was running straight up the pitch with our ball. Our... FUCKING BALL.

We had fought like there was no tomorrow to get that lineout and get into position to tear Leinster's heart out of its chest.

It was our turn.

But Elsom had taken everything in the lineout all afternoon long... and now he had just taken the one ball that we felt was the most precious ball of the whole game.

We were shocked by what had come before that lineout.

After that lineout, we felt sickened.

Devastated. Worse, we were emotionally drained, and none of us knew whether we could wipe away that sense of devastation.

The swing moment in the game had slapped us hard in the face.

CHAPTER 9

WE HAD IT all in our pack, we thought.

But we didn't have a Leo.

Leo Cullen is lineout obsessed. He'll go through everything and then go through everything a second time, and he will have a very fixed thought on anything that might present itself in the line and, at any time, which throw will be made in every position on the field.

It's all there in Leo's head.

He'll know where the other team have been throwing the ball in their last three games, five games, and he'll keep looking and logging information until he knows that he has the opposing lineout sussed.

Leinster wiped Harlequins in the lineout that afternoon in The Stoop. We were on top of them in the scrum but, unfortunately, there were an awful lot more lineouts in the game than scrums.

IT WAS ONE of the most physical games I ever played in.

We all felt broken after it.

There was so much close quarters stuff, so much banging into one another... last ditch defence, and us pounding away at their line.

Cheika gave most of the Leinster guys the following weekend off. He knew they needed to restore themselves, but Deano took his first choice 15 up to Sale one week later and I ended up getting tossed around by Andrew Sheridan.

I was shattered, physically and emotionally, after the defeat to Leinster and the last thing I needed was Andrew Sheridan. He was the nemesis of tightheads in England and all over the world during his career.

Sheridan was beyond me.

He was the only opponent who forced me to admit to that.

Incredibly, his career only included 40 Test caps for England and two for the Lions, as Big Ted had to retire at 34 years of age after four operations on his shoulders. He finished his career in Toulon which was handy, as he was studying to turn his love of wine into his future career. But he had spent nine seasons at Sale before all that, and I discovered the very first time that I scrummed down against him that he was someone who was not the same strain of mankind as the rest of us.

Stories of his prowess in the gym are legendary. He had a deadlift personal best of 700 pounds, and qualified judges stated that if he had switched to weighlifting as a career he would have been a dead cert for an Olympic medal. Not many people in Sale or Toulon wanted to train with him. There was no point. What's the fun, ultimately, in standing back and watching a man do parallel bar dips with 130 pounds tied around his waist? Or applauding him for doing chin-ups with 22 pounds added on for good measure?

For me, for someone who was a mere two year old in the gym in comparison to most of the men I met in England when I first moved over, Sheridan was super-human. All my angles, all my timing, all my footwork and tricks of the trade were usually ineffective, two out of every three times I faced him.

He was the undisputed strongman of the game.

I did not want to see him too often. Every time, I had to get it exactly right against him, and I had to be lucky every time. He never had to be lucky! I had to try and win all of the advantages, in every scrum.

Otherwise?

If he was planted? If he was tucked under me, and anyway comfortable? It was like having a monster settled beneath my body. I had my good days against him in the end, but that was often because the referees did not like what he was doing rather then me actually dominating Big Ted.

On pure technique, I was his equal.

On absolute bullish strength, he was too much.

AFTER BLOODGATE, I didn't talk for very long with anyone from Leinster. There was no need to say anything to Cheika. He had seen from up close what I was made of and, therefore, he must have known he had made the right decision to sign me. I had ticked that particular box during the afternoon.

But, the defeat hurt. I joined the rest of the Quins' players and had a quick bite in the cordoned off area in the ground, and then I went straight home. I still believed Leinster were lucky to get past us.

I thought they would be in even bigger trouble against Munster in Croke Park, but of course I was wrong. They had played 'backs to the wall' in The Stoop and that defiance which characterised their performance more than anything else gave them a huge shot of self-belief as a team. That, and the sudden, unexpected appearance of the magical Johnny Sexton in that same semi-final against Munster after Felipe Contepomi had been taken from the field.

Johnny and a barrel of self-belief was all Leinster required.

By the time I joined them they were Heineken Cup champions, and also there were plenty of questions from my new teammates about the whole damned Bloodgate business.

However, there was not much I could tell them all. That defeat at The Stoop had been like a death in the family, and the shenanigans that followed for months and months was never going to titillate anyone associated with Harlequins RFC. In Quins, through the remaining weeks of the season that ended with another surprising and dispiriting semi-final loss to London-Irish in the semi-final of the Premiership, we did not go there in our conversations.

The men getting questioned and hauled over the coals, and being hurt, were all my friends. Williams was a perfectly good, normal working professional. And Deano? Dean Richards was my hero, and I was shocked and upset for him.

What happened to Deano was warranted. He should have been made an example of, but, three years? It's a long time to exclude a man from his livelihood. And Steph Brennan? Two years?

It was not like they all woke up that morning determined that they were going to do something wrong and bring the game into disrepute.

FIVE YEARS LATER I would be back at The Stoop. It was strange playing again in the old ground. I hadn't run out onto the pitch since the semi-final defeat by London-Irish in the Premiership, and thankfully there was a good cheer from the home supporters when my name was called out.

For Quins, it was an evening that consigned Bloodgate to history, finally. We met in Pool Two of the old Heineken Cup, now titled the Champions Cup. They won 24-18. Quins were now… *they!*

Even a 'flashback' early injury to Nick Evans, who was still doing his business in the famous jersey, did not invite the humiliation of that afternoon in 2009 to make a cameo appearance. There were still many of my old teammates at work in The Stoop – Brown, Evans, Care, Robson, Robshaw and Easter, and also about that evening was Joe Marler, who had been a young buck and wannabe legend with the club when I was in their ranks.

Easter was 36 years old and Robshaw was playing his 200th game for the club against Leinster, and the pair of them were magnificent that evening. Easter scored the opening try of the game after 53 minutes. The deciding moment in the game came later, when Rob Kearney's short pass to Zane Kirchner was snaffled by Quins' Fijian wing, Aseli Tikoirotuma who made 80 metres up the field before touching down.

Danny Care's left-footed drop-goal left us for dead.

Danny, who would have been eminently capable of hitting a similar drop-goal five years before if he was asked, and which would have seen to it that Bloodgate never became a password for cheating in the proud game.

That evening, however, Bloodgate was far from my thoughts – by the end of the game revenge on Joe Marler was front and centre. I was looking forward to seeing him in the Aviva Stadium a week later. Marler had been very chirpy. He had pissed me off royally.

We'd had a fair battle in the scrum, though the newspaper reporters deemed him a convincing victor. I felt that was harsh. Reporters and referees are very often wrong and act in concert together to give a joined-up explanation, when in fact the pair of them regularly second-guess what just happened in the scrum.

They thought Marler had stuffed me.

On the balance of things, he'd edged me yes, but it wasn't like the media were making out.

There are excellent referees in the game, of course. I got to know Nigel Owens pretty well, and he was exceptional in the manner in which he interacted with the game. Owens, obviously, knew his stuff. And I think he liked refereeing Leinster and Ireland, because he understood that we entered the game with the intent to be legal scrummagers. Unless we were provoked, there was nothing dodgy up our sleeves. We also knew what Nigel Owens wanted from us.

Owens wanted a straight, long bind. That was his single focus, and anytime I was playing I would make sure to show him that. I might have taken the scrum down in the end, but I would have made damn sure my arms stayed up.

'Can't be me Nigel… look, I have my arm right here!'

Even though I might have just dropped my chest down!

And we could talk to Owens. I'd no trouble explaining to him that I dropped my arm down onto the ground to save myself from an injury. He did not want to see any of us land on our necks. Across the front row of an international scrum there is two tonnes of pressure. Every man has to channel that, which averages 600 kilos per man. We carry that pressure on our shoulders, but we are looking to channel it fast. However, there are five really fit and strong guys pushing as hard as they possibly can behind us, and behind the opposing front row there are another five hardy bulls doing the exact same thing.

Referees are watching this up close. They know they have a ringside view of something amazing, almost freaky, and very dangerous.

There are some referees I could always talk with, and with Owens I always knew that I could chat with him and explain myself before he made his decision. Wayne Barnes would chat as well. The lawyer in Barnesy was open to more information before making his decision. Roman Poite?

Nothing.

Poite did not want to talk, full stop.

'Yes Sir... No Sir... three bags full Sir... and Sorry Sir!'

IT HAD BEEN great to go back to The Stoop, until Joe Marler decided to start chatting to me.

Quins are a special club. They never forget their own, and once you have played for them they will always remember and receive you fondly. There is quality and a depth to the club. You are always... a Harlequin! And I had so many people come up to me before and after the game, telling me it was great to see me back.

I had not played well.

During the game Joe had too much to say for himself.

I had worked my arse off in the game to keep our scrum up. I hadn't played well, but neither had I played badly. Their tighthead, Will Collier who would make his England debut a couple of years later, was getting between Jack McGrath and Sean Cronin, and the scrum was piling over on top of me. As a result, Marler was enjoying himself.

But, most of the time we were getting fractured by Collier. We started getting ratty with each other in the front row. I was shouting at Sean... 'Nugget... YOU GOTTA KEEP HIM OUT!

'KEEP HIM... TO FUCK OUT!'

It was Ronan O'Gara who had first christened Sean Cronin 'Nugget' and like many Rog witticisms, it stuck on Sean, unfortunately.

Collier kept getting in between Jack and Sean, and if the tighthead comes between the hooker and the loosehead it is game over. Collier was getting in there repeatedly and I should have started coming across to counteract what he was doing, so part of it was on me.

The French referee, Jerome Garces singled me out the most though and the team paid for it.

It pissed me off. Though, afterwards, I told myself that I had not played well and that I was over-thinking my whole performance. Coming *home* to Quins was a much bigger deal than I had imagined it to be, and it hit me when I walked onto the field for the warm-up. Marler, in particular, left me in a rage.

When I was wearing the Quins' jersey Marler was in the academy and he was always asking myself and Ceri Jones questions. I gave him plenty of my time. He did not have the war-like hair and the full-on tattoos at that stage. He was no showman, though I knew enough about Marler to fully accept that when he gets on top of an opponent 'the chat' usually starts up pretty quickly.

'Rossy... HOW'S IT GOING?'

He was into that too early with me.

We'd be about to bind and he'd start again... 'HOW'S THE FAMILY, MATE?' He was trying to make it out to everyone, both packs, and Monsieur Garces, that he was having it so easy that he had time for a chinwag.

I said nothing back to him.

But, I was thinking... *You fucking b*****!*

I could not wait for the following week. I could not get out of the ground fast enough and get back to Dublin fast enough, in order to lie in wait for him.

I was ready to talk back to him in Dublin.

I wanted to cheap shot him, and come in with no arms, and see if he would come up with the same brainless shit that had resulted in him being banned repeatedly. Looking back now, this is precisely what he was aiming for but I couldn't help myself.

Joe has all of the physical gifts any prop would have on his Christmas and birthday wish lists and, whenever I met up with him after games, he was decent and personable. But he can be his own worst enemy, and he's fallen victim to the red mist plenty of times himself.

The second game went better, we squeaked home in the end. I did get an opportunity to put a shot in on Joe, after a turnover, and we had some words on the floor. That was about the size of it though, but it wasn't to be the last time we locked horns.

CHAPTER
10

MY THREE YEARS with Quins were at an end.

As I've said, I didn't want to leave when I did. Dean Richards and myself were both on our way, as it happened, within months of one another. He'd put his faith in me and given me a huge opportunity in life. He wasn't a man who'd bring you into his office and have long chats. Deano was a big figure who did not have to say very much to players in order for them to deliver for him.

He is a good man, and Bloodgate did not alter my opinion of him by even the tiniest fraction. It was not a question of Deano being found out by what happened. The entire game in England was *found out!*

Nearly everyone was at it. Harlequins were the only team who wouldn't think of nicking one of their own players with a blade, using the joke shop instead. It was seen as a method of getting another player onto the pitch. It was not right, and it was cheating, but nearly every team was doing it and, what's more, everyone knew that nearly every team was doing it.

A blade, or some cotton wool that would be dyed a bit red and placed up to a player's nose! Was it cheating? Yes. But was it the ruination of the game? No, it was not, and the truth is that it did not have very much impact on games.

People in the game knew that, and they decided to live with it... until Bloodgate.

THE THREE YEARS had flown by. Right from the off they just *took off*, as I landed in Mike Worsley's house in Twickenham with my suitcase to begin my initial three months trial contract. Ugo Monye was there too, and the pair of us would head off to training together to Quins' base in Roehampton.

It was a hectic three months in my life.

I was over with Quins for July, August and September and ready to impress. And I was also getting married in August, right in the middle of the biggest opportunity of my rugby career. Kimberlee's understanding was amazing. I took one week off from training and we got married and spent a three-day honeymoon in Newport, Rhode Island, before I travelled back to London alone. We had a proper honeymoon the following June in St Lucia.

Kim and I decided there was no point in her giving up her job and joining me, not unless I was offered a permanent contract from Quins. No contract, and I would be back in the States and starting the rest of my life with Kim there. A solid contract, and Kim was coming over to me.

Those three months were incredibly tough.

I was about 134 kilos when I landed into training with Quins in July, and I was down to 118 kilos when the three months were up. It was my first time to do a serious, professional pre-season. Over the next couple of years I eventually settled in or about 125 kilos.

I loved it, even though I was wrecked most of the time, and I suffered from a lot of soreness the first couple of weeks. That was not a good thing at all. We had Phil Richards in charge of strength and conditioning. He was a former PT instructor in the British Army and was one of the first full-time conditioning coaches in the game. He is now a legend in his business.

He was one of the very best. He had all of these low carb and high protein diets and, for some people like me, it can literally strip the weight off your body. Richards was also into 'leopard crawling' which meant that you were down on your belly and crawling the length of the pitch using only yours arms for propulsion.

On dry, sandy pitches it was a recipe to leave knees, arms and elbows skinless in no time. The sheets of the bed would be sticking to so many parts of my body. But everyone was crawling, backs and forwards, fatties and skinnies.

MY FIRST GAME in the famous Quins' shirt was over in France, where we played Bourgoin and Clermont in warm-up games. There was no shallow end in the professional game, not even during pre-season.

I know this guy... I told myself before the Bourgoin game.

Where the hell do I know him from?

Fuck!

AHHHHHH.... FUUUCCKKKKK!

As I got closer to him I saw that it might be... it was...

... definitely... Milloud!

Oliver Milloud, the first choice French loosehead. He'd been to World Cups. He'd a truckload of French caps. Milloud was one of the best in the whole game. And me? I was a professional for what... *six weeks, or was it seven by now?*

He caught me a couple of times.

But I got him in one scrum too. We each popped one another up and drove the other man backwards. On paper, it should have been a no-contest, but I survived. He was not the biggest guy I would ever meet on a pitch, but he was stocky, explosive and extremely powerful, a bit like a prototype Cian Healy. There was not a word between the two of us the whole game.

We shook hands at the end of it, and left it at that.

It was like my career was fitted into an hourglass, and the sand was slipping away. There were only a couple of weeks left.

I still had no idea where I stood, and next thing we had our first Premiership game of the season. London-Irish. In Twickenham.

Twickenham, for chrissakes!

I was in the squad.

I was on the bench!

Quins had three tightheads. Ricky Nebbett, Lorne Ward, and myself.

Nebs had a cap or two for England. Lorne was a huge South African. I was on the bench in front of Lorne. That surprised me. I knew they were better scrummagers than me, and they also had the jump on me in their conditioning. I was squatting 140 kilos and benching 120, and the pair of them would have been up around the 200 kilos mark. It was a substantial difference.

But, rather than worry about what was going on in Deano's head, I decided to enjoy every minute of it in case it was all about to end and Deano was not going to turn the hourglass over and give me a longer contract. I tried not to be a starry-eyed kid walking around Twickers, but I failed completely to carry off that one. I was mesmerised once I sat down in the huge dressing rooms.

I was sent in midway through the second half.

Nobody killed me, which was a nice surprise. We lost. And then we lost to Wasps, and third game into the new season Deano started me.

There was still no shallow end.

We played Leicester, and luckily the game was in The Stoop and not at their place. My first start and I did not have to take a second glance to confirm the name of my opponent.

Castrogiovanni... Martin Castrogiovanni... *YEP!*

The full walking and talking legend, who had the cut of a maniac with all that hair covering half of his face. After losing the first two games, Deano wished to mix things up. He must have believed that I would not disgrace myself.

I didn't.

Though we lost once again. Loosehead was not Castro's natural position, but loose or tight he liked to chat away to his opposite number. He liked to warn that it was going to be a long day for you. Nothing too original, though I found in my time with him that when Castro's early prediction looked like going off course he usually decided to leave the pitch.

If he wasn't happy, then he wasn't chatting anymore. When Ireland played Italy and things were going south for them, Castro had a habit of getting out of Dodge fast, with 20 or 30 minutes still left on the clock. If Italy were flying, he'd stick about. But, that first day against him I wasn't quite able to work him out.

He is a big strong man, and awkward in how he applies himself in the scrum. I made an early decision in my own head.

I'm not going backwards…

If I had to go up, I went up.

I went sideways if I needed to.

I did not care where I went, in truth, but… *I'm not going fucking backwards!*

I hit the floor a few times in order to keep that promise to myself. He was giving me a lot of crap and I was taking it. I knew I was in the classroom, and that I had to pay attention.

I'M GOING DOWN…

I quickly discovered, even in the professional game, that the best referees have no idea half the time what has happened in the scrum when it collapses.

Good… good… I told myself, as I got away with a couple of dives.

I'M NOT… GOING… BACK!

It was not that the referees were completely clueless. But in those days of maximum impact in the scrum, when we'd launch at one another, it took only the tiniest thing to go wrong with the engagement and the scrum was instantly destabilised.

TIME TO GO DOWN… AGAIN!

Castro tucked himself in quite tight to his hooker aswell. He left me with only half of the space I needed. He also tried lots of old tricks, like getting his head across and wedging it under my chin. Castro had been a tighthead for long enough in the past. He knew what tightheads disliked the most. With less room I had little or no chance to get my shoulders down, and through. I was bent into position.

And with a rounded back, I was not going to be able to transmit all the power I had mustered.

Castro had a big book of tricks.

Finally, the lesson ended.

I was quite pleased with myself.

Very pleased, but another two weeks passed.

I think I had good instincts, even at that early stage. I could always recognise whenever I was in trouble, something a lot of props struggle to understand when a scrum is about to devour you. A really good prop will sense something. He'll figure out that it's not right, and he'll bail out before he gets the blame.

That's often what I look for in a young promising prop now – does he know when he's in trouble? Tadhg Furlong had no problem recognising trouble. He might not always be able to do something about it, but he knows! You'll see him resorting to Plan X. We all know in the first couple of seconds of engagement how it is going to go. You can see which guy is going to be taken to the cleaners. He might be a little bit high, or something... and BOOMMMMMM!

It happens.

Maybe he hasn't quite got his foot planted in the ground, and you can see his opponent smelling blood and gathering himself for the kill. There's no way you are going to get control of your opponent, not if he has taken control of you first. First two or three seconds... it's very hard to get it back once you've lost the initiative. Once that momentum builds on one side?

There's no reversing out of big trouble.

MY THREE MONTHS was long up, and I was still waiting for a contract that might give me some idea of my immediate future.

Kim was still in the States.

Waiting for me, or waiting to come to London?

Deano, finally, gave me the remainder of the season.

It was another short contract, but my agent told me that was good. The following year I signed another one-year contract, and before I knew it my three years with Quins had finished. My education was complete long before then. I had been to every single rugby ground in England worth visiting, and a handful that were dreadful places that I hoped I would never see again.

I was nearly 30 years of age.

I had quickly discovered that the value of a prop can sky rocket very quickly, and it is smart to take it one year at a time. I've since offered this advice to many young players who are looking to settle into a club long term.

'Cool it,' I tell them, '... stay calm. There's no big hurry!'

One good season and a young lad can go from a value of 50 grand to 100 grand or well beyond that figure. Why sign a contract and be valued at 50 grand for two years? Wait, and sign that second contract for 200 grand!

'There's... NO RUSH...

'ONE YEAR MIGHT BE BETTER THAN TWO!'

I LEFT LONDON in the early summer of 2009 ready to immediately announce myself to the Irish rugby public, though it didn't quite happen like that, of course.

Michael Cheika ended up pressing pause...

And I was left to reflect for 12 months on the teams and the grounds I had left behind.

THE RECREATION GROUND.

Beautiful, amazing Bath. The most beautiful place in the whole of England in which to play a game of rugby, though the pitch could be hit and miss and, invariably, in the middle of winter it was an absolute mudbath. I went back there to meet them in Heineken Cup battles with Leinster, usually around Christmas time. It remained magical. It's a classic place, and I don't believe anything gets past planners that is not honey-coloured stone.

One Christmas, Kim also came over and the evening before the game the pair of us went for a stroll through the town and found a Christmas market. It was lovely while it lasted, but it was not my cleverest move because, next day, that tight, sticky pitch awaited, with the crowd encroaching and, as always, the Bath pack was bruising. The beauty and the charm of the place does not materialise on the pitch. Bath were always a typical West Country pack.

Think, Beauty and the Beast, and do not be fooled for one minute that you are there for recreation of any kind.

BRISTOL, WHEN I was over there, had a Dad's Army of a pack but they were still fully intent on spending the entire 80 minutes trying to beat the shit out of you. Mark Regan was 34, 35... Darren Crompton who made his comeback for England at 34... Dave Hilton who was older than the pair of them… if you were caught on the wrong side of a ruck in the Memorial Ground, no God could help you.

I NEVER MINDED the shed in Kingsholm Stadium. It was where the hard-core, cider-swilling farmers and Gloucester supporters stood and roared abuse at us. And good for them! I always loved it, but then I'm from north Cork! They were real salt-of-the-earth people. It's called the shed, because that's what it is. It's where I'd love to watch any rugby game.

NO OTHER GROUND in England offered a full physical examination, at no cost other than possibly ruining your reputation, like Welford Road. It's the ultimate bear pit, and given a choice of spending a Saturday or Sunday afternoon there, or somewhere like war-torn Afghanistan or Syria, I'd choose to turn up at the airport most times. Leicester is not the most cosmopolitan of cities. Its people are not soft. And its rugby team do everything in their power to perfectly mirror the city and its people but, as I say, if you want a free examination of your worth as a rugby player, play the Tigers. You'll know everything at the end of the day.

LONDON-IRISH AND the Madejski Stadium wasn't a weekend off, but it was the next best thing. They broke Quins' hearts in my three years but they never did it with venom. The surface of the ground was nice and immaculate, as a football ground should be, and there was never any need for danger signs to be dotted around the perimeter of the pitch, not like in Welford Road or the Memorial Ground.

I SCORED MY first try as a professional in Adams Park. And unlike my days playing for Fermoy when tries came fast and even faster, those individual moments of glory were like winning lottery tickets for me when I reached adulthood. There were only two.

I was there with Leinster in a Challenge Cup quarter-final. Isa Nacewa caught the ball and made a break. I followed. He kicked it on, and the ball could have bounced left or right. Left, and Leo Cullen would have got it and downed the ball. It went right, thankfully, and Kevin McLoughlin and Dev Toner made sure to bundle me over the line once I had the ball in my arms like a Daddy bear.

The second try came against Scarlets in the RDS, two years from the end of my career. Cian Healy was stopped short after picking up. I was on hand. I fell over the line. I would have liked to score more tries.

I was held up so many times.

It was said more than once in the Leinster dressing room that I was exceptional at making 60 yards up the pitch with the ball and falling six inches short of the line. I'm not sure how often I made the 60 yards, but the six inches? That much is true, and how many times did I wait for a ball carrier to look left instead of right, or right instead of left?

Too often.

KINGSTON PARK IN Newcastle, simply put, was a bollocks of a trip. Win or lose, there was a six hours drive back down to London. Play them in an evening game, finish after ten o'clock and arrive back in London at five or six in the morning. Kingston Park was one good reason to say goodbye to England.

NORTHAMPTON, FOR SOME reason, never got it into their heads that Harlequins were no longer a bunch of posh boys from London. Second to Leicester in the 'Hard-Nosed Bastards' league table they delighted in taking a chunk out of any one of us any time we went up to Franklin's Gardens.

It was like they were never sure that we had a backbone.

And, every time we went there, they seemed to want to locate that backbone just as much as they wanted to win the precious game.

Admittedly, a lot of other clubs also fell into that way of thinking at different times during my three years. Curiosity got the better of them, and they just had to try and find out for themselves, and that meant that they decided to come for us as a pack. They'd summon up that extra ten per cent it seemed to me that they were not too fussed about calling up most other weekends.

It pissed us off. They'd keep the ball an extra second or two, just to see what they might be able to do with it. Instead of moving it out to the backs, they'd hold and see if they could inch us backwards.

And teams like the Tigers and Northampton, if they happened to luck out and find a weakness in our pack, they'd keep going back to it, and back to it. There was no subtlety. No apologies. If we had one bad scrum, you could bet every pound in your pocket that they'd get all excited and be immediately back for more.

In ways, it was funny. Just how moronic they acted, holding the ball and holding it and trying to punish us, when it would have been far smarter for them to let the ball out. I believe this was one of the reasons why Quins' wanted Dean Richards. They realised that a former Leicester man would be able to finally dispel the thought that Harlequins was a soft touch.

It was so ridiculous. You just had to look at Quins, and look at someone like Andre Vos who was finishing up with the club when I arrived in. He'd played in the back row for Eastern Province in South Africa, for Queensland Reds in Australia, and for The Cats and The Lions back in South Africa, before arriving in London and signing up for Quins. He played 33 times for the Springboks, 16 as captain, and Andre had a habit of putting his head in places where nobody else would even think of placing their boot. He was the hardest practitioner I witnessed on a rugby pitch.

The loveliest man, but his face told the story of his career. It looked like it had been used as an anvil. He was fearless. He'd get up off the ground, blood streaming down his face and he'd get right back into the defensive line, asking us all if we were ready to go again.

We always said a fast yes to Andre.

EDGELEY PARK, THE home of Sale was another football ground and had the smallest changing rooms in the Premiership. Even though it was a football ground, for some reason the pitch was rubbish. For a prop it is pretty important that you have good, sound footing underneath you, otherwise a lot of the time you are going to end up eating lots of grass. Though we all did a lot of eating grass there because Andrew Sheridan was always present.

SARACENS ALSO FOUND a home in a football ground, Vicarage Road and they had a loosehead, Nick Lloyd I could never quite get my head around. He was not that big or strong, and he had no big international career, but the stuff I tried on most other props with a reasonable amount of success never seemed to work on him.

Usually, if I got my opponent's elbow to touch the ground, it was only a matter of counting down the seconds. It was game over. But Lloyd would get back up, somehow, and repeatedly. He was like someone from a crazy Marvel movie... before my very eyes the man would be getting himself back up and righting himself, as if he was made of rubber or some substance from an alien planet.

AND THEN THERE was Worcester.

Famous for its sauce, and also for a pack of grizzled rugby players who were completely fixated on going to war every single Saturday or Sunday, and never even thinking of taking a weekend off.

Every single time we went there they tried to go route 1, and route 1A if that wasn't on offer.

One of the perks of retirement is that I'll never have to play there again!

PART THREE

CHEIKA THE TERRIBLE

CHAPTER 11

THERE WAS THIS patch of cracked, dead skin on my knuckle. It was there for a few weeks, and I was thinking… *what the hell?*

How'd that get there… where'd that come from?

I was looking at it, as you do, and just trying to figure it out. I wasn't doing any punching… I wasn't thumping bags in the gym. It had grown into a fairly rough callus.

It was early into 2010, over halfway through my first season back in Ireland. And then, suddenly, it dawned on me… as though someone hit me on the back of the head and shifted a nugget of knowledge from the back of my brain to the very front.

Fuck!!!!!

This is from… holding… THOSE

… FUCKING

… TACKLE BAGS!

I understood that I had reached the lowest point of my professional career, and I sought a meeting with Paul McNaughton, the Irish team manager.

'This isn't working out,' I told him.

I explained, as calmly as I could, that I had come home from London in order to make a career for myself with Ireland. And, then, still trying to remain composed, I asked him… 'If I am not getting picked for Leinster, then…how am I ever going to play for Ireland?'

He told me to hang in. He asked me to wait a little longer before making a decision I would not be able to undo.

I nodded my head.

I was a rugby player, not a rugby trainer. I wanted to be playing the game. That's the be all and end all of being a rugby player.

I didn't leave Harlequins and come home to do nothing but hold tackle bags during Leinster training sessions.

LEINSTER HAD GIVEN me a two year contract. It was good. I was on a provincial contract, I was getting some starts, and the coach was talking to me.

Michael Cheika appeared content with me.

Then CJ got fit.

Then I gave away the most stupid penalty of my life against London-Irish in the first game of Leinster's Heineken Cup defence.

Then Cheika closed the door on me.

Actually, the door was slammed shut. Locked. Key tossed away. There was only one prop sitting on the bench in those days, and Cheika had CJ back. He was happy that Stan could play loose or tight for him, and he also had Cian.

I'd go into his office every few weeks.

Knock on his door on a Monday or Tuesday morning. Ask for a minute? I knew his demeanour would depend on whether the team had won or lost the previous weekend. It looked to me like my career in Ireland was over before it had even started. I was looking around elsewhere for another club and a fresh start. It's a small world, and I knew that Cheika might get to hear about it, eventually.

I also knew he was going at the end of the season, and I had a year left on my contract after that. I decided to wait.

I'll see how I get on with this new fella.

Joe Schmidt?

Fingers crossed.

THERE WAS A large bunch of us new boys at the start of the 2009-10 season. But Rocky Elsom was out the door. He wanted to stay with Leinster for another season and help defend their place as the No.1 team in Europe, but the Australian Union told him he needed to get back home if he wanted to be considered for the 2011 World Cup. I came in the door, with Nathan Hines, Shaun Berne, Richardt Strauss and Eoin Reddan.

Cheika had us all in Nice for a training camp and I thought... *Cool... I'm going to get used to this life!* But it was the first and last time Leinster ever went to a sunny spot on the world map for pre-season while I was there. After a week in France we had a game lined up against London-Irish at Donnybrook.

It was time to get to know my new teammates, and especially the other new boys. Straussy was 23 years old and a virtual newbie from The Cheetahs, while Hinesy was 32 and just off the Lions tour to South Africa where he'd played five times. Originally from Wagga Wagga in New South Wales, he'd over 50 caps with Scotland and had joined Leinster on a two-year deal from Perpignan.

Hinesy was a great teammate. He was one of those hard, seen-it-all vets you see stomping Germans into the ground for the Marines in war movies, but he was the last of the new signings I got to know because he had a wife and kids. I had no kids. People with kids tend to stick around together more often. Their schedules mesh more easily.

New boys tend to keep a closer eye on one another all the same, just to gauge what's happening? I hit it off with Eoin Reddan fast enough and we became good friends, though all of us became part of the Nathan Hines fan club very quickly. Hinesy, immediately, was a huge character in the dressing room, though he was not all that loud. He was a calm, confident individual and on the pitch he was an absolute pest for us. When I ended up playing against him, I found it an equal displeasure to be in his company.

He had a habit of always pulling me into a ruck, or holding me down longer and it wasn't just me. Hinesy was able to get a piece of everyone around the place and would hold several players down at the same time. Years later, after he left Leinster, I saw a clip of him on TV playing for Clermont.

They were playing Ulster.

Hinesy was clearing out a ruck. But the clip caught him lying on top of one Ulster player, while he was holding another by the jersey, and he also had his arm around the leg of a third Ulster player. You could see them all shouting at the referee to do something about him. But Hinesy, on an average working day, did what he did and didn't get very much grief from referees for some reason.

I think he must have had the refs half-enthralled as well.

Straussy was living with CJ, so I didn't get to see too much of him in the beginning. The pair of South Africans were holed up down in Wicklow and it was tough for Straussy. He needed CJ's company but he was struggling to get his starts and integrate himself within the squad. He was a strong young man. He could bench 180 kilos and while he was quite short, he had bullish power and once he got his arms around a ball, well, good luck to anyone who thinks they might be able to take it off him.

In that first game against London-Irish nearly everyone got a run and I came in for Stan after 60 minutes. We were 21-5 down at half time, and Johnny Sexton and Ryan Lamb swapped penalties in the second half. It was a poor performance. We coughed up a strong 16-7 lead in Parc Y Scarlets a week later. We lost 18-16. I didn't play, but got my first start in the then Magners League the following weekend, joining up with Cian Healy and John Fogarty in the RDS for the visit of The Dragons.

The RDS is obviously an odd looking ground. It's not your traditional rugby ground. It's the Royal Dublin Society, and it happens to have a rugby pitch in it now. I also thought it was a cool place from my first day out there. It's so different, totally family-friendly, and I got to love its nooks and crannies. The sight of kids kicking a ball around in the warm-up paddocks is not something you get anywhere else. Everywhere else, like The Stoop, you've got those corporate boxes but the RDS keeps its foot in a different age and that is so important.

Leinster's training base, in Riverview, also looked its age, but not in a good way. However, I didn't mind that. With Quins we were nomadic with our training bases and during my time there the club had taken a local school and put in a gym in an old handball alley. We trained in Aldershot, moved to Roehampton Vale in Wimbledon, and Quins are now out in very salubrious surroundings in Guilford. Leinster's daily dressing room was small and grim, with photos and pieces of paper and pages from magazines sellotaped all over the walls, lampooning the last player who may have struck a certain dodgy pose or who was talked into putting a few extra quid in front of his own sense of dignity.

I could see from day one that, in that room, nobody would ever be allowed to get away with anything. It was indeed a tiny room, and the gym that the club had built for itself was extra grim, but I loved it. It was the perfect place to do the hardest and most thankless piece of your day's work. A gymnasium with post-apocalyptic grimness is what the doctor should always order. It's not a place you ever want to hang around in either.

It's also a place where you have to be aware of the mob at all times.

The mob is always looking to aim itself at some poor dozy soul every single day. It helps pass the time to pick on someone. And you've also got to be aware of the mob when it's your turn to play your music. Knowing how utterly disgusted Cian Healy and some of the younger crew would react, I would always enlist the support of some of the older guys before whacking my 80s and 90s stuff into everyone's ears.

The mob are listening, and the mob are watching you lift.

And any new boy in the room, especially a 30 year old 'new boy' like me, was under the microscope from day one. It's the same as any job. You move from an environment where every person knows you and is comfortable in your presence, to a place where, quite naturally, nobody knows you or 'gets you' and you are being scrutinised. You are also asking yourself questions.

Why did I come here?

Have I a right to be there?

But, if there is something I love above all else in a professional environment it is the one basic tenet that is present in every club... the simple beauty of meritocracy.

If you are good and you are doing your job very well, then, straight away nobody gives a damn where you have come from or who you are!

Not once you are performing.

It's the complete flip side to any other working environment, where you get unhappy people, people who call in sick, and people who are 'lifers' and are doing the bare minimum to get by one more day before going home.

None of that exists in a professional sports environment.

Back in the gym, I was more aware than ever that I was 10 years behind most guys with my training age. I had catching up to do. I was quickly informed, for instance, that I was not using my glutes sufficiently.

In other words, I was not benefitting enough from the size of my arse. And that surprised me because my glutes are massive.

Glutes are a team, made up of three parts. There's the gluteus maximus, gluteus medius and gluteus minimus, but the gluteus maximus is the most important of the three. Maximus shapes your butt, and gets to work when you raise your thighs, rotate your legs or thrust your hips forward. I was three years literally working my butt off in the English Premiership with Harlequins but now I was being told I was not getting best value from that butt.

I was given an eight-week glute activation programme that was one hundred per cent torture. Ninety minutes blowing out those glutes under the watchful eye of Stevie Smith, who was our rehabilitation coach at the time. Standing up on a box with a weight, standing on one leg and lifting my body up and down. Simple enough for 90 seconds… try 90 minutes. There were lots of specific exercises, and all for the benefit of what Jamie Heaslip would one day dub 'The Toilet.'

CHAPTER 12

WE BEAT THE Dragons, 23-14, and Stan came in for me after 60 minutes. Quickly, this became the pattern in the opening months of the season... 60 minutes here... 20 minutes there... another 60 minutes. It was so staccato and it didn't suit me. As previously mentioned, I'd done 14 Premiership games for Quins in-a-row the previous season where I'd stayed on the pitch for the full 80 minutes. I liked to stay out there.

It worked for me.

Stopping and starting did not allow me to get into my stride. And coming in for the final 20 minutes was totally alien to me. Everyone on the field has their second wind, but you are there, gasping after 10 minutes and, before you know it, the game has ended.

By the middle of September Leinster's four Lions were back in, and CJ was also getting close to full fitness. He was back in too. We played the Ospreys, won 18-11, but I got no game time and by the end of September, as the season was set to heat up fast, with Munster coming to the RDS, and then London-Irish arriving for the first game in the Heineken Cup, I was not as physically or mentally tuned as I would have wished.

The RDS was a sell-out for the visit of Munster. I was gagging to play, but Cheika had started Stan three out of the four previous games on the tight side and he was hardly going to have a change of mind.

I felt as desperate as a little kid who wanted to get picked for his very first game. I was crying out for my start.

Games against Munster were massive. They were central to the whole giddy, ambitious dream I had of coming home. As Cheika called out the team I hoped against hope that I'd get the start but I ended up on the bench.

I came in for Stan after 67 minutes. We were 23-0 up by then, and four minutes later Shane Horgan went over for the final try of the game and Johnny kicked the points, and Munster had been well and truly stuffed. The only time they looked like they might score, Ronan O'Gara duffed his penalty from 40 metres. Kicking into the wind in the first quarter he barely raised the ball the height of the crossbar. Whether carrying or tackling, we dominated the collisions. Leo and Kevin McLoughlin tore apart Paul O'Connell's lineouts, an uncommon occurrence. Munster lost five of them. Their scrum was also shunted back and penalised, and by the time John Hayes was red carded in the 55th minute Munster were perilously close to giving up the fight. The referee, Simon McDowell sent The Bull off the pitch for stamping on Cian Healy in a Munster maul but it never looked to me as something that was intentional. I believe Hayes went to legitimately shoe Cian and got unlucky, and stood on his head. It can happen.

Whoever thought they would witness such a thing? The Bull found guilty of such an offence, or Munster losing heart?

But I wasn't part of it. I was watching it mostly, like everyone else. Munster had suffered their heaviest defeat in well over a decade and, truthfully, I had no hand, act or part in it. To reinforce that belief there was the 20 minutes run-out after the game with the other replacements, to give all of us a proper blowout. I hated subbing for the last 20 minutes, and I hated those 20 minutes of training in an emptying stadium even more.

Traditionally, the game against Munster is also the warm-up for the first game of the Heineken Cup. It looked like I was going to be on the outside and looking in at the first two big games of the season, until the news came through that Stan was in trouble. His efforts against Munster had left him with pectoral muscle damage. Since arriving in Leinster three months into the 2006-07 season Stan Wright was clearly a man that Michael Cheika believed in and he had played in 66 of the team's previous 73 matches. He had started in 58 of those games.

Suddenly, it was my chance.

To prove to Cheika he had done the right thing in bringing me into his squad, and to additionally let everyone else around him in the dressing room know that I had what it took to be a regular starter.

In Munster, it so happened that Hayes' suspension was giving Tony Buckley a similar opportunity. The Bull had started an incredible 67 Heineken Cup games in-a-row for Munster. Buckley and I were side-by-side at the start of a race that, ultimately, might also have one of us in the green No.3 shirt too. That's how I saw it. The opportunity against London-Irish was massive in size.

I KNEW LONDON-IRISH better than anyone in Leinster.

It was the perfect game for me. Additionally, I was still feeling a little sore, maybe even rightly pissed, for the manner in which they had beaten Quins in the Premiership semi-final at the tail end of the previous season.

I knew Bob Casey really well. I'd rented a house from him when I moved to Dublin where I ended up staying until 2013. He was a good guy, but one tough competitor. I knew their whole pack, and I'd had lots of tussles with Clarke Dermody, their loosehead. He was a New Zealander, who'd made his name with the Highlanders and played for the All Blacks a handful of times before moving over to London.

Any time I'd mixed it with Dermody I'd come out on top half the time; other times he had me. I'd knocked him back on engagement a few times. He'd popped me up now and again. He was a typically tough Kiwi scrummager.

He was my equal really.

And, for me, that vitally important game against London-Irish went just fine, almost exactly as I had planned it in my head, until the very end.

Until the 79th minute.

BOB AND THE Irish guys played well that evening.

They were flying in England and they were well up for it against us from the very beginning. They also benefitted from Roman Poite having an off night. The French ref missed a lot of off-sides, and even more fringing and spoiling.

When Sean O'Brien came into the game near the end of the third quarter it helped to give us an edge. We were keeping the ball in hand and running hard, and clearing out with far greater intensity.

The lineouts were not great for us, however. John Fogarty was throwing to the tail of the line in order to stop Bob and Nick Kennedy from pilfering too much ball, but they managed to mess up three of our throws in the first half, and another two after half time. Our scrum was better. We were well on top.

I was happy.

It was six points each at half time, however and we had not stretched away from them that little bit. Johnny Sexton kicked two penalties in the second and 12th minutes of the game, but their full-back Peter Hewat had them back level in the four minutes added to the first half. That half was also feisty. Jamie Heaslip and David Paice were yellow carded after one free-for-all which had been kicked off by a former Quins colleague, Chris Hala-Ufia. Another old Quins' teammate, Chris Malone never got his kicking game together and they had little to work with. We should have made it count. We didn't.

It was one day when it would have done my career the world of good to be taken off after 60 minutes.

But, unfortunately for me as it turned out, Cheika decided to keep CJ on the bench. Lamb had kicked them 9-6 in front. Johnny got us back level on 76 minutes. The game was almost up.

I WAS RUNNING back from a previous ruck, and the ball squirted out from the side, 50 metres from our posts.

Before I knew anything.

Before I even had time to think…

I poked my toe at it.

As soon as I realised what I was about to do I immediately tried to stop myself. But it was too late. My toe struck the ball.

I knew I had given away the dumbest penalty of my life, but I did not know that Cheika, repeatedly, would use the same phrase for days and weeks when he lamented the loss of the game.

'Dumb…

'Dumb… DUMB…

'DUMB!!!'

Hewat had kicked the penalty to put them back in front again. They fumbled the restart and allowed us one last, furious attack to save the day. Everyone in the RDS thought they saw Hala-Uifa high tackle Johnny Sexton. Poite signaled for play to continue. Eoin Reddan, who had also got his start, thought it was indeed a penalty and that we could have a free shot at them. He chipped the ball. It went into the deal goal area. Poite blew his final whistle.

It was over.

I knew I would be crucified for what I had done, and I had no doubt whatsoever that I deserved to be and, once we got back into the dressing room, I found myself apologising to all my teammates. They were having none of it. They told me we win as a team, and we lose as a team, and that nobody has to ever apologise.

Cheika didn't appear to agree.

I had not set out to mess up the game at the end and kick at the ball like some crazed idiot. It was a reflex. A millisecond passed and I knew I was doing the wrong thing.

Cheika was unforgiving.

He started me against Brive the following week, basically because he had no other choice.

After that?

I was persona non grata.

CHAPTER 13

MICHAEL CHEIKA DID not lose it with me in front of the other players.

Neither did he bawl me out of it personally.

Thinking about it now, I would have preferred a trial in the privacy of our dressing room, or a one-on-one execution.

That was not Michael Cheika's way, however.

He did not have to lose it with me because the simple truth of it was that I was losing it with myself.

After that, he only picked me when he absolutely had no other choice. I went from playing week-in and week-out with Quins, and being named on the Premiership team of the season, to becoming Mr Nobody.

Mr Nobody gets to play for… Nobody.

Maybe 10 minutes here… 20 minutes there. It was tough to get my head around my new life circumstance. Cheika, for starters, had the ability to go stone cold.

You were in his good books, or else… well, actually, there were no other books! I was well aware that I needed to do something fast, and hopefully something spectacular to get back into his books, but I did not know the man. I did not know where to start with him, apart from looking to have a word with him formally in his office every now and again on a Monday or

Tuesday morning.

Cheika's temperamental nature would remain a characteristic of his as he moved back to France and then back down to the Southern Hemisphere and eventually took over the Australian national team. At the same time, Cheika could be massively inspiring.

Later in the season, our schedule tightened and we had a tough corner to get around; we were playing Glasgow on the Saturday and Connacht on the Thursday. Cheika needed to pick two squads. He loaded the first team squad up against Connacht. The rest of us were sent to Glasgow.

It was a B squad. I did not have to guess which squad I was part of, of course, but Cheika got every one of us up for the game ahead of us. He was in a frenzied mood in the dressing room, and we all fed off it. We went out and we beat up a damned good Glasgow team for 50 minutes, and we did that because Michael Cheika made us believe we could do it. Dominic Ryan, a young lad at the beginning of his career, absolutely levelled Chris Cusiter perfectly legally and promptly got sin-binned for it! In the end, their best players turned the game to their advantage.

But we had beaten the crap out of Glasgow for that 50 minutes and Cheika had made us believe that we had every right to do just that. Up close, I saw that evening that he was a brilliant coach.

My only regret is that I never got to see him up close all that often and that, the rest of the time, the man who had come over to London to talk me into coming to Leinster showed me his unforgiving side.

I PERFORMED AGAINST Brive in the next round of the Heineken Cup. Cheika had no choice. He had to select me. CJ was not right. It was a big victory for us in a do-or-die scenario in Stade Amedee Domenech as defending champs. They were well up for it.

Brive had won the European Cup in 1997, but had not played in the competition for a dozen years. They were back alright, and they had 10 English speaking players in their starting team. Brive had invested heavily to get back into the big time.

Davit Khinchagishvili, their loosehead, was Georgian and together with the former English hooker, Steve Thompson I knew I had lot to think about.

I had never played against Khinchagishvili before, but we were soon hurting them in the scrum; Cian Healy, Bernard Jackman and myself leading the way. But the French are the most illegal shower of bolloxes going when they wish to be and my opponent was soon boring into me.

They had a huge pack. Massive power, and he kept coming across me. I'd expected this and more from him after studying him on tape. None of his tricks surprised me. Each one, I countered.

We won, three tries to one, 36-13 which put the kibosh on their big day of celebrations. Cheika put Malcolm O'Kelly in with Leo, and used Hinesy at blindside in the back row, so we had massive weight coming through. Jackman's throws were on the money and he had plenty of choices, and left us with all the possession in the world. Brive had a kick and chase game but Shaun Perry was overcooking those kicks and Rob Kearney won lots of ball in the air unimpeded.

Brive coach, Laurent Seigne took Khinchagishvili out of it early in the second half, before he bought a yellow card from the Welsh referee, James Jones. He'd been penalised four times for boring in before he was taken off. Thompson was losing the rag a fair bit too. There were a few scraps in the second half as they saw the game moving far out of their grasp. Brian O'Driscoll didn't like the look of Andy Goode stamping on Jamie Heaslip's arm but before he could do much about it he was blindsided by another Brive fella.

It was all a bit ugly out there in the end, but we kept our cool. And Cheika, amazingly, was amongst that number.

CJ came in for me after 61 minutes.

There wasn't much left for him to do, in truth, and I had no idea as I took myself off the pitch that I had just finished up my biggest contribution to Leinster's season. CJ was in for good.

I was out for good.

I HAD DONE a good job in Brive.

I did not expect to be completely frozen out of it, and left with dribs and drabs for the remainder of the season. But Cheika must have made his mind up, and believed that he could not trust me. That mind was not for turning.

He gave me the odd game. But, any game of any importance I was out – once Cheika had two able bodies to call upon! There was nothing I could do about it. Our chats never led to anything.

The tiny opportunities were doing me more harm than good.

His personality was difficult to gauge. He showed himself to be a fiercely passionate man, and even though he had made a small fortune for himself with his fashion business, there was no doubt that rugby flowed through his veins, and flowed in torrents.

Some of the Leinster players absolutely loved him, and they had no trouble with his style of management. Others, like me, who had ended up on the wrong side of him, had different opinions. Bernard Jackman has told the story that when he went into Cheika's office to inform him that he was retiring he was told, in no uncertain manner… 'You don't get to decide when you retire… I decide!'

The human response to someone rejecting you is to say… *fuck you too!* But I could not afford to take that attitude. I needed to add value wherever I could. I had decided to see out a second year and try to work with Cheika's successor, Joe Schmidt. I did not want the rest of Cheika's management team to see me as somebody who had thrown in the towel. I did not want anyone reporting such a judgment to Schmidt. My second season, if such a report was reached and dispatched, might be over also before it actually started.

So, I started writing even more data on the opposing front rows. I doubled down on my data. I also worked really hard to put a smile on my face and tried to come to work each morning with a fresh intent to improve things for myself.

My Dad asked me many times during this period … 'Why are you giving all of this information to lads who are keeping you out of the team?'

But I still believed that I needed to help. Somehow.

In any way. You have to still do your job. You never know what might happen next. Maybe CJ's toe goes again? You have to be ready, prepared, one hundred per cent on top of what might be needed from you.

CHAPTER 14

WE CALLED THEM… Sappuccinos. I picked the term up in Harlequins where a few of us including Ceri Jones, Tani Fuga, Olly Kohn, Jim Evans and Nick Easter would meet at a nearby Costa after training and have a good humoured old moan, whether it was about training, coaching, selection or whatever dreary away ground we had to travel to that week.

Sappuccinos existed in Leinster too but they didn't call them that. Those of us not in the thick of things ended up spending a great deal of time together, on the edges of training sessions, and in coffee shops.

We'd have extra weight sessions, because we had the time on our hands and we needed the extra workouts because we weren't getting our game time. Invariably, we started drinking too much coffee.

Sappuccinos was an appropriate term. Once that unhappy group sat down in a coffee shop and we all started talking about ourselves, we were definitely sapping ourselves of whatever remaining positive energy we may have had to begin with that same morning.

It wasn't the most positive thing in the world, but there was a lot of gallows humour and I'd always leave them feeling a bit better about my situation, knowing that I wasn't the only man having difficulties. It was one of those things that players do. For me, not knowing too many players all that well in the Leinster squad, I found myself in the company of other troubled souls too often. Some of the others had had Cheika for a good few years.

They had more than I had to get off their chests.

MICHAEL CHEIKA'S FIFTH and last season as Leinster coach was by no means a failure. The team reached the final of the Magners League, where we lost to Ospreys, and we also went to the semi-finals of the Heineken Cup. There, Leinster lost to Toulouse in their Municipal Stadium which is a ground in which every team has to fight for their lives. But it was a long season for everyone.

Cheika had made it known long before the end that he was on his way. Midway through the season, in December when everything was still to play for, he gave one of many interviews and spoke with an honesty that I have to admit, despite his tantrums, was one of the fine characteristics of the man.

He knew that defending the Heineken Cup would be incredibly hard. Only one team in the previous 14 winners in Europe (Leicester in 2001-02) had managed to put two titles back-to-back. Of course, even in that same interview, he cited the 'dumb penalty' against London-Irish.

He wasn't letting that one go.

But in the interview Cheika spoke about players in Leinster being happy to see the back of him. He admitted that any player might find it punishing to have to listen to the same man for so many years.

Despite the defeat at home to the 'Irish' we had finished top of our group in the Heineken Cup, winning our four games and drawing one. We scored 156 points and conceded 60, and with a total of 22 points in the group we were five points clear of second-placed Scarlets and 'Irish.' We beat Clermont (and Joe Schmidt) by a point in the quarter-final in the RDS. Then we ran into that wall in Toulouse. We were top of the table at the end of the regular season in the Magners League, took Munster in the semi-final, and then we failed to give Cheika the send-off he definitely deserved in the final against Ospreys.

I'm writing 'we' in all of this out of loyalty and also because I was also receiving a pay cheque at the end of every month.

But there was no 'we.'

It felt to me that I was mostly watching with everyone else who supported Leinster. It was tough to watch, especially that loss to Toulouse. I felt that I could make a difference. In *The Daily Telegraph* match report the following morning the former English lock, Paul Ackford called our scrum a 'shambles' and it was a view I knew was shared by some others in our dressing-room.

That was something I thought that I could help with.

The Toulouse scrum was magnificent. They hosed us. Toulouse had perhaps the best scrummaging hooker I had ever encountered on the field, William Servat. He was unbelievably strong, a hooker the size of most props. Benoit Lecouls (nickname 'The Butcher') and Daan Human, massive men, true scrum legends. It was a front row of absolute quality and power. Patricio Albacete in their second row is one of the biggest human beings I have ever seen up close.

Watching that game I fully realised how short-sighted it was for a brilliant all-round team like Leinster to place so little emphasis on their scrum in terms of preparation and coaching. Too much was left to chance.

We lost the hit to them in most of the scrums. We needed to get out of the blocks a bit earlier. They were pile-driving us and, of course, there are things that can always be done to counteract that but we had not done our homework sufficiently. There was no Plan B. We had no full-time scrum coach in Leinster. Reggie Corrigan would come in from time to time but he wasn't there all the time. No Plan B, no Plan C or D... there was nothing in our back pocket.

The scrum work in Leinster was taken a lot less seriously than at Harlequins. Too much was left to chance and to what might happen on the day, which is unfathomable when every other facet of the game received meticulous levels of attention.

I would have loved to have been out there against Toulouse and, if I was, I believe I could have made a difference, but I'm writing this to underline the lack of preparation in the scrum that riddled through Leinster in Michael Cheika's years as coach.

We lost to Toulouse 26-16.

The lads out there, including every forward, were brave and gave everything. We were without Johnny Sexton remember, but Shaun Berne brought his game up to the highest level after a shaky start. However, Toulouse were a magnificent team and close to the height of their powers and they had so many talented players on the pitch, none more so than the mesmerising centre, Yannick Jauzion who scored the game's decisive try, when the teams were locked at 9-9, to more than hint to the rest of his teammates that they needed to put their heads down and wrap up their victory.

THE SECOND HALF of my first season with Leinster did not skip by. It crawled. It was agonising. In the return fixture in the Madejski Stadium – one of those grounds in England where I had earned my spurs as a prop – I came on as a blood sub for CJ against London-Irish but 10 minutes was all I got. In March, I started against Connacht in the RDS and grabbed the opportunity, taking their scrum for a walk a few times, but I wasn't in the squad when we inched by Munster by one point in Thomond Park in April.

But, there was a moment down in Thomond that I grasped at. I was in the extended squad and warming up with the rest of the Leinster boys. We had finished our workout before the game and we were walking off the pitch.

Paul O'Connell walked past me.

He walked past and, then, Paulie reached out.

And he squeezed me on the shoulder.

He did not say anything.

Just a squeeze.

And I was like… *Why'd he do that?*

I did not know him well at all, and I started analysing that small moment, wondering what it meant? We'd been in a couple of Irish squads together but had hardly said two words to one another.

Paulie is one of those men who knows how to lead, both through his words and by example. He was a tough customer in his earlier years and was hard on others, but as he got older he seemed to realise there was another way to get the best out of teammates. Maybe he meant nothing much by squeezing my shoulder.

Maybe it was just a quick hello.

But it mattered to me. I was walking towards the tunnel when it happened and it was over in half a second. Our players were turning left for the Leinster dressing room. The Munster guys were turning right.

I went into our room and got showered, and got back into a fresh tracksuit. I settled in to watch the game and, all the time, I could only wonder?

I came to the conclusion that that squeeze on my shoulder, whether Paulie meant anything by it or not, had told me to hold on in there!

IT WAS A five months roller-coaster, but a ride with no real highs.

The lowest point? That's easy.

We met the Dragons in Rodney Parade. It was the first week in December. A Sunday. Cheika chose to leave out 15 full internationals from his selected 26-man squad. Ireland player protocols were kicking in before the Six Nations. Stan was injured, and the team was a mere shadow of the Leinster team.

Just over a week later I was due to celebrate my 30th birthday and little did I know that Kimberlee had organised a surprise party with all of the Leinster guys invited. Fair play to them, most of them showed, including Brian O'Driscoll and Leo Cullen and most of the leaders on the team.

I wasn't unduly worried about turning 30. Because I had started so late in the pro game I'd always figured that I would be able to keep playing until I was much closer to 40, but the clock was ticking and after waiting for so long to get a professional contract I did not wish to be hanging around the place.

Kim wanted to have my birthday in Ashton's in Clonskeagh. I did not think that was a great idea. Nothing against Ashton's, I've spent a few happy hours there since but I also knew it was the 'local' for our CEO in Leinster, Mick Dawson. I did not really want him to see me drinking when I was not playing. In my head I was… *Ashtons? Really?* But I had no idea that Kim was organising an actual party. I was caught stone cold. I'd no idea that my whole family had come up from Cork. I walked in and… SURPRISE!

I enjoyed the evening. It helped me to fully understand that I should not be feeling too sorry for myself. I was a professional rugby player and living the dream. It was not all bad, was it? I was not on the street, starving. My family had a roof over their heads in a nice home.

And people showed up, like Drico, who did not have to show up but made the effort anyway. That lifted my spirits.

Our whole family together in Ballyhooly in the autumn of 1997. Mom and Dad, Alistair and Matthew, Kate, and Andrew on my left shoulder

My Mom and Dad hold my son Kevin for the first time

Me and Kate

Alistair and Matthew doing the honours for me (above) at my wedding and me having the honour (below) of wearing the Cork Con jersey with the two of them

Taking down my future captain and coach, Leo Cullen when Blackrock met UCC

Celebrating Con's victory in the AIB Cup final with my Dad, Frank

Me in a Munster jersey, a rare sight indeed

April 12, 2009 was christened 'Bloodgate' and was a bitterly disappointing day for me and everyone in Harlequins as we went down to Leinster in the Heineken Cup quarter-final at The Stoop

It was a day when myself (far right in this photo) and the Quins pack was left chasing down Rocky Elsom, and when everything went wrong with Nick Evans coming back onto the field and missing with a final drop goal to win the game

Rodrigo Roncero giving me a little cuddle after a scrum breaks up against Stade, with Ceri Jones looking on, in a big win for Quins earlier in the competition that same season

These were the reasons why I came home and joined Leinster. Getting to run onto the field (top) with someone like Johnny Sexton and also getting to run into Ronan O'Gara and Munster (middle). A rare night out as parents, Kim and I at a Leinster end of season dinner

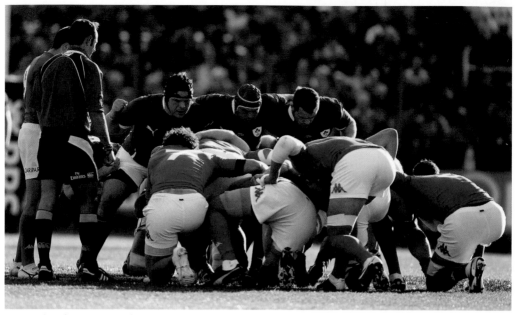

Scrumming down against the Italians in Rome in 2011 during my first game in the Six Nations

Leaving the field after narrowly getting out of jail on the day

The toughest and greatest day of my career came when we defeated Northampton in the Heineken Cup final in 2011, and I had to overcome the amazing man-mountain Soane Tonga'uiha

Celebrating our victory with Heinke van der Merwe and Richardt Strauss (top) and Gordon D'Arcy and myself introduce my son Kevin to the Heineken Cup

My first World Cup in 2011 in New Zealand ended in disappointment, but there was fun along the way as we had down time in Queenstown rafting and fishing, and I got to test Brian O'Driscoll's nerve for heights

Because I entered the pro game late, my 'gym age' was always lower than most of the lads and I had plenty of catching up to do

Casey Laulala could step his way out of a phonebox, but I manage to get hold of him here in 2012 (top) and the year ended with Leinster retaining the Heineken Cup after beating Ulster in Murrayfield

South African born Richardt Strauss won his first cap against his native country in 2012 and I never saw a prouder man in an Irish jersey

Referees broke my heart a lot of the time, but Wayne Barnes was always prepared to talk about it

Those South African boys liked to try to get their hands on the ball

All in a day's work

Cian Healy and I ended up serving
our time together, with lots of lads
in between the two of us – Sean
Cronin (left) and Straussy

I had my ups and downs with Declan Kidney and Matt O'Connor in my career, but with Joe Schmidt (below) it was nearly always plain sailing as he was a man who trusted me and never left me in any doubt about what he wanted

Taking the field in Thomond Park was always one of the greatest experiences for me as a Leinster player as I knew we would have the battle of our lives

If Munster was the ultimate club opponent, there was no team on the world stage I loved playing against more than the All Blacks, like here in 2013

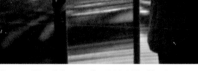

*Kim and I celebrate the 2014 Six Nations
in the quiet of the stadium*

*Enjoying our moment
after lifting the trophy,
with Rory Best and Cian*

*On the occasion of my
50th cap I had the ultimate
honour of leading the team
out against Wales in a World
Cup warm-up game in 2105*

Passing on the baton to Tadhg Furlong was a huge honour for me

I finished my Ireland career in South Africa in the summer of 2016, and left with remarkable memories on and off the field

Myself and a bunch of fellow retirees playing our last game in the famous Barbarians colours... Patricio Albacete, Thierry Dusautoir, Corey Flynn, Horacio Agulla and Chris Masoe

I had the best of company, my son Kevin (wearing one of my shrunken caps) for my last Leinster game in 2017, and leaving the field in that game against Glasgow in the RDS

How lucky was I to get a send off evening with Leinster, and have Kim, Kevin and Chloe there with me on the field to make our final goodbye together

I was also beginning to understand and accept that maybe, just maybe, I was one of the lucky ones.

MANY OF MY good friends, like John Fogarty, had greater reason than me to wonder what it was all about?

Fogs ended up having to stop playing.

He was one of those who had to spend time in darkened rooms because of concussion issues, and that's tough. That's real tough, compared to me not getting a game of rugby. Fogs and I would become a pair, and even when he stopped playing and ended up coaching in Leinster I still felt like we were equals because we would discuss everything.

We'd fought hard against one another before we ended up in Leinster together. When he was with Connacht and I was with Harlequins he was on the receiving end of me coming across him on the angle. But we had respect. Fogs knew what I could do for the team. He'd felt my head under his chin in games. And it's pretty obnoxious for a hooker when a tighthead starts doing that. I gave him a hard time and he never liked it, but he respected me.

And I hugely respected Fogs.

He later admitted to me that he passed out in a couple of those scrums against Toulouse, simply lost consciousness for a couple of seconds. The pressure coming across him was so great. It is not uncommon for hookers to pass out in games. If that blood supply is cut off for even a second under all of that pressure?

Goodnight.

BUT CHEIKA DID not start me against the Dragons.

I was a sub on a shadow team that was beaten 30-14. I came in after 47 minutes. Richardt Strauss was on the bench with me... one of my sappuccino buddies. We'd stayed the night before in the Towers Hotel near Newport, a regular spot whenever we went to Wales.

Talk about my most 'unfavourite' ground in the world?

Welcome to Rodney Parade.

It's a tough little ground at the best of times. In the depths of winter the pitch was a morass and the crowd would lean over the barriers and jeer at you for any mistakes.

Sitting there in Rodney Parade for that first half?

The roller-coaster stopped riding. And I had nobody to talk to. Cheika was still ignoring me. He was the angriest coach I had in my professional career. As a matter of fact, when I first saw Joe Schmidt in action in the Leinster dressing room I said to myself... *this lad is too nice!*

Little did I know.

I was so used to listening to Cheika for that 12 months. Cheika was more vocal than Dean Richards or Joe Schmidt. Always loud and kicking things about the place, that was Michael Cheika. Deano was far quieter and he'd make his displeasure known without any histrionics. Deano would never yell, but you'd know when he was not happy, and you would know immediately.

One look was all it took.

Joe, however, never left anything to chance.

Joe was different to the pair of them. Joe would be at pains to let you know exactly what he was thinking, good, bad, or something in between. Joe, unlike most coaches I've known, was always prepared to talk.

I SHOOK HANDS with Cheika when it all came to an end.

I actually thanked him for trying to make me a better player. I'm not sure I meant that, and I was certainly glad to see the back of him. We had a quick interaction in the Café en Seine bar on Dawson Street.

It was Leinster's end of season "refreshments".

Cheika and I had 30 seconds, maybe 40 seconds, and that was that. The next time I saw him was when Ireland defeated Australia a couple of years later and we had a scrum penalty against them. I nodded in his direction at the after-match dinner.

He was not someone I sought out to talk with. It was a period in my life that I was happy was over, and desired to leave it at that.

PART FOUR

DARK ARTS

CHAPTER 15

SATURDAY THROUGH SUNDAY, October 17 and 18, 2015 was the only night I can ever remember struggling and failing to sleep solidly before a game. Until then, no opponent had ever kept me awake most of the night. No other team.

Sometimes I might be a little fitful at night, but that depended on who I was playing against directly the next day and how comfortable I was expecting to be in the scrum.

On this occasion I was meeting Marcos Ayerza.

He was no stranger to me. I had played against him so many times, and he was one of the very best. He was always a handful, easily in the top three looseheads I had ever come across.

Ayerza was 32 years old. He'd played for Argentina since 2004, and he had joined Leicester Tigers two years later. Before finishing up, he'd play in six successive Premiership finals for the Tigers, winning four of them, and he'd play his part in two European Cup finals. At the World Cup in 2007 Ayerza had helped the Pumas to a third place finish.

He played the piano, and he was also a polo player. He liked his horses. His family owned a stud farm. I knew everything I needed to know about Marcos Ayerza on and off the field. He was from Buenos Aires, and one of 10 children.

He spoke English perfectly well, having lived in our half of the world for nearly a decade, and he was proud of his Irish heritage. When I was with Quins we'd often have a few beers together after games. His great great grandfather was an Irishman named David O'Connor and Marcos told journalists that his grandmother would always beam with extra pride any time he played against Ireland.

I knew his thoughts. I knew his tricks.

The next day we wanted to become the first Irish team to make it through to the semi-finals of a World Cup. The previous Sunday we had beaten France, 24-9 in the Millennium Stadium but at a great cost. Johnny Sexton, Paul O'Connell, Peter O'Mahony and Keith Earls were injured and would not be able to play against the Argies. We were also without Sean O'Brien who was banned from the game for punching Pascale Pape. It looked more like a slap to me, but whatever it was, Pape had it coming.

Thoughts of Marcos Ayerza and him alone were not keeping me awake. Neither was the regret that we were without Johnny and Paulie and the other three.

I felt history weighing down on me. I knew there was a chance that I might be pulling on an Irish jersey for the last time in a World Cup.

I was telling myself that that could not happen.

But, all my worst fears through the long night that preceded the game came through in the very first scrum in the game.

They shunted us.

It set the tone for the remainder of the game and although we recovered in the scrums that followed, and won a couple of penalties ourselves, we were left on the back foot after that very first hit.

Ramiro Herrera, their tighthead who played in the Top 14 with Castres, came straight across into Rory Best and the whole damned thing went awry. In the scrums that followed I started going across more as well. The only way to stop an angling tighthead is to start angling yourself.

But they had shunted us to begin with.

We were like a boxer who had received an early blow on the point of his chin. We knew it, and we had felt it. It gave them extra belief in themselves.

It left us extra wary.

IS THERE ANY other team that loves their scrum as much as the Argentinians? I'm not sure there is. The Argies and their special… Bajada!

Which means… locked… low and forward!

That's what they call their own personalised scrum technique that was pioneered by a man, Dr Francesco Ocampo who had a love of physics and scrummaging, and brought the two very different sciences together. He saw no reason why the scrum could not be built into a devastating weapon. The Bajada is all about eight men making themselves one single, powerful arrow. It began in the San Isidro club. Then it transferred itself to the Pumas and became central to the personality of the national team.

Locks don't bind by putting their arms through the legs of the props. They bind, instead, around the props' hips. The props are pinned inward toward their hooker. Their scrum-half gives his first call.

'PRESSURE!!!'

Every man in the pack tightens his bind and fills his lungs with air, and waits for the next call.

'ONE!!!'

Every man sinks to a point where his legs are at 90 degrees.

'TWO!!!'

Every man comes straight forward – not up or down, not left or right – while violently expelling all the air from their lungs.

Nobody moves their feet, not an inch, until the pack has forward momentum. If the first drive does not impact on the opposing scrum, they call it again. All Argentinian forwards are schooled in the Bajada from an early age. They know to direct all their power through their hooker.

One imaginary arrow.

But, sometimes lethal.

In the days before the game, Marcos Ayerza spoke of the Bajada as a cult and promised us a battle. 'Argentina have always tried to be a force there,' he stated, '… and we love the scrum. We love to test ourselves and we don't like to have to be putting the ball in and out for backs to attack.' He was immensely proud of their Bajada.

Neither was Ayerza afraid of telling us that we did not have a dominating pack. He told us our scrum was 'efficient.'

He name checked Cian and myself, and Rory Best.

'We want to have a battle up front,' he had warned.

I NEVER HAD much to say for myself on the morning of games.

I liked to sleep in until around ten o'clock, unless the kick-off time demanded I get out of bed before that. I liked games at 5.0 pm and 7.0 pm, therefore, and not 1.0 pm or 1.30 pm. There's nothing better than a long sleep-in the morning of a game, and then a good decent breakfast.

I liked my bed.

Most professionals spend a lot of time there.

Sleeping.

Resting… waiting and thinking.

I tried to abstain from the coffee a couple of hours before the game. But I like my caffeine. I drink too much of it. It heightens my awareness. All through the week when I was playing I was always topping myself up with too much coffee.

A good breakfast the morning of the game had me looking into a bowl of porridge, followed by a plate of eggs and bacon. If the game was in the early evening, I'd have my pasta for lunch, and more pasta for my pre-match filler, which is one reason why I intend never again eating pasta and chicken, or spaghetti bolognese, in my life. Four hours before a game I stop eating.

We kicked off against Argentina at one o'clock!

I had less food in me, and got into my music earlier than usual.

Headphones on.

Playlist called… MATCH!

Anyone and everyone was there… shuffled… and ready to go.

Doves.

Mumford & Sons… Queens of the Stone Age, and The Prodigy.

Marilyn Manson, and Ministry.

Radical Face.

Nirvana. Anyone and everyone, all of them busting a gut to get the hairs standing up on the back of my neck.

Listening to my playlist.

Reading Joe Schmidt's play sheets.

JOE LIKED TO have every little thing that might occur on the pitch covered on his sheets. Joe had needed you to know your role inside and out.

We'd have a set of plays for every game.

They would be tailored to the opposition, weaknesses that had been spotted and were waiting to be exploited. The plays would cover the first three or four phases, and then it was up to us.

Those phases needed to be completely nailed down in my mind. What rucks I had to hit, and when I needed to act as a decoy. My every movement in those phases was down on Joe's sheets and if I missed one, Joe would be ready to eviscerate me. Joe Schmidt loved precision.

There might be a hole there.

But if there is a hole there, it will only be there for half a second and if you did not go through it in that half a second then, that hole would close.

Everything on Joe's sheets needed to be enacted, and done exactly so.

Of course, Joe was a coach who also liked players making decisions but, like all coaches, he had time for good decisions and no time for bad decisions.

All of us knew individually that if we were to make a decision and depart from a play, then that decision had better work out! It had to, if it was to match or outdo what lay on Joe's sheets.

On Joe Schmidt's Leinster and Ireland teams you could back yourself, but... man oh man... you had better be right!

Therefore. Me?

I always thought it smarter to stick to Joe's sheets.

Because Joe had worked on his script all week long, night and day, he was hard, and merciless even, when we messed up. He would never do so in public but at the next video review or team meeting, Joe would be ready and never had any interest in holding back on anybody. He had pored over that script. All we had to do was learn it by heart.

We had the easier half of that bargain.

We needed to concentrate.

And stop visualising, that useless mental game in which you fast forward and imagine how you will feel if you've won the game... or imagine how you'll feel if you've lost the game. Hours before you have won or lost, there's no point going there. There's no point weighing up a victory against a defeat.

Anytime, once I found myself visualising – wandering subconsciously into the hours after the match – I stopped myself. I always told myself to stay in the present.

That was the biggest message shared by every last man on the Irish team.

Be rooted in the present. Win the moment that is in front of your face. If you have messed up, you have messed up!

Move on.

You can't go back and change it... MOVE ON. There's another moment right in front of your face... RIGHT NOW!

What's happening in front of your face is the only thing that is important though, occasionally, I'd find myself on the ground and getting back up on my feet, and watching the big screen in the ground to see what had just happened?

Paulie or one of the other lads might be shouting at me!

Maybe I had conceded a penalty, and they were shouting at me to move on, but I still wanted to see how I had messed up... I needed that data.

My brain especially required that data more than most of my teammates!

I needed some replays.

They helped me.

'The moment in front of your face... ROSSY!' I'd hear someone shout at me.

'Fuck off!' I'd shout back.

Sometimes I needed to see that big screen, and I needed to sign off on the moment that had concluded, before concentrating all of my being on the next moment about to jump in front of my face.

MOST REFEREES NEVER had a rashers.

Most of them were backs in their playing days and all of those years the scrum was a mystery to them, and unravelling it and understanding its strange dynamics was none of their business.

The likes of Argentina were always tough, and they were never tougher than in that 2015 World Cup quarter-final in Cardiff. But it always wound me up when I was playing against them, or playing against South Africa, or any team that had a big scrummaging reputation, that the referee would take the easy way out and give them the decision.

Referees decided by reputation too often, rather than make a decision on what had just happened in front of their faces.

A scrum goes down... Ireland and Argentina, and the referee thinks... *It can't be the Argies, can it?*

Nah... and, instinctively he gives it to the Argies.

I lived with that thinking for too long in my professional career, though not that early afternoon in Twickenham in October of 2015. Argentina hit us early, and they finished up winning 43-20.

All my worst daydreams from the long night that preceded the game.

CHAPTER 16

PLAYLISTS.

PLAY SHEETS.

Four years earlier I was reading Joe's sheets on the morning of the game that might have killed off my whole career. That same afternoon in Cardiff's Millennium Stadium I survived the first half. In the second half I was one of Leinster's heroes. I went from zero to hero in my personal journey in the game.

It was May 21, 2011.

It was 5.30 pm when we kicked off against Northampton Saints in the Heineken Cup final. More to my liking! I had a good lie-in, and everything I wanted to eat. I'd filled my head with my rock music.

I needed it all, and more.

My opponent was Soane Tonga'uiha.

Yes, him!

As monsters of human beings go, Soane Tonga'uiha was the total package, not that that worried me in advance of the game. Big men, bad men, absolutely crazy looking dudes, I'd really seen them all by then and the important thing was, I wasn't meeting them in some dark alley. It wasn't a fist fight. Or a wrestling match, or some snarly mixed martial arts contest in the UFC.

It was a scrum.

Soane Tonga'uiha...and me.

147 kilograms...and 124 kilograms.

23 stones and one pound... and 19 stones and seven pounds.

6 feet and 5 inches... and 6 feet and 2 inches.

Most rugby journalists were of the opinion that Tonga'uiha could probably wreck a fast moving train all on his own. Same jury would consider unleashing a search party to pick up the bits and pieces of yours truly if I sought to deal with the same train.

Soane Tonga'uiha was one thing, but on top of him Northampton had decided to act out their own interpretation of the Bajada.

THE MAN WAS Tongan-born.

In Franklin's Gardens they called him 'Tiny.'

Tonga'uiha, in truth, was a pretty poor scrummager when I had first played against him a couple of years before the Heineken Cup final. He moved over from tighthead to the loose side. It was Dorian West, the former Leicester hooker, who took him under his wing at the Saints and worked a particular brand of magic.

All through the 2010-11 season the Saints' pack was handing out severe punishment to every single team they met, and Tonga'uiha became pretty damned good on the other side of the scrum. They were destroying every other team. Their loosehead was lifting people out of his way and depositing them on the side of the road.

In the run-up to the final he was definitely occupying a lot of my thoughts. If anyone had told me at some point before the final that the Saints and ourselves would have the sum total of 18 scrums in the game, then I might have started to worry. As it was, my opponent was taking up enough of my mental space. There's no doubt he was the biggest loosehead I ever faced.

And, if we were not on a rugby pitch, he could break me into two pieces. If it was a bar fight, I doubt that I would come out of it looking particularly well.

But it was only a scrum.

Right?

Before the game, we'd consulted with the match referee Romain Poite and it seemed to be agreed that the Saints would not be allowed to try their hand at any arrowhead against us.

With Poite, however, we might as well have been consulting with the dressing room door. He was the worst referee we could have had for that final. Poite sees what he sees, and for the first 30 minutes of the game Poite saw nothing wrong. In the next 10 minutes before half time our pack started turning the corner.

At half time, we were like men who had been helicoptered out of a life and death situation and had a brief reprieve before being returned to a jungle or a ravine or a war zone. We took our deep breaths.

Me?

Everyone was looking at me.

Leo Cullen was asking me what the hell was happening? Actually, Leo had been asking the same question a few times out on the field as the Saints' pack, and Tonga'uiha in particular, had been manhandling us and driving us in every direction of their choice. It was not exactly like that, but I could not explain to Leo at half time. I told him to give me a minute.

I needed to think.

In the sanctuary of the dressing room I quickly came to the realisation that I had been thinking through the whole situation far too much. I had made the decision from the very first scrum to go after the monster, before he came after me!

As a result, I had separated that bit from Straussy.

I had tried to hit and chase Tonga'uiha. A lot of their scrums started with him powering into me, and I thought it would be to my advantage to get him on the back foot. But that had given Dylan Hartley, their hooker the time to isolate me from Straussy.

It was the first huge final I had ever played in as a professional.

Of course I was guilty of over-thinking. It was the Heineken Cup final, a game I had dreamed about all of my life. I wanted it so badly and I thought…

If I can get across the mark quickly… get him on the back foot?

… we'll be off!

I ended up too far ahead of Straussy.

Greg Feek told us at half time, and showed us on his iPad, that the two of us needed to stay closer. Feeky warned me and Straussy... 'Don't let Hartley through between you two!'

Joe was also being typically Joe and telling the whole team that there was very little that was going wrong. Joe liked to keep his words on the money, his messages easy to get into our thick, sweaty, near panicky skulls.

'Just hold onto the ball!'

Joe kept repeating himself

'Hold onto the...BALL...

'HOLD ONTO THE BALL... just do that!

'Don't give them the ball...

'Hold onto it!'

He also reminded us how to retain possession... 'Make sure your rucks are right...win the collisions...don't give any fifty-fifty passes.'

And... 'Don't try to force things.'

All that and... 'We'll be able to cause them problems!'

That was Joe.

Right up to the last precious seconds, reminding us, as though our skulls were suddenly clad in the thickest of steel.

'Just hold onto the ball...

'HOLD ONTO...

'THE BALL!'

MY CAREER WAS hanging by a thread.

As we walked back onto the pitch I understood that, the same as everyone watching. But I felt emboldened by my own understanding of what had gone wrong in the first half and, furthermore, in the faith shown in me by Joe and Feeky. They had Stan Wright and Heinke van der Merwe on the bench. Nobody would have faulted them for making a switch. Even though we had come through against Leicester and Toulouse in the quarter-final and semi-final, they would have been excused for even the mildest form of second-guessing in our dressing room.

But neither man had switched an inch in his thinking. They backed us as a front row to flip the game on Brian Mujati, Hartley and Tonga'uiha. All 22 of their first half points, in the opinion of most journalists afterwards, had come from their superiority in the scrum.

Their devastating ownership of it.

They led 22-6.

They had crossed our try line in the seventh, 31st and 39th minutes. Dawson, Foden and Hartley had enjoyed those honours, while two penalties from Johnny Sexton in the 14th and 38th minutes had kept us barely alive.

There were 10 scrums in that first half.

Eight more would follow.

THE FIRST SCRUM in the third minute of the game had been our put-in, but we were back-pedalling before we knew it. Jamie Heaslip made yardage off the base and, holding the ball in one hand, was tackled low by Wilson. He knocked it on. I put it down to an opening feeler. The scrum went up one side and back another. Once it was over, I thought… *They didn't mangle us!*

I felt okay 60 seconds later crouching for scrum two.

We were dealing with their pressure, and both front rows popped up. Wilson picked up and off-loaded.

Early days… I thought.

But scrum three led to their opening try. They went arrowhead for the first time on us. Tonga'uiha and Hartley had us in trouble, and Poite signaled for a penalty. They played advantage, attacked our blindside with Clark who put Dawson over for their first try.

Scrum four was unsteady. We were inside their 22 and Jamie had to pick the ball fast and early and get it to safety. We earned our first points of the game after scrum five, but I wasn't happy for the first time in the game. I got myself into a horrible position. I over-extended and found myself on my knees and I thought… *I'm fucking dead here!*

I was in the worst position possible in scrum five.

I was gone. Useless.

But I was not thinking that there was anything fundamentally wrong. I had made a poor decision in scrum five. My mistake. *It's going to be a tough day*... I thought. But... not one of those days!

Some days there are not a lot of scrums. If someone had told me after scrum five... 'Sorry Rossy... there's another 13 of these coming your way!'

Then, maybe, I might have been a little bit concerned.

We'd had five scrums in the first 11 minutes. Scrums six and seven were the worst of the whole amazingly confounding day! They came on 18 minutes and 23 minutes. Count in scrum eight on 27 minutes. That was bad aswell. By then they were down to seven men after Mujati had been sin-binned.

'THREE BLUE'' Poite shouted after scrum six.

For the whole world to hear! And Myler, from wide on the left, made it 10-3 for them with his kick. Brian O'Driscoll was away before scrum seven but was stopped brilliantly by Ben Foden. In scrum seven Tonga'uiha had me up and out of the scrum, and searching the heavens for help.

After scrum eight, Poite had a few harsh words for Leo.

'Your team is coming up under the pressure,' he informed Leo, '... speak to your players!'

I had just experienced the three toughest scrums in my whole career. I felt a sense of panic circling my head, and that was the first time I had ever experienced real concern in my whole career about what was happening on the pitch. Even in Andrew Sheridan's company panic has never taken a grip but, now, I was seriously worried that it might happen. I feared... *My worst nightmare!*

I was surprised at how good they were, and how effective Tonga'uiha was proving to be. I'd been watching them for months, studying them more than any other team. I'd always felt that we'd meet.

I thought I knew them, but it was another thing entirely being on the receiving end of it. I was prepared for it. But I was not prepared for it to happen... to me!

None of my mental preparation included this happening... TO FUCKING ME! However, I knew that I was helping them doing what they were doing to us. I already felt we needed to start working as a complete unit. I knew that I should have been going after Hartley a lot more from the beginning. I should have kept him stapled down.

But, now they were a man down, and they were still powering through us.

Scrum nine was bad again.

What can I do here?

Foden had shrugged off Drico for their second try. They had hooked us against the head in our own 22 and… *What the fuck… they're down to seven men, and they're still at it!* What they were doing was not entirely legal. But we were hopeless at stopping them. As much as anyone watching in the stadium and in their own homes on television, we were in shock and awe.

I was being man-shamed in front of the whole world. Luckily, however, I never thought of my family in the stadium watching me being dissected. If that thought had landed in my brain?

Holy Fuck.

After scrum 10, after Hartley had gone over for their third try in the right corner, I did not feel quite as bad. Scrum 10 was not a disaster.

Scrum 10 felt solid.

Scrum 10, despite the try, said… *Wait a second here… this might not be one-way traffic, Rossy!*

SCRUM 11 WAS FINE.

It was rock solid.

The second half was six minutes in and Johnny had gone over for our first try 60 seconds earlier, and converted. It was 22-13 to them before scrum 11, but the game had changed. They had a victory that they imagined was all wrapped up. We had nothing to lose, not a damn thing.

On the pitch, everyone knew.

We were two different teams. Thinking differently, and acting differently. Feeky had also told us at half time that we were winning the hit in the scrum and then stopping. We thought the job was done, but they were counter-punching. They were waiting… waiting and waiting, and as soon as the pressure eased off from us they were hitting us back. We all saw it on Feeky's MacBook.

Now we were seeing it on the pitch.

And putting it right. We had stopped going back in the two scrums before half time. We were still getting beaten, but we were not being pummelled.

That understanding, and Feeky's clear breakdown of what was happening, had us ready to put our scrum to proper working order.

Scrum 12 changed everything.

Scrum 12 was the game-changer. After scrum 12 Johnny went through Clarke, after a clever Jamie screen, for his second try. Scrum 12 was over, and they were winning by just two points, 22-20.

We'd settled in at that scrum. They, also, were not the same team from the first half in scrum 12. Scrum 12 put doubts into their heads that would never shift and scrum 13 turned the screw with those doubts. All of a sudden we were marching them up the field and winning penalties.

We won a penalty off scrum 13, and Johnny kicked it. We were in front. All of a sudden in scrum 13 Hartley was standing up and we were walking through them. We knew we had taken their best. Equally, they knew we had taken their best. I went in after Hartley in scrum 13 and gave him no room to work with. I kept him low, and down.

Scrum 14 came on 63 minutes, a whole eight minutes after scrum 13. We laid waste to what was left of their pack. Heinke sent Mujati airborne. Hartley was left gasping for air. A blooded Wilson went off. Dawson was in the bin. Poite raised his hands for advantage, as Jamie picked and charged up the field. O'Brien, Straussy and Leo also carried, and Hinesy went over to make it 31-22.

It was all over.

Scrum 15 was ours. Scrum 16 was theirs, surprisingly, but who cared and scrum 17 and scrum 18 on 77 and 78 minutes no longer mattered.

I HAD LISTENED to Joe at half time, but it was a voice in the distance. My own voice, in my head, was charging around the place.

This can't be happening.

We've been in holes before... how'd we get out?

We have to work a way out of this!

How?

We have to get out of this... we CAN get out of this!

We were trailing by 16 points at half time.

We're going to get out of this!

Fuck... I hope they let me help them get out of this!

Joe had faith in me.

It may have buckled for all I know, but it was never lost. He knew and I knew that I was not operating in a vacuum. The implosion in our scrum was not all on me, and neither was the recovery all about me.

It's just that tightheads are typically asked to carry the can for everyone else in the scrum. People were looking at me getting beaten up. They figured I was getting murdered, that I was dead meat.

We were all close to dead meat, but people were looking at me more than anyone else in the scrum. They had heard all about my ability to lock the Leinster and Ireland scrum and, now, they were looking at me getting... mangled, destroyed. With most people not knowing what the scrum is really all about, people must have been confused at half time.

They must have been looking at me, thinking... *Mike Ross... con job!*

If we had lost that final it would have been an opinion that I would have shared. The greatest season of my rugby life would have been rudely beheaded.

Finally nailing down a spot in the Leinster team, followed by playing my first Six Nations with Ireland, that too would have counted for nothing much.

Ending the 2010-11 season by surviving against Soane Tonga'uiha and then defeating Soane Tonga'uiha, and ensuring that Leinster won the Heineken Cup had impressively bound one long season together.

Irish rugby supporters had watched me come back from the dead.

For 40 minutes they had felt only pity and sympathy.

They had every right.

And then they watched me become Lazarus. *The Irish Times* wrote about me and compared me to Sylvester Stallone in one of his many *Rocky* movies.

But Rocky didn't have Joe Schmidt and Greg Feek in his corner, and he didn't have Cian Healy and Richardt Strauss and a whole gang of men in blue duck between the ropes with him.

AFTER 67 MINUTES, he had left the pitch.

Soane Tonga'uiha was taken out of it and I never saw the man after the game. I never shook his hand, and I never played against him, ever, after that.

I never met him.

That afternoon he had looked the most formidable and impossible opponent I might ever have to face. Up close, he looked huge in the Millennium Stadium, and far bigger than I had remembered him from two years earlier.

Anyone looking at us and comparing us that afternoon would only have seen one winner, but scrummaging is not that simple. I could not squat 300 kilos like him. I was not as tall or as heavy as him. Luckily scrums are not decided by measurement tapes. Or weights. More often they are decided by technique and intuition, and also a collective.

One man never won a scrum. And one man never lost a scrum.

All of the Northampton players were lost in the depths of misery after the game. I was not in the best of moods myself. The madness of what had happened had descended upon me, and the realisation of a dream left me ecstatic, but I had gone into the game with a partially separated AC joint. My right shoulder was in bits before the game, and I had taken a dose of painkillers to numb that throbbing pain.

Within an hour of the game ending, I started being hit by waves of nausea. I was wanting to throw up. I began to feel physically ill. In the scrum the codeine had taken the edge off the discomfort, and adrenaline had also played its part.

Eventually though, the pain receded, and I was able to properly enjoy the night. Many of my family were at the post match celebrations at The Burlington Hotel, and we continued long into the night. I finished up in a taxi coming home from town as the dawn broke and the birds began to sing. I crawled into the bed next to my wife, who had the good sense to come home hours earlier, and I was asleep before my head hit the pillow.

PART FIVE

MEETING MR SCHMIDT

CHAPTER 17

IN MY EIGHT seasons with Leinster I had four head coaches. The two Australians, Michael Cheika and Matt O'Connor weren't the best for my career, while Leo Cullen, good friend that he is, walked me respectfully into retirement. Truth is, my Leinster career was all about Joe Schmidt.

When Joe replaced Cheika in the summer of 2010 I had no idea what lay in store for me. I certainly would never have dreamed that I'd be part of two Heineken Cup winning teams, winning the two of them back-to-back and at that point in time becoming only the second team in the history of the tournament to actually retain the trophy.

But not everybody loved Joe.

As I've always explained, in any professional dressing room, it's usually the case that one third of the players love the coach, one third don't love him all that much, and the other third sit somewhere in between.

Unashamedly, I can say I loved everything Joe Schmidt brought to the job.

When the time came for him to move onto the Ireland job, I had to accept it. In a perfect sci-fi world I would have liked to have had the man cloned, and keep one Joe Schmidt back in Leinster.

But that's pro rugby.

Everyone's voice goes stale after a few years. There are not many Arsene

Wengers or Brian Codys to be found in our game, men who hit a 20th anniversary as team bosses. Besides, Joe had a greater calling in his career and the Irish team was waiting for him to bring it to places people in rugby in this country had only previously dreamed about.

IT'S NOT LIKE I totally disgraced myself any time I had the ball in my hand, but Cheika favoured forwards who could run around more with the ball.

Joe saw things differently.

Joe needed to see in the first instance if I would become a vitally important part of his system. Joe was building a machine, if you like, and he arrived at the judgment that the machine was stronger with me in the middle of things.

But I could still carry the ball.

Some people forget that I played most of my professional rugby in my 30s, whereas Tadhg Furlong, who is phenomenal when he takes possession, is in his early 20s. Tadhg is ready to tear around the place.

When I was his age, I was also a little faster on my feet.

SO, SCHMIDT WAS amongst us.

What now? I wondered.

A new coach brings everything back to Ground Zero.

He can't be any worse for me than Cheiks… can he?

What's he going to do?

Play me less than Cheiks… that's not even possible!

But they started bringing Jack McGrath over and tried him out at tight, and while Jack was not having a whole lot of fun there, I was thinking… *Shit!*

He's such a good loosehead… why on earth would they want to bring him over?

I knew they were also scouring the whole damn globe looking for a tighthead. Greg Feek was sent on a mission to bring one home!

I was in my 30s.

And Stan was in his 30s.

Underneath us, what did they have? Jamie Hagan was there, but he ended up going over to Connacht. Leinster were not producing too many tightheads at that time. Stewart Maguire in the academy was a huge man, 6' 5" and 130 kilos, and he was doing well for Old Belvedere and had a handful of Ireland under-20 caps, but it did not happen for him in Leinster either. He also travelled west. Jack O'Connell, who was more of a loosehead, went over to Bristol to restart his career. Then there was Marty Moore, but Marty was injured a lot and Marty too, despite having things lined up nicely for himself here a few years later, also went to England. Marty had asked me for my thoughts several times.

I advised him not to go.

It was tough advice for me to give him, because it was in my selfish interests for Marty to leave Leinster! He had massive potential, and he might have taken my place and a lot of my contract. My value went up after Marty left. But, I still told him to think long and hard before making the decision to go.

Excellent tightheads are hard to find.

Feeky had his Wellington association and was searching about the place in the Southern Hemisphere, but most of the players of international standard were already spoken for, I knew that for sure. I knew who they all were, though when the rumour started doing the rounds that they had found who they were looking for in Toulouse, and had lined up Benoit Lecouls, I held my breath for a little while.

They could still have come around the corner with anyone! But I could not worry about it. I reminded myself that I could only control the controllables. I could not enter either Feeky's brain or Joe's, and reprogramme them, could I?

I still probed Feeky.

New Zealand was not a scrummaging powerhouse but they had a good selection of props at that time. *Stop worrying… stop… don't even think about it…* I repeatedly advised myself.

At the same time, I was enjoying working with Feeky. He was capped 10 times by the All Blacks between 1999 and 2001 before moving into coaching with the Super Rugby franchise, the Hurricanes. He was an outstanding coach and he picked up on the simplest things. We had a habit of setting up on our toes, so that we'd get across the mark faster. At the very first session with Feeky, I remember he said that he wanted us on the balls of our feet.

'You're going to generate more power through the balls of your feet,' he informed us all, '… than you do through your toes!' We all had this idea that tilting forward would get us across quicker. On the balls of your feet, what you lose in speed, you gain in power.

It made sense.

We'd talk about everything, almost from day one. We also had some running arguments. I felt we should cheat more in the scrum. Feeky was adamant that we would get more out of it if we were straight and legal.

One-on-one, we'd have these big discussions.

Ultimate nerds. Deep in discussion, while everyone else was changing and showering, and wanting to head home. But we'd be on the laptop, looking for things. At home in the evenings I might find something on YouTube, and I'd get the clip and send it onto him on my phone. We were kindred spirits when it came to the scrum.

Feeky's mentor was Mike Cron, a legend back in New Zealand. Cron is better known as 'The Scrum Doctor' and it's not just his knowledge that makes him the best. He's been through six World Cups in one capacity or another, but he also looks at other sports and picks up bits and pieces. He's studied sumo wrestling in Japan. In the United States he's looked deep into football and basketball, even ice hockey. He's been to cage fighting. And he attended the New Zealand Royal Ballet. 'For their lifting,' Cron stated last year to quickly explain his new interest.

Like Cron, everything with Feeky began and ended with physics. If everyone's spines are in a line and everyone is at the same height in the scrum, exactly, then that scrum is equipped and fully loaded to transfer the maximum amount of power.

'If everyone is lined up,' Feeky would tell us, '… then the power can only go in one direction!' He never wanted anyone pointing in a whole different direction, not even by half an inch.

IN AUGUST, IN a warm up match against Wasps in Donnybrook, I have to selfishly admit that things fell into my lap.

I started the game

Stan came in for me, and blew his Achilles.

I came back in, and I strained my calf, but while I missed the first game in the Magners League against Glasgow – and Joe started with Heinke, Straussy and Simon Shawe – I knew that my misfortune was temporary. Shawe was my age. He was playing for Ballymena in Division Two of the All-Ireland League after not getting his break with Ulster years before. He lived in Lisburn and held down a day job, but we needed cover and Shawe answered Feeky's call. I didn't think Shawesy was going to overtake me. Shawe was more than decent.

But the opportunity was only in my hands.

Stan's bad luck was the serious break I needed. I knew Stan was looking at a solid six months. It was my opportunity… my time, and I knew that if I failed to take it… then… I could pack my bags in Leinster and look back with fewer regrets.

Joe got off to a slow start. We lost games. He was bedding in new systems and defensive structures, and you can't rush these things. Besides, from week one, the training pitch with Joe Schmidt calling and whistling was like a place I had never encountered before. It was new to everybody.

All the lifers in Leinster, from Brian O'Driscoll down, could not believe what was happening. It was like every single man was going to get a second chance at becoming a far greater player.

The easiest things, but things that made us all think faster, and think faster on our feet and think faster with our hands than we had thought possible. He still does these things, basic things, like lining up five players in a line and calling out a sequence of numbers… 3…6…4…1…5… and you have to pass the ball in that sequence. He doesn't call a second time. On the fly, players must adapt, react, think… think and think harder. At the same time, Joe empowered us.

Two years later, when we defeated Clermont in Bordeaux in the Heineken Cup semi-final, we had a smart move planned off our lineout and we went for it straight after half time. The lineout did not go to plan. I ended up with the ball at the back but instead of trying to formulate a Plan X and putting my head down, I passed the ball off to Isaac Boss.

Not one newspaper the next morning questioned what had happened.

Brian O'Driscoll and Rob Kearney punched a hole in the Clermont defence and Cian Healy had an easy run through to the sticks for a vital try that brought us back from six points down at half time. The move was quickly reworked, and it *worked*!

Joe, from day one to his very last day in Leinster, made sure that we all had faith in the system. If you do this… and this and this, he'd repeatedly tell us… 'Then you will be rewarded fellas!'

He'd predict that stuff would go wrong.

'Stick with it…

'Make it happen!'

WE LOST THE opener to Glasgow 22-19.

And we kept losing. In the middle of September we were the first Irish team to lose to Treviso. It was rainy and skiddy over there, as usual, but we lost big time, 29-13 and even when they lost their hooker and captain, Leonardo Ghiraldini when he was sin-binned near the finish we still could not score.

A week later we had our third away defeat on the trot, to Edinburgh, 32-24, and we had our first match against Munster right around the corner in the Aviva Stadium, and then Racing Metro in the RDS in our opening match of the Heineken Cup a week later. Cheika would have been very unhappy looking at us, but Joe remained absolutely calm those first few weeks.

He just kept collecting his thoughts.

BUT I WAS in the team.

And I was getting ready for the two games that would surely determine for Joe and Feeky my true worth to their team.

I was not taking any chances.

Against Edinburgh, I'd come up against Allan Jacobsen, a lifer with the club and someone who had been on the Scottish team since 2002. They called him 'Chunk' because he was a short, little guy. When he finally retired they took a cast of his outrageous looking cauliflower ear and they still give it to the Player of the Year in Edinburgh.

It's something I'd be proud to have in my home.

We had Dominic Ryan in against Edinburgh, and I had noticed that Jacobsen was one of those looseheads who liked to do a 'walkaround', which meant he liked to swing his hips out in the scrum and come at me from a different angle. I told Dominic, who we preferred to call Dippy, to keep an eye on him, and told him that if Jacobsen went for a walkaround then he needed to feel Dippy's head in his ribs to straighten him out.

Dippy understood me perfectly.

Dippy was also young and extremely enthusiastic. And he gave Jacobsen a right good dig every time he moved outside in the scrum.

Jacobsen was soon spitting nails.

'Tell that young fucker,' he told me, struggling to catch his breath after another dig had been received, 'that if he wants to come to the front… and scrummage… come to the front!

'But if… he does that… ONE…

'MORE… TIME.

'I'm going to

'…put him…

'IN THE FUCKING GROUND!'

I was trying not to burst my arse laughing.

When Jacobsen had finished I politely advised him, 'Keep your hips in man… and I'm fairly sure it won't happen again!'

CHAPTER 18

THE 30-0 DRUBBING in the RDS 12 months earlier was the third of four successive wins we'd had over Munster. In league and cup meetings we led them 10-9. But meeting them at the beginning of a whole new season was a game in which Joe Schmidt and every single one of us would be measured.

Queenslander, Tony McGahan, who had come in after Declan Kidney in 2008 was Joe's opponent. Mine was Wian du Preez, from Bloemfontein. We would win in the Aviva 13-9. The following April down in Thomond Park they'd take their revenge, 24-23 and they'd end up top of the table. We were right behind them. In the final of the Magners League, back in their neck of the woods once again, they beat us again, 19-9.

Marcus Horan was back in the front row by the final. I had done fine against du Preez. I got a couple of penalties off him, he got a couple off me. Horan was a whole different customer, and he had his tricks. I also brought my own box of tricks any time I was in Marcus' company. I've had it out with him since we retired and we landed in Legends squads together. I've asked him about that... round, so innocent face of his?

Marcus was not a massive man. But he was clever, and he did like his 'hinging'... where he bends at the hips and nothing more... and his opponent falls flat on his face. Marcus, meanwhile, would stand back up and look down at the human wreckage in front of him as though he had not the foggiest notion what had just occurred.

But the 2010-11 season and Joe Schmidt's first was not defined, on this occasion, by Leinster and Munster and our bittersweet but great rivalry. While Munster won the league, we got our hands on the bigger prize of the Heineken Cup.

And it all began in the RDS, for Joe, and for me personally, with our 38-22 victory over Racing Metro. It was, at that time, the most pressurised game I would ever play in. I felt all eyes were on me.

That's because they probably were, and when I looked into the mirror I also asked myself, just in case… *was Michael Cheika right?*

Or… am I right?

It was that sort of game. Career defining. Simply that, and I needed to make sure that Andrea Lo Cicero would not be able to forget the game for a long time. Simply that, nothing less.

He's Sicilian, Lo Cicero, and he was already well on his way to over 100 caps for Italy. I ended up playing against him so many times in the following years and I remembered almost every single one of them. We always seemed to have big battles. He was a strong scrummager, but that first time I met him, in the RDS, we were that bit quicker than their front row, and we went that bit lower. The ball was in and gone before they knew too much about it.

I wanted to make sure Lo Cicero was kissing his own knees.

I knocked his head down.

I made him adjust his feet all the time, and I kept changing my stance to get inside him. Our first big battle was over, and it was my victory. No doubt about that. I had everything to lose while he was in the process of counting down to the final season of his brilliant career. He quit in 2013.

The game went so well for me that Joe name-checked me afterwards, and Joe usually avoids name-checking individual players, but myself and Richardt Strauss, who had also grabbed at his biggest opportunity in a Leinster shirt, shared that honour. Joe knew that both of us were in the same boat, in the same saloon if you like… both of them labelled Last Chance… or Second Last Chance.

Whatever the name, we were both in places in our careers where a huge performance was demanded of us, and we had a new coach who was placing an enormous amount of faith in us – and in the process seriously doubting the wisdom of his immediate successor, who didn't play the pair of us, but had still proved himself a Heineken Cup winner!

I did the job for Leinster right through the autumn, and I felt that I would also have Declan Kidney rethinking about what I could bring to the Ireland team.

John Hayes was 37 and people in the game were craning their necks to see who would be his successor. I believed that person should be me. I also knew that lots more people believed the rightful successor was Tony Buckley.

In the November series of 2010, however, Declan did not give me one minute of game time in the four matches. He still loved The Bull. Everyone did. And Declan knew so much more about Buckley as a Munsterman.

The 2011 World Cup was my ultimate target.

The clock was ticking.

By the time that World Cup came around, I had played through the 2011 Six Nations and it was not a contest between Tony Buckley and myself for The Bull's magnificent old shirt. It was Tom Court or me! And Tom was not a natural tighthead. He had a shot-putting background and his strength in the gym was jaw-dropping. He was quick. He had athletic gifts, but Tom struggled to become an outstanding tighthead whereas, on the other side of the scrum, when he was of a mind he could simply demolish tightheads.

By then, Tony Buckley's performances had slipped. People were talking about his inconsistency, and because he was the biggest man in the Irish dressing room they were also demanding more aggression from him.

They wanted him to be aggressive all the time. Tony got a reputation for not quite hitting the mark on either front, consistency or aggression, and reputations usually stick like damned blood-sucking leeches. It was unfair on Tony.

The Bull, in his formative days, lived through seasons when people foolishly agreed he was not a very good scrummager. It may have been true at the start but in his latter years he was as good as anyone out there. It took The Bull a long time to remove that label that was stuck tight to his name.

WE SCORED FIVE tries that amazing day against Racing.

We also took down Chabal early, which is something that every team sets out to do. Sebastian Chabal was Racing's talisman, same as he became his country's talisman. He's the sort of individual that queues of people would probably line up behind anywhere he went.

He looks mesmerising, that hard and dark stare, and those flowing locks that are stuck to his face. He could be a cult leader. He could be a caveman. Chabal is made of iron and after 74 seconds he whacked into Jamie Heaslip and sent him onto the broad of his back, though Jamie held onto the ball.

In the tunnel, as we waited to come out onto the pitch, I could not help looking at them out of the corner of my eyes and I could not help thinking... *Fuck!*

They're... fucking HUGE!

It was Isa Nacewa, typically, who took the first chunk out of Chabal with a death-defying tackle, and then the rest of us followed with any chance that came our way. We had conjured up the first try of the game after 30 minutes. And I was in the middle of it. As well as dominating them in the scrum, I had put on my running shoes for this particular match.

Straussy ran a great line.

Gordon D'Arcy showed his fastest feet to break their line.

Sean O'Brien carried the ball.

I carried the ball.

We were within a metre of their line and from the resulting ruck Seanie had repositioned himself, and he took the final pass and went over.

After the game, Joe mentioned in particular that I had taken a step forward in my workload around the field.

A small part of me was hoping that Michael Cheika was listening. A bigger part of me, far larger, was sincerely hoping that Declan Kidney was listening. That was far more important.

But Kidney was not tuned in.

The following month the South Africans, Samoans, All Blacks and Argentinians all came to Ireland and I was in his 34-man squad but when the trimming started to the edges of that squad, I was gone. Every time.

JOE HAD A six-match unbeaten run that came to an end in the Liberty Stadium at the very end of November. Clint Newland started. Newland was a 30 years old New Zealand Maori prop who had featured for Hawke's Bay 94 times in the NPC, and for the Highlanders in the Super 14/15 he had a further 24 appearances. Feeky had found him and brought him in as cover until February.

I came in for him after 42 minutes. We lost the match to the Ospreys 19-15 but, worse than that, we gave away a penalty try on my watch.

They got us under our posts.

We had a fairly inexperienced team out and they took full advantage of us. As a prop, a penalty try is one of the most emasculating things that can ever happen to you.

I was not happy heading back home.

To have genuine ambitions of playing for Ireland I knew there was no way that penalty tries against us could be deposited on my doorstep.

It was the first penalty try on my watch in eight years.

It had awful timing, however.

In the back-to-back Heineken Cup group games in early December we lost to Clermont in their place, 20-13 but turned them over 24-8 in the return match which left Joe buzzing. Any time Joe got one over on his old pal, Vern Cotter whom he'd backed up as forwards coach in Clermont for three years he was especially happy. The rabid competitor in the ice cool coach would pop his its head up in the air and say… that feels good, fellas!

We sealed home advantage in the Heineken Cup quarter-finals when we went to Colombes where there was no Chabal, no Lo Cicero, and we romped home 36-11 with five tries from Isa, Seanie, Drico and two from Johnny. I was playing well, and for the first time I felt that I was starting to put a lot of pressure on to get picked for Ireland. People were asking why I wasn't featuring in squads.

I liked those questions, but at the same time I didn't want to get used to it, I didn't trust it.

It was nice to have a bit of support out there though after years of indifference.

My contract was up that June too, and of course as is usual the rumour mill started up, linking me with a return to Munster. It was never going to happen, I was too well settled in Dublin.

But it received headlines in the media. And perhaps the speculation helped me to nail down a central contract even though I had only amassed seven caps by the end of March.

I was enjoying a spell of good form, and I wanted to be more than a part of Declan Kidney's squad, I wanted a shot at the starting jersey. Not many play past their mid-30s, although front rowers last longer than most. I was just about to turn 31, and a World Cup was months away.

And that same month, rather than come back and restart with Leinster, Stan Wright signed a two-year contract with Stade Francais. Stan was heading back to his old coach, Michael Cheika.

I could only wish him well.

ALL OF MY concentration was reserved for Leicester, who were coming to the Aviva for a Heineken Cup quarter-final.

In the absence of my old pal, Marcus Areyza their coach Richard Cockerill put his faith in his Kiwi loosehead, Boris Stankovich. They had their bench loaded with Martin Castrogiovanni and Julien White. Stankovich sounds a tough customer and he was, and just for effect he possessed a very leaky ear that I had encountered in the past.

A lot of the time that ear was leaking over me while I was scrummaging. There was fluid pouring out of the damn thing. But that was the least of my worries. I had him and if we defeated the Tigers, probably I had Jean Baptiste Poux of Toulouse to consider.

Stankovich and Poux.

They stood between me and my first Heineken Cup final. They stood between me and Soane Tonga'uiha!

But... one at a time.

Leicester lost to us in the Aviva and, as they fondly do, the Tigers ripped every ounce of energy out of us before they finally fell. It was 17-10 in the end. I was never so tired after a match. I sat in the dressing room and I remember wondering to myself... *how long can I sit here... before I have to actually move...*

Before I have to lift a limb… stand up
Walk?

We won the only way you can against the Tigers. We did not flinch in the scrum, we dissected their lineout, we defended stoutly despite wave after wave of relentless hard running from them, and we contested the ball in every single bloody tackle… and the tackle count must have been in the thousands! Yeah, and we also counter-rucked them and managed to rip the heart out of that famous jersey occasionally, which is a wondrous thing on a rugby pitch.

Poux was an extra strong boy who could play either side of the scrum. He helped himself to 42 caps for France and nearly reached the magical 300 number for Toulouse.

With him and Servat, who was a scrummaging hooker with few equals, I had no room for error, none whatsoever against Toulouse. Servat was always like an extra prop. I'd see it on his face. He'd take the guys under his arms and there would be absolute relish on that face.

Every scrum for William Servat was another feast.

We won 32-23 after making every mistake in the book in the opening quarter. But, as Joe had preached for almost nine months, all we needed to do was work that little bit harder at getting his system right. We were imperious at times in the second half as we strode to our victory but, in that first half, it was scratching around the pitch and trying to get Joe's system in action.

Shane Horgan had chased and caught Johnny Sexton's kick off. After that, it was error after fumble after indecision, and back to error again.

Leo was beaten to the first lineout by Yannick Nyanga.

Straussy overthrew the second.

The first scrum was a penalty to them, and their first attack into our 22 resulted in a penalty for David Skrela.

It shaved an upright and bounced in the in-goal area.

As if to prove nothing could go right for us, the bounce cleared all of our heads and landed back into the arms of Florian Fritz. We got out of jail, but we needed to do more than that, and Johnny's penalty kick gave us points on the board and concentrated our minds, finally. Johnny would kick five more of them. Jamie's try put us in front. Drico got binned. He'd come back onto the field to score and give us a huge nine-points advantage but, before then, two props laid down the law.

Cian charged up the touchline and it took a desperate tackle from Picamoles to deny him a stunning try. Soon after that he was replaced by Heinke who, first time of asking, heaved Census Johnston high into the air.

It was a long and worrying afternoon.

But Joe Schmidt had told us all season long that things would go wrong. And he'd told us to stick with it.

'Then you will be rewarded fellas!'

Joe's words, his promise.

'Stick with it…

'Make it happen!'

IN OUR FINAL game before the Heineken Cup final, in a 'demolition derby' with Ulster in the Magners League semi-final in the RDS, I had damaged my AC joint. Also in the A& E were Brian O'Driscoll, Isaac Boss, Richardt Strauss and Seanie O'Brien, but Seanie was fine. Three stitches inserted into a wound in his head was almost playful by Seanie's personal measurement of bangs and bruises.

All thoughts centred on Drico's damaged knee.

On my mind, however, was Soane Tonga'uiha. The Northampton front row was quite a mixture of treats. A naturalised Kiwi hooker in Dylan Hartley, and either side of him a Zimbabwean Springbok in Brian Mujati and one Tongan in Tonga'uiha. On the Tuesday before the game I was asked to speak to the media on behalf of the team.

I spoke about Northampton's arrowhead formation.

Why not?

I spoke about Mujati and Tonga'uiha tucking themselves tightly into Hartley and trundling forward. 'It can be fairly hard to stop at times,' I forewarned.

It was hard to believe that I had arrived at a Heineken Cup final, that I had survived Cheika, that I earned Joe's trust and, what's more, that I had also finally won over Declan Kidney in the Six Nations that spring.

I was about to play in my first Heineken Cup final, and little did I know that I would also move past Tony Buckley and Tom Court, and I would get to anchor the Irish scrum in the 2011 World Cup in New Zealand. Get to visit that country for the first time. And get to play in the tournament of all tournaments.

The only time I had been at a Heineken Cup final before 2011 was way back in 2002 when I was over in Cardiff supporting Munster, and myself and my Dad and our friends did not have enough tickets. I was wearing an old UCC jersey. And we came across this guy who wanted my jersey. And I gave him my dingy old UCC jersey, and he handed me a ticket to the game.

TALKING TO THE media before the Heineken Cup final the last question asked of me was about my direct opponent.

And... 'Soane Tonga'uiha?'... a journalist enquired.

The 22-stone loosehead had cut loose on Ulster in the quarter-final and also Perpignan in the semi-final. Before replying, I took a deeper breath than I did for any of the other questions through the afternoon.

'Tonga'uiha?' I was reminded by my questioner.

CHAPTER 19

THE 2011 WORLD Cup, and the weeks and months preparing for it, and its disappointing aftermath, meant that I was away from the Leinster dressing room for almost three months. I was one of 14 Leinster men on duty with Ireland in the tournament.

Being an accepted part of the Leinster team and the Ireland team was so good. All my dreams, all my planning in London had worked out, just about in the nick of time. I nailed down my place on the Ireland team close to midnight on the big ticking clock. It was a close-run thing.

Having two team bosses to answer to was also part of the plan, but it took a little getting use to, having Joe in one ear and Declan in the other. Each man's wishes, and each man's game plan and its most intricate details, had to be deposited in two separate boxes in my head.

The 2011-12 season would also see the two coaches head in different career paths, however. Kidney was in his second last season as Ireland coach and already the memories of 2009 and Ronan O'Gara's Grand Slam winning kick, and the gratitude that the whole country felt for Declan and his team, was beginning to recede. In the 2012 Six Nations we would start and end with defeats to Wales and England respectively.

Whether he fully realised it or not, Declan Kidney had already started making his long goodbye as a successful and famous Ireland head coach.

Joe, on the other hand, despite one Heineken Cup at his back, was still only starting. He'd win a second Heineken Cup in 2012 and a Challenge Cup in 2013, succeed Declan and win two Six Nations Championships, defeat all three Southern Hemisphere nations for the first time, including the little matter of finally bringing the All Blacks to their knees in front of us and, then, he'd see to it that Ireland didn't have to wait very long for another Grand Slam.

OUR DEFENCE OF the Heineken Cup started in the Stade de la Mosson in Montpellier, in a soccer stadium that was built for the 1998 World Cup. It was a mixed day for me, and the team. Repeatedly, I was on the receiving end of some damned smart chop tackling from their tighthead, Max Bustos an Argentinian who had me on his radar for some reason.

I conceded a penalty at an early ruck that was also annoying. We knuckled down and spent a five-minute period hammering away at them, and just when we got to 10 metres from their line and were set to reward our hard work with a try we turned over the ball. Instead of us going over their whitewash they hacked the ball on and their flanker, Fulgence Quedraogo helped himself to five points at the other end of the field.

We trailed 16-6 at one stage.

Sean Cronin scored a great try to complete a sweeping move, and Johnny grabbed the draw with the last kick of the game. It was 16-16, but we bulked up for our Heineken Cup defence with five straight wins after that in a group that included Glasgow and Bath. We finished second in the final seeded table to Munster, though Ulster surprised them in the quarter-final down in Thomond Park, winning by six points.

YESSSSSSSSSS.

THAT WAS the first, long word out of my mouth the first time I packed down for a scrum with Brad Thorn directly behind me.

Yes...

Yes...

Yesssssssssss.

There were a lot of yeses. But the first day that Thorn arrived and said his hellos there was an excited air in the dressing room, and there are not many times in a professional environment that you can sense that slight change. In Leinster there was no greater legend than Brian O'Driscoll. Someone coming in and grabbing everyone's attention was a rarity.

Lots of the lads were eager to chat with Thorn.

We wanted to pick his mind, and we also wanted to impress him. And how often does a 'new boy' have a whole team wanting to do right by him.

That was the Brad Thorn effect when he joined us on a three-months contract at the beginning of March of 2012. One look at the man informed you that he was an exceptional human being. Besides appearing to be made of granite, he also had a career that spanned both codes in rugby with equal brilliance.

He joined us from the Japanese club, Fukuoka Sanix Blues where he had been playing since winning the World Cup with the All Blacks. But Thorn had made over 200 appearances for the Australian rugby league giants, the Brisbane Broncos before beginning his 59-cap career with the All Blacks that also included three Tri-Nations titles. The man did not quit playing until 2015, when he turned 40!

There are tighthead locks!

And there are loosehead locks! Though Paul O'Connell was equally strong on either side. In Leinster the previous season we had Nathan Hines as my tighthead lock but he'd moved on to Clermont. Steven Sykes had come to us from South Africa but he'd struggled with his fitness, and Damien Browne, who was brilliant behind me, had a shoulder injury that left him fighting a 12-week fitness battle. Leo Cullen, who was a loosehead lock, was also on the injured list with a damaged Achilles. On a few occasions, Joe had used Dev Toner as my tighthead lock but against the bigger teams, and especially the French, more muscle mass was simply required.

Thorn was not a massive size of a man, and he wasn't the tallest, maybe 6' 4", but when he hit people... they stayed... HIT! What he had was total power. In the gym he was never too bothered taking the requisite rest period between different sets. When Brad Thorn was 'resting' he would still do some core exercises. And we'd be there, looking at him. And watching him stretch… he stretched for about an hour every single day.

He could also scrummage brilliantly and his technique was exceptional. He stayed connected with me the whole way through the scrum. It was not just… BANG… and nothing else.

Thorn was a constant force in every scrum. He stayed connected to his tighthead, and after a few hits on the machine I came to the conclusion that Carl Hayman and Owen Franks, New Zealand's respected tightheads, merely served as a human scrum sled for him.

Some locks give the impression that scrummaging is just another part of their job description, but Thorn loved it and in Leinster he had an influence that extended way beyond the three months he was with us.

He loved every second of the scrum.

When we defeated Cardiff in the quarter-final of the Heineken Cup, I came into training on the Monday and found him there, in the video room, and he was watching the game. He was viewing the compilation of scrums. Everything else in our fairly magnificent 34-3 victory was of far less interest to him. In the scrum we'd made them give up a small truckload of penalties and free-kicks.

Nobody else ever got into our video room and watched a scrum before me!

But Thorn was sitting there, and he was chuckling.

Just smiling and chuckling away to himself, with nobody else in the place, and the particular scrum he kept pausing and rewinding, and playing over and over for his own amusement, had been one very satisfying effort where we'd managed to get the nudge on and disrupt their ball.

THEN, ONE FINE morning, one newspaper officially named me as the most valuable player in Irish rugby.

It was an amazing thing to see in print, in black and white, for two good reasons, and probably a few more. To start with, nobody in the country – and not too many people deep within the game – had been all that bothered about giving the scrum the time of day for decades. And, to finish with, I was the same tighthead who had been told for years and years, up to my 30th birthday and beyond, that I just wasn't quite good enough to make it at the very highest level in the Irish game.

Shit... I thought to myself... *zero to hero.*

And another... *shit... there's always one fast moving elevator that brings heroes back down to earth.*

But, I told myself I could enjoy it for one morning at least... and also enjoy the thought that there might be a few people saying novenas for my continued good health.

TOM COURT, FOR starters, might have a view on my prized elevation, I warned myself. Tom was my opponent in the final of the Heineken Cup. My roommate in Ireland camps and trips – since we were first introduced on Ireland's 2008 Churchill Cup tour of the US in 2008 - and one of my best coffee buddies when we landed in a different city and wanted to sit back and relax, and watch the locals go about their business.

Ulster had taken Edinburgh, 22-19, while we had gone to Bordeaux and taken the scalp of Clermont, 19-15. We'd watched the Ulster game in our hotel the evening before. And we all noted something that we thought was interesting once the final whistle blew. Ulster went a little ballistic with their excitement. They were into a final for the first time in 13 years admittedly, but a lap of honour and some serious interaction with their celebrating supporters seemed, to us, to be excessive. There's a long way from a semi-final to a final.

And an even a longer way from the kick-off in the final to the last whistle from the referee. Finals are merciless games.

An All-Ireland final for the whole of Europe to sit back and enjoy was our mission, but Clermont were as physical and relentless as ever, and I remember at one stage trying to crawl out of a ruck and being dragged back into the pile for a nice helping of shoe pie, their pack obviously having come to the conclusion that I did not get my share first time around.

That All-Ireland final looked a busted flush close to the end, as we watched Wesley Fofana celebrating a try. It looked good to all of us, and having fought back from a 12-6 deficit to go four points to the good it was sickening to have the game ripped out of our grasp.

The only try of the game up to then, from Cian Healy, had been one of those classic Joe strike plays that he had us practice and practice and practice all week long – just like he'd worked over and over again on the CJ Stander try that helped Ireland to the Grand Slam victory over England in Twickenham. Joe had used that same set piece that led to CJ's try only once before, three years before against England in Dublin, when Robbie Henshaw was through but unluckily got taken down by Billy Vunipola. Joe kept the move in his back pocket all that time.

The TMO in Bordeaux, however, deemed that Fofana had fumbled the ball over the line. I could not help thinking in the dressing room that if Fofana had spent half an hour less in the gym working on his biceps we would have been out. The ball had nudged off his bicep.

Thankfully, I had Tom and Rory Best to think about, as that All-Ireland final was put back on the table. I knew what Tom would be like, and I knew for sure that I did not want to take him on in any areas where he could utilise his superior strength. I wanted to try and get inside and on top of Besty, and keep Tom down that extra little bit. Keep him compressed.

Get him to work that incredible strength of his on correcting his body position, and not have him directing that strength straight at me. In a contest of pure strength, Tom was going to have me, nine days out of 10.

I needed my angles.

And I needed my wits about me all the time in his company.

He knew me as well as I knew him, however, and he knew what I was thinking and planning with as much devious intent as I could muster. Even if he was a friend. Knowing one another was okay with me. I'd prefer that every day rather than face a complete stranger.

I would not have to spend 30 minutes figuring out Tom.

I needed to keep him under me

I needed to stop him driving me up.

And I knew how to do both. I wanted to beat him across the mark, and catch him with his feet forward. I wanted him to have to take a step back, and re-gather. And while he was doing all of that, I wanted to keep going and get inside him. At Besty.

That would be half the job done.

After that there was Besty to deal with, who's also a great scrummager and a teak tough competitor. I go a long way back with Besty, my first memory of him was playing against Belfast Harlequins for Con. A scrum popped up, and I found myself face-to-face with him. Besty had a little think, and then promptly head-butted me square in the nose. We became very good friends since, but all that would go out the window for the final.

WE WON OUR second Heineken Cup with a bit to spare in the end. The first half was tight enough but we eventually pulled clear.

Five tries to one, coming in the 12th, 31st and 44th minutes, before they crossed our line for the only time on 60 minutes from Tuohy. Seanie and Cian got our first two tries, and the third was a glorious penalty try from a maul. Heinke and Sean Cronin got our last two in the 76th and 80th minutes.

Four tries courtesy of the props department.

Leo became the first man to ever raise the trophy three times though, typically, Leo shared the honour every time with chosen teammates and did so again in Twickenham with Shane Jennings after our 44-14 victory.

It was like a victory that was pre-ordained and it was entirely different to the final 12 months before. This time, my biggest and proudest memory was not taken from one of the scrums. It was something small that went unseen. Eoin Reddan had box kicked and Dave Kearney competed for the ball. It bounced free.

I managed to get down and scoop up the ball to Straussy, half a second before getting opened up by Stefan Terblanche. I took my punishment, happily. Straussy streaked up the pitch before he was finally hauled down.

It was a swing point in the game in which Ulster needed to find the tiniest snatch of daylight. That movement snuffed them out.

My first encounter with Ulster had been way back in 1999 on the day that they were crowned kings of Europe, and UCC were honoured at half time as student kings of Europe.

They were infused with serious South African pedigree, and nobody in

Leinster anticipated a walk in the park. It was no such walk, despite the final scoreline. It was their first big day out, and they made more mistakes than us. That was no big surprise. The game was close enough for 60 minutes, and our two late tries definitely did their contribution to the game a disservice.

While it was a kick up the backside to lose to Ospreys in the Rabodirect 12 final a week later, it was no more than that... a sudden and unexpected kick. We went into the summer as champions of Europe, well and truly.

Two years standing.

We were top of the heap. But someone was higher up than the rest of us. Joe Schmidt was the greatest coach in Europe. Every player who worked with him for a week understood that. Everyone wanted Joe.

In Ireland we were lucky that he chose to stay in this country.

CHAPTER 20

REMAINING THE TOP dog is gruelling.

In professional rugby, pre-season is where everyone, including the very best, have to pay their dues. Every single damn season. And, if you get injured and have to restart your season then there are extra dues. It's the way it is.

Our pre-season, as we aimed at conquering Europe for a third year on the trot, was excruciating. There was six weeks of it; weight sessions, conditioning sessions, skills and functional sessions. Of course, if you needed more, you were invited to add to the long list. From the start to the end of the week there was not a muscle or limb that was overlooked.

Monday began with lower limbs. That always meant that the main dish on the menu was squats, with a dessert of high-clean pull and weighted step-ups. After that there was a functional circuit, which was often tougher than what came before it. All of the programmes were always tailored individually, with our head of fitness, Jason Cowman not neglecting skinnies or fatties.

Then there was Tuesday, Wednesday, Thursday…

It worked.

Some of us would gain up to five kilos of pure muscle in our six weeks of pre-season. And for those who had been on Ireland duty, pre-season just seemed to last that bit longer, as if elasticated, until our player protocols allowed us back out on the pitch. The 'repatriation' of players was not complete until the middle of September in 2012, when Brian O'Driscoll, Fergus McFadden, Johnny Sexton, Eoin Reddan, Jamie Heaslip, Kevin McLoughlin and myself all landed back with Leinster.

We were all back, just in time for a rude awakening in The Sportsground where Connacht treated us to a five-try rout in a 34-6 victory. I came on in the 46th minute for Heinke so I had to stomach my fair share of the embarrassment. We had the excuse of having one full session as a 'full team' but there could be no excuse. Next up we had Munster, which was supposed to be our 'wake up call' at the start of every season. We had conceded 18 tries in our first five league games.

Munster helped us to get on track, as games against Munster nearly always did. We won 30-21 but in the season ahead there was so very little between the pair of us and when the final Heineken Cup seedings were completed for the knockout stages the following spring we were both locked on 20 points, though they squeezed through to the quarter-finals of the tournament on a points difference of +60, compared to our +28. We were... Out!

We won four of the games in our group that included Clermont, Exeter and Scarlets, though significantly the two losses were to Joe's second favourite club team. Going down back-to-back to Clermont in December hurt, but if there was a team we would have chosen as our slayers it might indeed have been them. I'd hit the ground running in the tournament. In the opening fixture against the Scarlets in their place I was voted Man of the Match, courtesy of Alan Quinlan. The scrum had been a highlight, we shunted them back 'half a postcode' according to one commentator. I did carry the ball plenty, and had a tackle count that was into the double digits.

We won our first two games. However Clermont kept pace with us, and they had a maximum of 10 points from their two games, while we had eight.

The coffee machine at training took a fair hammering the week before the two games. Also, Joe wanted us absolutely prepared for the noise that the Stadium Marcel Michelin was able to generate any day of the week. It could be deafening. Friday was our final preparatory session of the week and we worked mainly on defence and Joe decided that we should do so in absolute silence.

No one was allowed to speak a word.

Joe wanted us prepared for the maddening noise of the Clermont supporters, and he wanted us to react to the positioning of the man next door to each one of us. Generally defensive sessions are the noisiest of the whole week. Everyone is barking out where they are in the line and who they are marking.

This time, we had to prepare by scanning one another. No speaking, no shouting… no desperate late calls. On their sticky pitch, which always gave the distinct impression that we were all running around with five kilos of mud stuck to our boots, we lost by three points. A week later we suffered our first defeat in the Aviva Stadium when Clermont were superb in a 28-21 victory and Morgan Parra, who had struggled to find our jugular in previous attempts, was relentless slotting eight of his nine kicks for a 23-point haul. And it was Wesley Fofana, who had come so close the previous season, who also put us to the sword with a try five minutes before the break. They stretched their lead to 25-9 before Shane Jennings and Fergus McFadden added some respectability to the scoreboard.

The result left us needing two bonus points from our final two games, and also looking for favours from others. The defeat left me with some sleepless nights. I'd been pinged too often during the game and that cost us points. We'd done fine out in their ground, and they decided to target our scrum. I was not at all surprised at the amount of weight coming through on the first engagement. But there was a huge gap between the two front rows. We over-extended ourselves, our legs locked out, and we lost power and grip. The pitch also tore up fast, and I ended up eating more Aviva dirt than I ever had before on my plate.

THE NATURE OF professional rugby smacked me in the puss in the first defeat against Clermont. Actually my old teammate Nathan Hines might as well have grabbed one of my ribs and smacked me in the face with it.

'Can I have my rib back please?' I'd asked him nicely, after he had surgically removed it with his knee.

Friend today, foe tomorrow.

That's the business of professional rugby, though, in truth, I could never be sore with Hinesy for very long.

Wayne Barnes was refereeing that match. A lot of times our scrum was not going backwards… it was just collapsing. But Barnesy was convinced that I was at fault, and that it had nothing whatsoever to do with Raphael Chaume. I thought it was quite clear that Chaume was detaching himself a bit from his hooker and that I was falling through the hole. I was unhappy. I told Barnesy, and he quickly gave me a penalty the next time it happened. But, after that, I could not buy a penalty from the man for the remainder of the match.

Once it got into Barnesy's head that I was at fault, there was no convincing him otherwise. They had a bigger pack, and the bigger the pack the more momentum they were able to generate.

Wayne Barnes? He broke my heart for so many years. Sometimes it seemed to me that the friendlier he was with us in our dressing room before games, the harder it was to win a penalty from him.

But, I soon hated having the craic with Barnesy before any match. We'd have pints and chats together after matches at the official dinners, because I always liked to figure out what referees were thinking? I also figured that if a referee kind of liked me as a person I might also get the rub of the green from him some day down the road. No harm trying to be friendly, but I genuinely liked Wayne Barnes.

He was a good bloke. But he never stopped thinking like the lawyer he had been trained to be, and while he would always talk and listen, and appear to take the dialogue on the pitch into consideration, I never got much back from him in return.

AND THE NATURE of the paid game also smacked the whole of Leinster in the chops a month later when Johnny Sexton made it known that Racing Metro had made him an offer he would be unable to refuse.

We all had a bunch of beers with him at the end of season drinks and we wished him well. Sincerely. Anyone who can get someone like Jacky Lorenzetti to sit down with him twice, and who can get Racing's multi-millionaire owner to double his salary, gets my good wishes. I've no idea what Johnny was offered, but it was said that the IRFU were willing to put up half a million per year and it was not enough to distract Johnny from making the biggest move in the history of Irish rugby.

People also forget that Johnny was 27 in the spring of 2013, and he had waited a long time to earn the money he deserved in the game. He had only two years of an international contract, having sat patiently behind Felipe Contepomi for a few years.

Everyone was aware that the French were starting to flex their financial muscle, and as for any suggestion of disloyalty? Well, loyalty does not exist all that much any longer in professional rugby. You will get a few extra months handed to you if you are coming back from a serious injury and the club feels it is worth their while seeing what transpires, but bottom line is that rugby players are commodities.

Once you become less valuable, that's the end.

Nobody is going to give you an extra hundred grand out of sentiment or sympathy. Rugby is a cold-blooded business, like any other business.

Too many players had to try to entice Leinster into dipping deeper into their pocket in the past, and we always made a song and dance, and a joke, about it in the dressing room. On this occasion, there were photo-shopped pics of Johnny in French gear being thrown around the place, and lads brought in berets and baguettes to leave around his seat.

But Johnny Sexton was out the door at the end of the season. As a pro you have no idea when exactly the carousel will stop…

And you have to get off for good.

ONE MORE THING about the nature of the game.

We all talk about the 'afterlife', but rugby players get there earlier in their discussions than most people. We always talked about our lives after our careers.

Few of us get to herald that 'afterlife' quite like Brian O'Driscoll. However, I have never met a player who has ever begrudged Drico one day of his status as the 'superstar' of Irish rugby. He earned that status, and some.

At the end of March, after getting the green light from Kim, I boarded a plane with a few of the other lads in Leinster. We were heading to London for

Drico's testimonial dinner. The venue was the impressive Grosvenor Hotel in the heart of London which was familiar enough to me, as Harlequins always had their end of season gig there. I ended up sitting at a table hosted by Coutts Bank, one of the main sponsors and whose managing director, Harry Keogh was the chairman of the testimonial dinner.

At the table next to me were Bono and Prince William. How Kim would have liked to be in my boring rugby company, for once! At our table was one of the Prince's bodyguards. The poor man, I must have worn the ear off him asking him questions.

More interestingly, once the speeches were over and the charity auction had wound itself up, I was at the bar when I met up with Bob Casey.

Bob was already enjoying his 'afterlife.'

He was working for a major recycling company in London. Bob was one of the truly good guys in the game. Everyone wished him well, but Bob suffered from the after-effects of a long and honourable career. He'd just had an operation, I found out, to clean out one of his troublesome knees that had taken quite a hammering at the coalface that is Premiership rugby in England. When I'd last met him at Gordon D'Arcy's wedding he'd just had an operation to break his femur and reposition it so that there was sufficient cartilage in his knee joint. The operation was also due to be performed on his other leg a few months later.

Still, Bob was in great form that night in the Grosvenor Hotel, and there was not one moan from the man about his life or his rebuilt body.

I WAS THE only member of the Leinster team who had played in the Amlin Challenge Cup before. I'd fought for the 'second best' title in Europe with Quins in 2007, but in 2013 we were in good company. The final eight included former Heineken Cup winners in Toulouse, as well as Bath and Wasps.

Naturally, I had absolutely no idea of the historic day that was in it when we landed at a bitterly cold Luton Airport, but it was a little warmer in England and the snow had stopped. When we looked over Adams Park, Wasps' home ground, the place looked perfect.

Our quarter-final got off to a frenetic start. Christian Wade went over for a try after three minutes, despite all our talk and work all week long on stopping him. We hit back through Darce, but Wade then went in for his second. We replied through Ian Madigan, but it was all a bit too loose for Joe's liking.

We were 20-15 in front at half time.

I'd been a pro rugby player for seven years, and in all of that time I had never scored a try.

I'd come close lots of times. Inches on occasions, but the final pass never seemed destined for my waiting arms. When Isa Nacewa made a break after the kick off, I followed up on him, as usual. Leo Cullen was on my shoulder. With Isa, you never know what might happen. He's just magical. Isa benefited from a fortuitous bounce of the ball and gathered it five metres from their line.

Turned out, Isa's hands let him down. Instead of flicking the ball to Leo who would have been in under the posts unopposed, he had to find me.

Wasps had their cover back.

I thought one of my golden chances was gone. But in the nick of time all 120 kilos of Dev Toner and 104 kilos of Kevin McLaughlin arrived right on time, and they smashed me over the line.

Monkey off my back!

We also saw off Wasps 48-28.

We also beat Biarritz, and had a home European final to look forward to, against Stade Francais, and Michael Cheika. Joe had Cheika's number and we were three tries to the good by half time, all set-piece moves designed on weaknesses in Stade's defence. We ran out 34-13 winners. It was brilliant to see Isa and Johnny lift the trophy into the air together. They had both been at the heart of so many of our best performances and no pair of men deserved the spotlight more.

It was not a Heineken Cup, and I guess it was a bit like eating in the servants' quarters.

But who turns down decent food?

JOE SCHMIDT WAS done and dusted with Leinster, and had brought home a trophy each season. Matt O'Connor knew what was expected of him.

Though I would not have wanted to be in his shoes.

MATT O'CONNOR WALKED into an impossible job.

Matt, however, was his own man. And he backed himself, as someone who had won two Premiership titles with Leicester.

Matt O'Connor could be quite sarcastic and he was always prepared to level someone with a slag. Though he was also jovial. On the pitch he was very particular about how he wanted things to be done. O'Connor came into Leinster with his own playbook, and we had a multitude of new calls and phase plays to learn off, but he quickly came to understand that Leinster was not Leicester.

In Leicester, he had more direct control over his players, but in Leinster he seemed to happen upon and be surprised by an environment in which there were limitations around his access to all of his players. I think he chafed at that.

Matt O'Connor would last two out of his three-years contract with Leinster, and it would all end for him fairly quickly in the end.

Unfortunately, he nearly took me with him.

CHAPTER 21

IT WAS O'CONNOR'S second season that left me confused, and wanting a meeting with the coach. We had lost to Harlequins and then scraped by them in the second game of a double header in December 2014, and then O'Connor decided to give Marty Moore a start, and then he chose to give Tadhg Furlong a start.

All of a sudden I was not featuring in our next European game, against Wasps in the new year. I needed to have a chat with him. So, I went into his office and experienced one of the most unpleasant conversations I ever had in my professional career.

O'Connor ripped me to shreds.

He laid in.

All of our scrum shortcomings were left on my doorstep.

I was informed that I was not as good a scrummager as I was made out to be by most people, and I was also told that I was not all that good around the park.

He made me feel like one of the academy kids.

I was not thinking pleasant things as I listened to him.

I was also thinking that there was no future for me in Leinster.

It was that bad.

Against Quins I had a lot of weight coming across onto me from Will Collier, and I was telling Sean Cronin to keep him out. Looking back on it, I could have come across him more but I was trying to keep Joe Marler square and straight, which I knew I needed to do from the five or six times I had played against him.

Marler was a royal pain in my arse.

My chat with O'Connor was serious business. I never had such a discussion with a coach before. I was not expecting it either… I'd just gone into his office to ask him… what's the story?

That Monday, as always, there had been the starting team and the second team, and then the rest of the lads. I was with the rest! Third in line. I was Ireland's first choice tighthead so of course I had a big question to ask.

Marty and Tadhg had done well. They had both scored tries when given the opportunity and I was sitting watching this, thinking… *This doesn't look very good!* So I needed to know what O'Connor was thinking?

He told me… yes he did.

He blamed me for our scrums going south against Quins. In our first season together he had picked me throughout, solidly, and we had never sat down and discussed either life or rugby. When he started into me there was not much I could say in my own defence.

I was dumbstruck, I guess.

I began to defend myself, but then realised that it might not be the best time to do so. I decided it might be wise to just listen.

As I did so, I began to see the implications. Marty and Tadhg were younger men, they were only going to get better. If this was how Matt truly felt then a future of being left out of Leinster squads beckoned, and by extension I'd won my last Ireland cap.

This is the end…

I'm done!

No second World Cup…. it's all over!

Though I sensed that it all seemed to be brewing in Matt for a while. I think I must have pissed him off when I got injured a few weeks before, when I was troubled with my groin, and I ended up rehabbing for about six weeks. He had wanted me to play a game before the autumn internationals in 2014, but I did not think I was ready.

I told him I wasn't right yet.

And then, after being out for about six weeks... I went and played in those games for Joe, including 80 minutes against Australia.

It was no way for a coach to deliver his message. If Joe was ever unhappy he would always come in and let me know directly, in double-quick time. With O'Connor, I felt he was simply angry. Being a head coach comes with a huge amount of pressure. I still left his office absolutely raging. He'd talked to me like I was a kid. I don't mind being dressed down, it had happened more times than I liked over the years, but never in that fashion.

Luckily, he did not end my career.

Joe called me a few weeks later and told me he was giving me a chance against the Wolfhounds, and while the prospect of turning around and proving myself with Ireland A was not thrilling, I was thankful to Joe.

'I'm not promising you anything, Rossy,' Joe said, '... but I will give you a shot at the jersey.'

JOE WAS GOOD and true to his word.

But, at Leinster, I thought I might still be finished and I got talking to Rory Best in Ireland camp. And Besty must have had a chat with the lads in Ulster.

I was soon asked if I wanted to come up and finish my final 12 months contract out with Ulster, rather than Leinster? My contract was a central one at the time, so technically I wasn't tied to one province. Matt had another year to run I figured, so I needed to make a big decision. When he exited after his second year I was as surprised as the next person.

I heard the news on my car radio.

I had been quite close to moving. Ryan Constable, my agent got into talks quickly and the IRFU were not going to stand in my way. It made sense from their point of view to have someone with my experience playing regularly rather than gathering dust in Leinster. There was a decent offer from Ravenhill. It was attractive, but I knew that if I left Leinster would not have been too happy. I also thought that I might wish to coach when I finished up my career and I did not want to damage my career options in Dublin. My family lived in Dublin.

It's where we wished to remain living.

I did not want to torpedo lots of relationships.

I also thought of heading out to France. I chatted to Bernard Jackman, my old Leinster teammate who was then head coach in Grenoble, and he thought I would be a great fit as a player-coach with them. Playing in France and coaching seemed idyllic, compared with putting up with what looked like a future of holding more tackle bags.

Thankfully, the choice was taken out of my hands.

O'CONNOR'S FIRST SEASON with Leinster had been reasonable.

It was Brian O'Driscoll's farewell season, and with Johnny gone we knew we all had to dig deeper – to make up for Johnny's absence and to make sure Drico got the goodbye he truly deserved.

Jimmy Gopperth, who had played with Wellington and North Harbour, and also the Hurricanes and the Blues, had joined us from Newcastle. Ian Madigan also saw a huge opportunity present itself to him. Mads we knew and trusted, but Gopperth was a good guy, and he was confident. He played good stuff, and did not seem at all fazed by the massive pressure that was facing both No.10s.

There were a few faces missing, in addition to Joe and Johnny, and Isa Nacewa. Also gone were Damien Browne, Andrew Conway and Fionn Carr. It remained surprising for a number of weeks to walk into the dressing room and not see so many people. Eoin 'Chubo' O'Malley was amongst the missing and that was the cruelest blow of all because he was one of the most popular guys in the squad and was in a prime position to succeed Drico. He was only 25 but a long-standing hip problem and then a ruptured cruciate knee ligament left him making his toughest decisions to call it quits.

In addition to O'Connor's new look on life, we had other forced changes. In the new scrum laws...HIT... was out! It killed the initial impact on the engagement and... we were into wrestling matches. The good news was that scrums automatically stopped collapsing as frequently as they did. More good news was that the absent... HIT... was kind to the spines of all of us props.

The bad news was that the most important part of a tighthead's armoury was gone. I could no longer hit the loosehead down on the initial engagement, and look to power through.

In a tough looking Heineken Cup group that included Northampton, Castres and Ospreys we did fine, winning five and losing to Northampton, 18-9 in the final game before Christmas in the Aviva when George North and James Elliott opened and closed the scoring with tries.

WINNING THE SIX Nations championship in Paris in the spring of 2014 was something that had to be marked and, with time off before reporting back to our clubs, some of the Irish guys took off. New York, Boston and Dubai were some of the destinations, but I had Fermoy in mind.

We'd been gone from our homes for the guts of eight weeks and I wanted to hang around, and reintroduce myself to my family. However, I'd also managed to get my hands on the Six Nations trophy and I headed down to my former schools and club back home, feeling fortunate and humbled, and absolutely delighted with myself. The cat was bringing the cream back home.

BRIAN O'DRISCOLL PLAYED his last game against Munster at the very end of March and he was in tetchy form that evening, giving referee Alain Rolland what's what on one occasion. But he also got in for the decisive try in the 22-18 victory, which was our tenth successive win in all competitions and our 13th league win in-a-row at the RDS. While some of us had been enjoying the highs of the Six Nations the rest of the Leinster squad knuckled down and earned 24 points from a possible 25. Our form one week out from a quarter-final in the cup in France was quite exceptional but, in Stade Felix Mayol, Jonny Wilkinson and Toulon were too hot. They won 29-14, and in every way it was bloody roasting out there on their pitch.

Our scrum held up well against them, but they played like the defending champs they were and handed us our heaviest defeat since losing 33-6 to Toulouse in 2007. Mathieu Bastareaud did most of the damage in a team that read like a World XV. But we didn't help ourselves either, missing 26 tackles.

They made seven line breaks to our two, and in offloads they finished with 17. We had just three.

La Marseillaise was being aired long before the final whistle.

But we had topped the table in the RaboDirect Pro 12. We won 17 out of our 22 games, narrowly beat Ulster in the semi-final, took Glasgow 34-12 in a four-try rout in the final, and made sure that there was silverware on the table for Drico in his last season in blue, and Matt O'Connor in his first season in blue.

All told it was far from a disastrous season.

At the start of the next season, going into 2014-15, O'Connor did not need to give the impression that half the world was against him, but that is what he did. He got the mood in Leinster, and the mood in Ireland wrong, from the very beginning.

He had a shovel in his hand.

It genuinely seemed his idea to start digging. Even at the end of the season he was not giving up on his displeasure with how the Irish game was organised. He talked about not being able to get his hands on his 'best blokes.'

I don't think he was making himself any friends.

AT THE END of my ninth pre-season as a professional rugby player I took a look around the Leinster dressing room.

There was no Brian O'Driscoll.

No Leo Cullen either anymore.

I was the oldest boy in the whole room. I was also about to become a father of two, Kim and I welcoming our second child, Chloe into the world at 8.30 am on a Monday morning in the middle of October. We had arrived at the Rotunda at 7.0 am. As lucky parents know, it is truly one of the greatest feelings there is, and for me it immediately put the trials and tribulations I was experiencing in my rugby career in a very clear perspective.

I had been in a strange place in my career.

And it was about to get stranger still with my big conversation with Matt O'Connor about my lack of playing time right around the corner.

October began with Munster coming up to Dublin and bringing to a halt a run of seven straight defeats to us in either the RDS or the Aviva. I was nursing a groin strain. We had the Heineken Cup coming down the tracks at us, and it would be the first campaign in 16 seasons that Leinster would step into Europe without Drico.

We had Wasps, Harlequins and Castres for company in our pool. Of course paternity leave is an abstract idea in professional rugby, even if you are unfit to play. Every morning I had to report for medical attention, and my phone was constantly buzzing with reminders of squad meetings and dozens of other things for which I was actually not needed. My new daughter did get a little more attention than she might have done otherwise. I was able to pick my wife and daughter up from the hospital on a Friday afternoon, a time that would normally be far too busy for me to even consider my amazing wife and beautiful new daughter!

Due to my groin strain I missed our opening European game against Wasps when the team's character shone through and they fought back from a 20-8 deficit, to win 25-20. I also missed the 21-6 win in Castres with Ian Madigan kicking seven penalties and showing himself as a real leader. Mads was such a dependable kicker, from 40 metres and inside, and to have an eighty-five per cent kicker from that range is a gift to a team. Out further, and Mads' percentages dropped a bit. That season, on reflection, neither Mads nor Jimmy really got enough time to settle into the position. We all knew that Mads was at his very best when he was confident, but there was so much chopping and changing between games. Too much, far too much, but then again who'd want to be a coach and it's always tough deciding who is the very best No.10 for a different opposition every weekend.

I was back in December for Leinster's much heralded and first return to The Stoop since the Bloodgate affair, when we lost 24-6, and I remained on the team with Jack McGrath and Sean Cronin when we took revenge in the return fixture by the slimmest of margins, 14-13.

IN BETWEEN THE pair of Heineken Cup games, I had done my part in a November series for Joe Schmidt that resulted in a perfect three from three win record against South Africa, Georgia and Australia. I was particularly worried about my match fitness before the Springbok game as I had been out for a month and a half, and most of my condition work had been on that damned 'Wattbike.'

That bike!

Actually, someone bought three of those damned bikes!

There's no mistaking the bike because it has 'Wattbike' emblazoned along the sides. When you start, the pressure is constant, with no let off when you remove your feet. My legs were soon cylinders of lactic acid, every single time. Twenty minutes lasted an eternity. The bikes are developed for professional cyclists and come with more data than any of us could dream up, right down to rudely analysing your pedaling to see how efficient you are! There's also the usual power output, and rpm. I managed an average of 330W for one 10-minute run on the bike, which left me pretty pleased with myself.

I later read that Bradley Wiggins averaged over 400W for a 50-minute time trial at the London Olympics!

The bike worked, however, and the magic treatment of Enda King at the Santry Sports Clinic finished the rehabilitation job brilliantly. Being back on the pitch felt great, though I was not entirely happy with our scrum against South Africa. It was my first time to come up against Tendai Mtawarira... the famed Beast himself and I was delighted I lasted 73 minutes, having begun the game quite wary of him. He caught me a couple of times in the first half, coming right across me. But I straightened things out in the second half. I started to dive inside him. I wanted to avoid that explosion of power and his ability to go from zero to 60 in two seconds flat!

Against Georgia we had our hips a little too high pre-engagement and we needed to follow through a bit more on the hit too. Joe kept me out there for 47 minutes. He wanted me fit, and against Australia a week later he played me for the full 80 minutes. It was the last 80 minutes game I ever played for Ireland. That was also the same day that Joe had an appendicitis and was on a heap of meds...and I told him afterwards he must have been on so many drugs he forgot to take me off!

There was one gigantic scrum five minutes from the end.

Up until then they had won some, and we had won some, but they now wanted one more. They were pushing for a penalty to level it up. We dug in...

It's not going to happen boys!

The scrum collapsed. Glen Jackson, the New Zealand referee gave us his vote, and we won 26-23. Truth is, Jack McGrath, Besty and myself had dropped our chests down and down further, and it was virtually impossible for them to push from such a low position.

Come on lads…

See if you like it down here… WITH US!

I had my bind.

I was making sure I was not going to hit the ground first.

It was risky.

I was playing with a suspension bridge… with physics itself.

Then… it went down!

But good old Glen Jackson!

That Australian game was one of the fastest I ever played in. One minute we were up 17-0. They scored three tries on the bounce. Johnny kicked us home, and I woke up the morning after feeling stiff and sore, and feeling just a tad sorry for myself for slightly over-indulging in the refreshments department.

But, I felt I was back and ready to lift my performance even more.

The Stoop, however, once the warm welcome was completed, had felt disconcerting. It was great to be back on my old stomping ground but a large part of why we lost to Quins in that first game was because our scrum was not good enough on the day. There was no point bellyaching about scrummaging angles when it was all over. If the referee does not see it on the day, then it is up to us as a front row to do something about it.

It took us too long to do that.

In the middle of the week, in our six-day turnaround before the return fixture, we laid into it in the scrums. We usually stopped at between 10 and 15 live scrums every week, but on the Wednesday of that week we did 30 of them… all on the one day. The game started with big hits. We'd about sixty per cent possession. We got home in the end, barely. Eoin Reddan came on and made the vital difference. Unfortunately, I could not say the same about our front row!

We scrummaged better, but we hardly got one crucial decision from

Romain Poite. He was like a man who had his mind made up and was not for turning. It looked to me that Marler had his arse out, 45 degrees or more.

Matt O'Connor had also made up his mind, as it turned out. Like everyone else, he was evidently convinced that I did not turn the tables sufficiently on Marler, who was voted the winner by both the match referee and our coach... in both matches.

IN JANUARY OF 2015, I was dropped for the final two matches against Castres and Wasps. By the end of the month we were top of the pool.

Matt had made his decision but, thankfully, Joe Schmidt chose not to accept his word for it that I was third choice for Leinster. I had performed for Joe in the November internationals, and I would also do mostly everything he asked of me as Ireland retained the Six Nations Championship the following March.

Watching those two games against Castres and Wasps was dispiriting. Marty and Tadhg both scored tries in our phenomenal 50-8 win over the French side, and it was Tadhg's third of the season! It was hard to watch. I was overcome by selfishness and my own desperate needs to get back onto the pitch.

I needed one of them to get tossed around in the scrum.

It did not happen.

I needed the two of them to stop scoring tries. I wanted the team to win, but I did not want Marty or Tadhg scoring any more tries.

And I was watching from the stands, in a suit, sitting there in freezing temperatures, with my three years old son wrapped up in my arms.

At the same time I know that everyone, or nearly everyone gets dropped at some stage in their pro careers, and the last thing the rest of the dressing room wants to see is that person throwing their toys out of the pram. Nobody else has any time for that carry-on.

Everyone wants to see you bury your disappointment, and put your head down. And work your arse off to get back onto the team.

So, I'd had a good look at the Castres' scrum technique in the video room, and I sought to replicate it against the starting pack on the Tuesday before the match. I needed to help, and be seen to help. I had noticed that both of the Castres tightheads had a fondness for coming across at a slight angle to try and get through the joint between our loosehead and hooker, so in training that's exactly what we did.

I tried to go through a few times, until every time I tried going in I was getting buried by Michael Bent.

Benty had learned enough from the session, that was clear.

Jack McGrath replicated their loosehead technique on the other side, swinging out wider than he usually would and trying to pop Marty and Tadhg.

One of the other drawbacks to not being named on the match-day 23 was that I did not have the Wednesday as an 'off' day. Instead, I was in the gym for extra weights and conditioning.

JOE STANDING BY me for the 2015 Six Nations changed everything.

Ireland were the best team in Europe.

And, once more, it looked like I was back on form.

Matt did not seem to have the stomach to argue the point as he named me with Cian and Sean Cronin for the Heineken Cup quarter-final. Six of the best from Ian Madigan in the Aviva squeezed us through against Bath, 18-15. In an epic struggle against Toulon in the Stade Velodrome we went out of the tournament after 20 minutes of extra-time, 25-20.

Matt was not a lucky coach.

That rain-soaked match should have been his, and Leinster's, as Jimmy Gopperth came within a whisker of winning it two minutes from the end of normal time with a drop goal. We had them on the ropes. They had Ali Williams sin binned. We went for their jugular, but they intercepted. Brian Habana touched down.

The back-to-back champions got out of jail.

We'd scrummaged them off the pitch when it mattered. And we'd defended as well as any Leinster team ever did, and the bedrock of our performance was a tackle count in excess of 100. We only missed eight tackles.

We were brave and strong, but we had not been able to finish the job and that's all that counts. We also failed to retain our league title. Eleven wins out of 22 left us in fifth place in the table and out of the semi-finals.

The season came to a fast ending.

We'd been in five straight Pro 12 finals, and there was a sense of failure about the whole season. Of course I was relieved to see the back of O'Connor. When he picked me for the game against Bath we'd had minimal conversation.

I'd no interest in going back into his office ever again!

He picks me... I play. That was the fullness of our relationship in the end. He told me I'd done well in the Six Nations, and asked me to do the same for the team against Bath.

He'd pulled out all of the stops to try to get over the line against Toulon. He'd special t-shirts made to give us extra focus on the match, and he had us writing stuff on the gym wall about what it was like to play for Leinster, and what it meant to us. That was a good idea, and they took it further the following season by getting a huge mural done with pictures and quotes from past and present players.

Like every coach I'd ever had, Matt left a dressing room behind him that had fairly different feelings.

One third loved him.

One third tolerated him.

One third weren't unhappy to see him go.

Yes, he was unlucky, but neither was he able to get into the business of manufacturing luck in tough times. It did not help him that Brian O'Driscoll retired, and Johnny Sexton left for France. It was a tough hand, and he had those impossible shoes to fill.

Last time I spoke to Matt was upstairs in The Bridge pub in Ballsbridge, where we all gathered to say our goodbyes to him.

I had two pints.

I shook hands with him, wished him well, and left it at that.

CHAPTER
22

IT WAS NO surprise that Leinster looked to Leo.

Through and through, Leo Cullen was totally Leinster rugby and his appointment to succeed Matt O'Connor in August 2015 had heads nodding in agreement in the dressing room. It was good to have one of our own as boss. Leo is also a very studious individual and, while the job of head coach had come much earlier than he had imagined, we knew that he would get up to speed. He also had Girvan Dempsey, another one of us, as his backs coach. He wasn't alone.

But Leo my friend was gone. That had to be the case. He was now Leo my coach, my boss and while we would have happily bled for him, none of us could help him in his first season. It was an awful campaign, there was nothing to cling to at the end of the 2015-16 season.

Apart form the fact, I guess, that things could only get better. The other great element to Leo Cullen's personality was that he did not suffer from any insecurities. He had been through everything as a player. He knew that pro sport does not have too many colours. It's black. It's white.

Leo wasn't afraid to have Graham Henry, the former All Blacks head coach, give him a bit of a hand and when the bigger question arrived at the end of his opening season as coach, and he was asked about Stuart Lancaster, the former English head coach coming in full-time?

Leo telephoned Stuart himself. Leo's arms opened to expert help.

We had been bottom of our pool in the Heineken Cup in 2015-16. It was embarrassing for us all. It did not help that so many of us were gone in the opening months of Leo's first season because of the World Cup. For the guts of three months we were away from Leinster.

And, as I've said, switching from Ireland back to Leinster is like switching languages. Plus, we were not just reprogramming our brains, we were also having to get to know the ways of a new head coach, even if he was an old friend.

But sessions were sharp and intense.

There was a buzz around the place leading into the Heineken Cup. We were sitting fourth in the table in the Guinness Pro 12. In our first game in the Heineken Cup we came up against Wasps, who were eighth in the English Premiership. We also had Bath and Toulon in our pool.

I was talking to Leo a lot.

I felt proud of him as our coach. We all genuinely loved the man because he was more than a former colleague... he'd been our inspirational captain, our greatest leader. None of us were prepared for a 27-point walloping from Wasps in the RDS. It ended 33-6. They crossed our line three times. Johnny Sexton kicked two penalties. There were excuses, like the loss of three of our forwards to concussion. Seanie O'Brien, Richardt Strauss and Mike McCarthy left us with no strike runner.

But, at the same time there could be no grand excuse.

In the scrum I recovered from a difficult beginning to get on top of their loosehead, Matt Mullan but when Tadhg came on for me our scrum was already beginning to disintegrate again.

Bath was a huge game for us next up. After that we had back-to-back games with the three in-a-row European champions in December. We knew we needed to catch a break but our fixture list before the end of the year showed... Wasps, Bath, Ulster, Glasgow, Toulon, Toulon... and Munster. At least we won the last of those games to rouse some Christmas cheer.

IN ONE OF our personal chats Leo asked me how we looked for Bath?

I told him we were... 'not on!'

He knew I was giving him an honest answer. We did better at the Recreation Ground but lost again, 19-16. We were done in by a 77th minute penalty. But this was a game in which our scrum was absolutely obliterated. In total, we were penalised seven times, if you included the penalty try that Jerome Garces awarded. George Ford also nailed a couple of scrum penalties.

Our scrum was to blame for 13 out of Bath's 19 points total.

The next morning was a Sunday and we were all so completely pissed off with ourselves that the whole front row and prop replacements came into the upstairs meeting room in UCD by noon. We met up in the video room. None of us wanted to wait until the Monday morning. We sat down and for the next hour and a half we went through every single scrum from the day before. All of us, and our forwards coach, John Fogarty.

I had been up against Nick Auterac. He was a kid, only 22 years-old, and it was inexcusable that he and his colleagues had their timing so much better than us. We could see what had happened. We were not aggressive enough in the engagement. We were waiting for people to do unto us... instead of us doing unto them.

Leo never looked angry, he didn't need to as we were angry at ourselves.

He was feeling it, for sure, but he never lost it. That would not be his style. He asked lots of questions, big questions and small questions. More big questions as the season continued. We lost both games to Toulon, and in the second of those games I tore up my hamstring. Our only win in the tournament was a 25-11 result against Bath at the RDS.

The nadir was our final game at the Ricoh Arena.

Johnny Sexton was making his 100th appearance for the club and captained us on the occasion but lasted just eight minutes before being concussed.

We lost the game 51-10. In the Pro 12 we won 16 games from our 22, and finished top of the table ahead of Connacht. We beat Ulster in the semi-final but in the decider, in Murrayfield, Connacht turned us over 3-1 in tries, and 20-10 on the scoreboard. It was a season that everyone for some time had wished to end, to see the back off it, but nobody wanted it to end like that.

LEO DID NOT know that I had spent a couple of months off and on talking to Bernard Jackman again.

I was thinking… *France*.

Kim was warming to the idea. We were looking at photos online of Grenoble. It felt good. Then, there was no offer on the table.

France had the appearance of a retirement package. The role of player-coach was appealing. I could get my French back up to scratch. We could go skiing as a family. Not too far from the Mediterranean, we could enjoy lots of sunshine.

All of that had been on the table too.

No offer meant no life in France.

When Leinster offered me another 12 months, I felt thankful.

I UNDERSTOOD MY career with Leinster, just like a human body, would start shutting itself down before too long.

How long that period of 'shutting down' would last, I'd no idea of course. My career with Ireland was further down that same line.

It may have been actually 'shut.' I was not included in the squad for the 2016 November series. It was the first time in six years. But then I was back in, briefly, when Finlay Bealham took a knock to his head against us.

He got the all clear a few days after.

I was out again… and not on the flight to Chicago for what turned out to be one of the most historic days in the whole amazing, roller-coaster history of Irish rugby. The All Blacks… flattened… at last!

I was in Zebre that same weekend. We won 33-10, and I came into the match after 45 minutes and left it again five minutes later with a torn hamstring. It gave me time to look at Leinster, and Leo and Stuart Lancaster. There was definitely a future dawning. Fresh blood, young men like Joey Carbery and Adam Byrne, and bigger men like Andrew Porter. And Tadhg Furlong now fully at home in the front row, and waiting to hit his 60th cap by the end of 2016!

Fresh, young blood and also Stuart Lancaster methods, gave everything a different appearance to Leo's first season as coach.

Lancaster came in at the start of September as 'Senior Coach' and it was a tricky one putting him together with Leo, and seeing how they might work. Lancaster had been head coach of England for four years and led them into the 2015 World Cup that ended badly for them as hosts. He still stood amongst us as a seriously impressive and ambitious figure of a man.

Both men, Leo and Lancaster, knew that they would be judged on how they worked together, and how the team picked up the pieces from the disaster of the Heineken Cup the season before. In 2016-17 we had Montpellier, Castres and Northampton in our pool and this time we got off to a flying start, sorting out the French in our first game by 33-15.

I came in for Tadhg after he got a knock just before half time.

And looking around me, there was the future of rugby in Leinster, in place and at work already. And winning. Rob Kearney was there, and Dev and Jamie, but there was also Garry Ringrose and Robbie Henshaw, Carbery, Luke McGrath, Dan Leavy and Josh van der Flier. We lost a week later to Montpellier, 22-16. But it would be our only loss, and we would end up topping our group with an incredible scoring average of +140.

I was in from the start against Montpellier.

But opportunities would be rare, and my hamstring tear in Zebre left me out of commission from November 7 until the start of February. The tear had been high up where the tendon attaches to the bone. The tear also tore a giant hole in my last season with Leinster, not that I knew that I was counting down the months and weeks.

I'd no idea that I would have a conversation with Leo long before the end of the season when he'd tell me that he wished we had a bottle of whiskey on the desk between us, and also inform me… 'There's nothing for you here!'

THE LONGEST INJURY of my whole pro career proved tedious.

It also left me isolated.

That's what happens when you rehab over a lengthy period, you end up in view and also viewing, but essentially detached. The bad news was that I had to be in and ready for the gym by 7.0 am every morning, as all of the injured needed to have their 90 minutes out of the way before all the others began wandering in around 8.30 am. The good news was that there was no traffic at that ungodly hour. A normal 40-minute journey was a 10-minute zip.

As I worked on my hamstring I walked a fine line between tiring it out sufficiently, and not causing any further damage. Our rehab specialist, Diarmaid Brennan had a programme tailored for us all.

I was assessed each week. I needed to progress through various running speeds until I was hitting velocities that are found in matches. Then my strength was measured and compared to my good leg, and when it was within ten per cent I was allowed back out on the pitch.

As I worked my way back I also wanted to be useful in any way I could to Leo and Stuart. As part of the prep for Northampton in the back-to-back Heineken Cup matches in December I agreed to look at their scrum and present to the group. I was delighted to do it. Even if it meant that I looked to be on the wrong side of the line that separates coaches from players.

I viewed scrums where the Sants did well, and where they did poorly, and I needed to devise a plan to make sure that we could nullify their strengths and magnify their weaknesses. Most front rows have a vulnerability. Some don't like to have their space crowded. Some are not good at going low. Some have weak joints with their hooker that you can disrupt and break.

There's always something to find.

With eight fully capped front rowers in the Leinster squad, there was always a lot of discussion after every presentation. It can go on for a long time, and I always enjoyed those discussions.

It usually ended when the guys in the back row had heard enough and told us to just get out onto the pitch, and get on with it. Back out on the pitch I never felt stronger.

Or fitter. I wanted matches, but as I waited for the conversation with Leo I kept getting denied and disappointed. Starts would become few and far between. One final 12-month contract to help me finally get my head around my imminent retirement would never be handed to me.

The team was in full flow by the time I had returned. A wild and amazing draw with Castres, in the biting cold of a French winter, was just about sufficient to secure us a home draw in the quarter-finals. It finished 24 each, but after moving into an early 10-0 lead there was less satisfaction in the final result than there should have been. We lost our way with knock-ons and missed tackles.

We did not make our chances count, and an injury to Johnny Sexton in the first half when he damaged his calf meant that the team's playmaker had less than 140 minutes of European action under his belt in the tournament.

Coming down the home stretch of the season we were top of the league, and preparing for Wasps in the Heineken Cup quarter-final, whom we beat 32-17 at the Aviva. I talked to Isa before the game and said I thought there was a smell of a European Cup around the place, and he agreed.

We were right, but just a season early!

I had my heart on getting on last run out in Europe in the semi-final. Against Clermont, in Stade de Gerland in Lyon.

One last game in which I might be able to suck up everything my career had been, and bring it with me into retirement. We lost 27-22 to Clermont. Tadhg started. Michael Bent replaced him. My last opponent would have been Raphael Chaume, my tormentor from a few seasons before, a man I would have loved to have one last shot at.

A man I would have loved to have forced down, one last time. Instead, five days after the loss to Clermont, my last opponent was Glasgow's Alex Allan. I was given 53 minutes against him after I had led out the team at the RDS. We won a thriller 31-30, with great drama in the last five minutes as the lights went out. Jack McGrath, of all people sliced a clearance kick to touch, his blushes spared by Adam Byrne who ran out of play to end the match.

It was Friday, April 28.

My goodbye game. Ross Molony was captaining the senior squad for the first time but he generously let me lead the team out.

Kevin was one of the mascots.

I got to hold his hand as we walked out onto the RDS pitch together, Kevin in one of my old scrum caps that had been melted and shrunk in the dryer.

When I put him to bed later that night he was still so excited by what had happened. He was buzzing.

So was I.

Over 300 club games as a professional rugby player in 10 fast years.

I too struggled to sleep that night.

PART SIX

LOCK AND LOADED

CHAPTER 23

I WOULD NEVER have made it to the top in the heavyweight division, either in England or Ireland. I was never fast enough with my hands. My speciality, I suppose, were 'haymakers' but they take too long to land when a row starts amongst a tight cluster of players on a rugby pitch.

Simply put, I was never the best fighter in the history of Irish rugby.

Unfortunately, there is also evidence to prove this, from a decade back when I travelled with Ireland A to the Churchill Cup that was being staged in the United States in 2008. There is a photograph taken by the Irish team doctor, Eanna Falvey of me with our entire family from my Mom's side. They had travelled down to Chicago to see me play.

There I am, surrounded by my smiling and proud American cousins, and I'm presenting one seriously blackened eye to the camera.

We kicked off the tournament by beating the USA 49-9 in the Kingstown Stadium in Ontario. There was a lot of talent in our party. Johnny Sexton and Tomas O'Leary were paired at half-back, and Keith Earls and Cian Healy were also out there. However, a week later in Fletcher's Field, still in Ontario, we went down 34-12 to England Saxons. That sent us in the direction of Argentina A, and a game to see who came third and went home with the absolutely worthless Plate.

It also sent me in the direction of a gentleman called Juan Pablo Lagarrigue, the Argies' lock. From early on he began to act the complete bollox.

I regularly was getting punched in the face and the more we stretched our lead – we would win 33-8 – the more the punches came. I was locked into the front row. There was damn all I could do to defend myself. I thought I might be able to kick him in the face, maybe… but I wasn't able to work out how I could do that. It was hard to get to him. His big head was sticking through, but I couldn't do any damage to him.

So I called in the troops. I actually called in Trevor Hogan, who was behind me, and told him to sort out Juan Pablo on my behalf.

'Right… SHKINNN!' Trevor shot back.

Trevor and Donnacha Ryan called everyone… 'SHKINNNN.'

Next scrum, I catch a quick flash of this big fist coming up between my legs and it lands right on my nose. Blood starts to pump. Then there is another fist… from the opposite direction. It gets me on the left eye.

'FUCK SAKE… WHAT THE FUUCCKKKKKKK!

'…TREV!!!

'WHATTTT….

'WHAT ARE YOU FUCKING DOING?'

The first fist that had smashed into me was Trevor's… the second was another one of Juan Pablo's.

As I tried to gather my senses, all I heard was… 'SORRY…

'SORRY SHKINNNN… SORRY SHKINNNN!'

WITH FIVE MINUTES left on the clock it was time for some payback.

I saw Juan Pablo idling around the side of a maul, and I threw what I thought was a decent punch at him. Quickly… of course very quickly, I discovered he had a much longer reach than me. He's a lock… of course he had!

And he started filling me in with fast punches. Two of them landed on my left eye again and I managed to get an elbow into his face. More luck than anything else. But I got him on the jaw and he felt it…and then everything took off from there.

Everyone wanted a part of it.

When the mass brawl was concluded myself and Juan Pablo were dispatched to the sin-bin.

Not only were my punching skills hit and miss back then.

My Ireland rugby career was hit and miss, thanks to Premier League Rugby, the umbrella group for all English clubs, who were not too worried about helping me advance and win that green jersey I so badly wanted. Unlike Ireland, where the Union rules, it was the call of the PLR as to whether the likes of myself, and others like Geordan Murphy, Bob Casey and Eoin Reddan could come home to play for different Ireland teams.

THE CHURCHILL CUP, which most of the lads referred to as the Churchill Stag, was my first involvement with Ireland teams at any level. Schools and underage, there was nothing for me!

With the Ireland A team at least I was on the radar... someone's radar, but I also knew I was not centre stage in anyone's thoughts, not while I was playing in England. Declan Kidney would look at me.

But I knew Declan might as well have been kicking tyres when he threw his eye in my direction. That's why I had to leave Harlequins. I was about to turn 30 years of age, and having amassed a big handful of games for Ireland A, and nothing else, it was time to get back home.

I was in Ireland training squads. I was added to squads... then cut from squads. In 2009, thankfully – and thanks in the main to Ian McGeechan and his Lions management team selecting 14 Irishmen for their battle in South Africa – I got my first chance of a first senior cap. It was Declan Kidney's first tour with Ireland, and it came just a couple of months after the Grand Slam, but he was without most of his first choice front row. Bernard Jackman and Jerry Flannery were unavailable, and John Hayes and Marcus Horan were given a rest.

The newspapers were immediately sizing up Tony Buckley and myself, and waiting to see which one of us would make the bigger shout for The Bull's jersey. We played Canada in Thunderbird Stadium in Vancouver, and then flew to Santa Clara in California where we met the United States in Buckshaw Stadium.

Declan had this saying, one of his favourites…

'You don't have to be talented to work hard!'

And the work that The Bull did around the pitch was never fully appreciated. People complained early on about his scrummaging, but they were unfair on him. I remember, once, trying to hit him off a ruck in training one morning and, well… I might as well have been trying to inch his car to the parking space next door to it.

Buckley was the heir apparent.

I was a little disappointed to lose out to him in selection for the Canadian game, because Tony had already been given a number of shots at impressing Kidney and Co. I just wanted one big shot.

Please… just one shot!

They put me in against the States, who had Eddie O'Sullivan starting out with them. Tony was switched to loosehead. We had Rory Best in between us. My shot, but it did not go great for me. We won the game 27-10. I was in against Mike McDonald, whom I'd played against before a few times. He was with Leeds at the time, and I felt ready to dominate him.

Then, for some knucklehead reasoning, I went and changed my studs the morning of the game. I felt the ground was too hard. At half time I swapped back, but it was too late by then. Too much damage had been done. I'd been slipping and sliding in the first half in front of too many people.

In my mind I had to dominate every single scrum.

It was… *MY SHOT*.

I'd changed the studs because I wanted to answer the critics who believed that I did not offer enough in loose play. I wanted to get all over the field, and I did not want to be crippled by blisters. It seemed a smart idea… but the downside was that it felt like I was wearing slippers instead of rugby boots in that first half.

When I called home after the game, I was surprised that my wife was even more upset than me. Kim was very upset indeed but she wouldn't say why. My Dad later informed me that one of the after-match analysts had seen fit to label me 'a donkey' and had said other unflattering things. I later found out that same man had form for doing that, so I was in some good company. I quickly shrugged it off though, when you win your first cap there are certain duties you must attend to, and certain traditions to be followed. Traditions like having a drink with everyone in the squad. I'm a good man for tradition, and I'm not sure if I knew my own name by the end of the night.

THERE WAS A pretty big mountain to be climbed.

I was home, finally… but I was looking up. At 30 years of age, almost, I was starting that ascent.

Pre-season and the first couple of months with Leinster were great, but then the London-Irish game happened and for the next 12 months I tried to put a brave face on it when I came home, but I knew that my whole career was being called into question. It was an overwhelming feeling that I would not experience again until the final 12 months of my career. It happens with everyone who plays a pro sport. I know that! Brian O'Driscoll even had to face it on a Lions tour.

You are told you are not wanted.One game even, it can hit hard.

One whole year? Michael Cheika did not want me in Leinster, and Declan Kidney was of the same mind when tidying up his Ireland squad. In the November series of 2010, I didn't get one minute of game time.

Four games, and I got nothing.

By that time, Cheika had left Leinster. Joe Schmidt was in. I was playing some of the best rugby of my life, finally, for Leinster. But Declan had his heart set on Tony Buckley. He also liked the look of Tom Court, but it was mainly Tony.

Tony got injured at the start of that four-game series, coming off after 50 minutes in the loss to South Africa and being replaced by Tom Court.

John Hayes started the win against Samoa, but came off after 63 minutes and Declan sent Cian Healy in and swapped Court over to tighthead.

Court started at tighthead in the loss to New Zealand, but Hayes came on for him after 63 minutes. But, when we beat Argentina in the final game, Buckley was back starting and was replaced by Court midway through the second half. See what I mean?

I had a mountain of men to climb over.

CHAPTER 24

IT WAS ONLY a small number of Irish journalists who formed The Mike Ross Fan Club. But, luckily, they wanted to be heard. Declan Kidney also got out of his bed one morning and decided that instead of being No.4 on his favoured list of Irish tightheads, I was No.1. Tony Buckley moved in the opposite direction, and in the middle of January of 2011 he did not even make the extended squad of 34 for the Six Nations.

Three of us would play our first Six Nations match against the Italians, myself, and Sean O'Brien and Fergus McFadden. We were on our way to the Eternal City. My fan club was insistent that the Irish scrum lacked stability. The club said only I could do the job. Simple as!

Except, now I was chosen to play against Salvatore Perugini, who was also going to be celebrating on the same day as me, except he was about to set an Italian record of 33 Championship appearances in-a-row.

I could say that Perugini was fair and decent in how he applied himself, but I'd be totally lying through my teeth. He looked a bit like a caveman, hunched over with a massive neck and thick shoulders.

It was a testing day for my fan club.

And it was a testing day for me with Romain Poite. What I said to that man… in my head! He gave them scrum penalty after scrum penalty, and it was not because we were getting dominated or driven back. It was because there were a lot of angles coming from them! All of them completely illegal.

I'd come across my share of looseheads who liked to go 'walkaround'… but Perugini! At one stage he walked around and was actually lifting me up with both of his arms. And I got penalised.

I looked at Poite… *mate, this is in front of your face?*

Perugini had actually left the scrum. He had departed. And he had lifted me up with both of his arms!

Are you admiring the view?

You are… TWO YARDS AWAY… how are you not seeing this?

The trained policeman in Poite, I always found, did not take too well to players talking to him and certainly not arguing with him. He was the opposite of Nigel Owens in that way, the complete opposite to Wayne Barnes.

We got there in the end for a 13-11 win, thanks to Brian O'Driscoll's try, plus two kicks from Johnny Sexton, and a drop goal from Ronan O'Gara. Near the end also, when they were about 15 metres out from our line, they went for a pushover. But we were able for them. We didn't give an inch.

And if Poite had even the faintest notion of what happens in a scrum we wouldn't have been under such pressure. He gave four full and three indirect penalties to Italy. He gave us just two indirect penalties.

Poite did not seem to care how either front row went forward. Once you went forward, he was giving you a penalty… even if you were going off to the side… even if you were standing up. Poite was still happy with you.

My new fan club was outraged by Poite.

Kidney was equally dissatisfied with him after the match.

My position in the team was safe, and Kidney made no changes for the visit of the French.

WE LOST TO the French, 25-22. But our scrum did well, and everyone seemed happy with how myself and Cian were doing. The two of us, and Rory Best, were in the early stages of forming a serious partnership.

Thomas Domingo and the magnificent Wiliam Servat were opposite me, and I never had anything but the height of respect for the pair of them every time I met them on the pitch. I had so many good battles with Domingo, when he was with Clermont and France, before I called it a day. He was not a tall man, but he was wide and had a bullish strength. I felt we shared the honours that first day in the Aviva, though three years later, when we won the Six Nations in 2014, I got a good few penalties against him and he was pulled off straight after half time.

I went into the French dressing room to see him. I knew he would be down, and I found him sitting there by himself. I knew what he was experiencing.

We'd all been there!

I sat next to him, handed him a beer and in my best French told him… 'Today you Thomas… tomorrow me!' He was always an honest opponent, and I hope he thought the same about me. He understood what I was telling him.

I never went into the opposing dressing room very often, not unless I felt it was necessary, like after what turned out to be my last game for Ireland. I thought it would be a good idea to go into the South Africans and chat with them. I had that slight suspicion that it might be my last chance to do so.

So, I sat there with them, and they offered me a beer.

And I sat there a bit longer.

MY FIRST SET of opponents in my first Six Nations were Salvatore Perugini, Thomas Domingo, Alan Jacobsen, Paul James and Alex Corbisiero. Quite an interesting and accomplished bunch of men.

I believe I came out of the Championship with a couple of wins, a couple of draws, and then that day against Perugini which should have been ruled a non-event. In the Championship table itself Ireland ended up with three wins and two losses, so I think I was a head, or at least a nose, in front of the team performance. I needed to be. A great deal was expected and, more or less, I met those fair-sized expectations.

We had a second slim victory over the Scots in Murrayfield, 21-18. I had another good performance, as I usually had when I played against Jacobsen. He was old school in his technique too. He suited me every time we met, but if I took him for granted then he was capable of catching me unawares.

That was always the danger he posed to me. Otherwise, if I was properly respectful of him, and made sure that I got across the mark quickly, then I beat him for size every time. I'd try to take him where he wasn't comfortable.

If I brought him up, he never had a lot of leverage.

I always sought to put him up, or behind me where he could not get to me. In Murrayfield, that afternoon, he was deep into his frustration early on and got himself sin-binned after 44 minutes.

BUT EVERYTHING WAS not rosy about our general performance as a team, and we'd lost the penalty count against the Scots 13-4.

We met up in Carton House for a mini-camp in our down week to discuss what was happening. We had Alain Rolland into the RDS for an hour with us, to give us a referee's view of what we were doing. The penalty count in Rome had been 13-5 against us, and it was 10-8 in the French match. We had outscored our opponents 7-2 in tries, but we'd barely won through in two games and lost the third because of our indiscipline.

And some questionable calls too!

We lost to Wales, 19-13 in the Millennium Stadium and did England in, 24-8 in the Aviva. It had been my first time in the Millennium Stadium since I had attended Munster's 2002 Heineken Cup defeat there. Paul James, and the Lions hooker Matthew Rees, were a formidable pairing and James was a tough customer. If he saw an opportunity to put a mark on you, he'd take it fast. A year later in the Pro 12 final against the Ospreys the scrum went down but instead of stopping, James pushed through and I strained my hamstring. He did not set out to damage me, but he was trying to make doubly sure that the referee had absolutely no doubts about why the scrum went down in the first place.

He's no different to the rest of us. Most players will put the hurt on one another if they can. The only thing, I guess, that makes every single one of us stop in our tracks is when someone's neck is under pressure.

We all know that is the line that can never be crossed.

But, the rest of the body?

It's part of the game of rugby to put that hurt on!

We conceded fewer penalties in the final two games, but we were still suffering as a result and not getting the maximum return from our performances. Declan Kidney never came down on us as hard over the penalty count as Joe Schmidt would have. With Joe, a penalty count anywhere close to 10 is deemed simply unacceptable.

Not giving away penalties frustrates the daylights out of the opposing team. It means they are not getting any easy yards. It means they are not getting access to the game. With Joe, we'd always get specific feedback.

Less so with Declan.

In my early days with him he came to me on one occasion and told me that he wanted more involvement from me, but I was not sure what exactly he meant by… involvement? I figured out he wanted a few more carries, and more impact at rucks. He also wanted some big hits in defence.

But he never spelled it out for me.

Joe would tell me directly.

He'd say… 'Rossy… your clean out is not good enough!'

Or… 'Rossy…I want you to move your feet quicker!'

Or… 'Rossy… stop turning your hips… you're letting guys get by you by turning those hips… stop it!'

Or, Joe's favourite one he liked to remind me of… 'Rossy… keep your feet alive… DON'T BE PLANTED!'

ENGLAND WERE IN the mood for a Grand Slam when they came to Dublin. And we knew what we were up against. A team led anywhere by Martin Johnson is all about serious business. But he probably got the English job too quickly and we held too many aces in the Aviva in 2011.

Corbisiero and Dylan Hartley also found out that afternoon, from the very first scrum, when we got a massive push on and set the tone for the entire 80 minutes, that we were absolutely ready for them. Tommy Bowe and Brian O'Driscoll got our tries, and while it was two tries to one at the end, it was a match in which we could easily have hit the 40-point mark.

I never enjoyed a day on a rugby pitch more up to that point in my career. I came off after 58 minutes and Tom Court came in, but it was of those matches that you never want to leave behind, no matter how tired you are becoming. Corbisiero, who I also knew so well from London-Irish, had one long and painful late afternoon. Hartley, of course, was one of those guys who everyone genuinely loved hitting.

His demeanour and attitude on the pitch demands it from opponents, because he's fiercely confrontational and you have to respond to that. When he first came onto the scene he was not thought of as a very good scrummager, and at Quins we'd go after him, though he did improve that part of his game. By the end, his scrummaging was his greatest strength and his use of the 'arrowhead', which he applied against us in the 2011 Heineken Cup final, became something of his trademark, always looking to pop the opposing hooker and create that space for his props to utilise.

I met him a lot too, and I thought he was a man who could not get out of his own way. Trouble followed him around like a pet dog. He could just not hold it together in his head and we knew that if we kept after him, and kept at it... he'd probably blow. And in the scrum to stop him in his tracks, we pinned him to the floor that day in the Aviva and pinned their Slam hopes into the bargain.

IN SO MANY ways 2011 as a year was a whirlwind.

I won my first Heineken Cup with Leinster, and I was welcomed onto the Ireland team as a man who had a right to remain there for several years. That meant I was also heading to my first World Cup by the end of the year, and getting to see New Zealand and play down there for the first time in my life.

I had it all in my rugby life, all of a sudden.

And in my private life, Kimberlee gave birth to our son, Kevin. He was born between the French and Scottish games in the Six Nations. A few days later, Kim almost died because of complications after the birth.

In 2011 I won almost everything I ever dreamed of, and almost lost the one person who is central to everything I am.

It made me understand by the end of the year that I was indeed a far luckier man than I had ever imagined myself to be.

CHAPTER 25

I NOW UNDERSTAND that rugby is part of people's lives. And that it is not life itself.

Professional rugby players live and breathe in a bubble. And from within that bubble we presume that the next big game, and the next big game after that, are also central to the lives of the people we see wearing blue Leinster jerseys and green Ireland jerseys on the street. For over 10 years I did not understand, or at all imagine, that the game is nothing more than that!

It's only a game to everybody outside of the bubble.

It's not life and death.

It's not even life!

It is entertainment, and it is part and parcel of people's social lives – and it is not dictating the emotional highs and lows, and the pace of the lives of those who watch the game.

Only now that I am outside of the bubble do I completely understand.

THOUGH I HAD an inkling.

At different times in my professional rugby life I wondered about the next game, and the game after that, being the be-all and end-all?

But only once or twice.

On occasions when the bubble was pierced, I guess. Back in the early spring of 2011 when I jumped from being fourth choice tighthead in Deccie Kidney's thinking, to first choice, was a time when my professional career seemed to be everything to me and my family. I had been ignored by Kidney during the November international series. But a couple of months later I got my first start against Italy.

I grabbed the chance of a lifetime, as it appeared at that time.

Then we played France in the Aviva eight days later.

And then we played Scotland in Murrayfield 14 days later and, the next game, on my list of priorities was... first, second and third!

But I look back on that game against the Scots now, and I genuinely wonder was I completely mad in the head wanting to play in it? *What was I thinking?*

Kimberlee was heavily pregnant with Kevin by the time of my first Irish cap, though I do recall her being well impressed by the French during the after-match banquet when we were wined and dined, and she was the centre of attention for many of the impeccably mannered Frenchmen.

Kevin was born in a 'down week' during that Championship.

He was a very considerate baby!

But, how considerate and aware was I as a new father? I wonder now, as I look back on those weeks, and I understand that I had my priorities completely wrong. Arse about face, in all honesty.

Kim was due the week of the French game.

Kevin was born on February 19. We played Scotland on February 27. The eight days in between were a matter of life and death for my wife. But, at the time, I also thought that playing a rugby game for Ireland was also a matter of life and death.

How wrong was I.

As professionals we accept that we have a good life and we have a great wage compared to talented people in so many other walks of life. And we accept that we have to pay a price for that, like missing weddings or family celebrations, and needing to put the team first during the Christmas period. Things like that. It's no big deal, and when I came back from my first World

Cup with Ireland near the end of 2011 and Kim was there, up front with the waiting families, and with Kevin in her arms, I knew that I had missed out on something special in our lives together as husband and wife.

While I had been in New Zealand, Kevin had taken on the world – my baby son had crawled for the first time, and I had not been there to see it.

THIS WAS DIFFERENT.

Something else entirely, but I was so wrapped up in my career that I did not see it as that at the time.

At about 5.0 am on the morning of February 19, Kim woke me up. The contractions had begun. We grabbed a taxi. And we were in the rooms in the Rotunda Hospital pretty fast.

Kim progressed just as fast.

By noon, she was ready to deliver our baby. Being the dutiful husband, I had the hand worn off me rubbing her back – and doing sweet damn all else of any value.

Kim's waters had been broken.

There was a monitor on Kevin's head.

All of a sudden, Kevin's heart rate dropped and, within seconds, there was an entire team of medical people on hand. It was action stations. I was chucked out of the room. An emergency C-section was underway.

Before I knew it, I was handed my son. Of course, he pissed on me straight away. I'm thinking… *what do I do with this fella?* I had been counting on Kim telling me what to do and she was unconscious in recovery. The nurses soon showed me how to swaddle him. And that was fine. He was happy. But he was soon roaring for some food. The boy was hungry as hell, but Kim was in the recovery room. I wanted to feed him, but the nurses refused me a bottle because they wanted him breast fed to begin with.

The C-section was a five-day stay in the hospital.

Kim was fine.

The morning after Kevin was born I was back at training. The back slaps and congratulations were coming my way, all of the men in the Irish camp agreeing that I had done a great job – as Irishmen do. I was in camp on the

Sunday evening. On Monday I was back in the hospital and Kim was not looking so good.

She had a lot of pain through the night.

Her stomach was bloated.

The consultant on duty decided on an x-ray, and we found out that Kim had developed a toxic megacolon, which is an abnormal dilation of the colon. They had to move her to the Mater. Kim and I had to get into an ambulance and leave our baby behind in the Rotunda. I rang my mother straight away and she came up and stayed with Kevin in the Rotunda. After one miscarriage and now having a baby boy to celebrate, Kim was not happy. She wanted her baby. To add to matters, the staff at the Rotunda discovered that Kevin had a protein allergy and had to be fed a special formula. They moved him to the NICU for observation while his mother was gone.

In the Mater, Kim remained in pain and in great distress. The staff at the Mater tried several treatments but no progress was being made. They suspected a reaction to opioids so the pain relief was a paracetamol drip, something I had never seen before.

Me? I went back training. I went to the Rotunda to see Kevin the next day and I made it to the Mater to see my wife, but I also trained with Ireland. However, I was concerned.

On Tuesday, Kim was still not well. Wednesday was our down day in camp and I rang Professor Arthur Tanner, our doc with Leinster. Arthur was taken from us too quickly, in 2017 on his 69th birthday, a few years after he was supposed to be enjoying his retirement. Arthur was revered in Irish rugby circles and further afield as a brilliant carer and friend to all of us on the team. I needed to talk to the 'Prof.' Arthur listened to my concerns and said he'd see what he could do. I fielded a call from the Mater later that day where they said Kim was improving, and they thought she'd be out of the woods soon.

I was still worried, but I went back to training the next afternoon and while I was on the pitch with the Ireland team, Kim crashed.

My wife looked to be on the way out.

Kim's life was saved by Ann Brannigan, a specialist in colorectal surgery in the Mater. When she started failing Ann rushed her into surgery immediately. I got the phone call to come into the hospital but by the time I got there she was in surgery. Ann did not wait around. She conducted a laparotomy. A large section of Kim's colon had to be removed. Gangrene had set in. Three or four feet had to be taken. If Ann had not opened up my wife when she did, Kim might have died.

I'D BEEN TRAINING.

While all of this happened, I was running around a rugby pitch.

Kim's parents, Kevin and Kathy, needed to be brought to Ireland. My Mom was up from Cork and staying with Kevin in the Rotunda. All hands were on deck. But when Kim came out of surgery she insisted that I should go and play against Scotland, which I did for 70 minutes before being replaced by Tom Court in our 21-18 victory in Murrayfield – but going to Scotland and playing in that game is something that I felt guilty about through the remainder of my career, and ever since.

Kim's Dad is a biomedical engineer. He was perfectly familiar with the machines his daughter was attached to. Kim knew there was nothing for me to do in the hospital. She said she wanted me to go and play rugby, and look after our family's future.

I don't remember much of that weekend, to be honest.

I did go to the House of Fraser in Edinburgh and I spent about 200 euros on designer baby clothes which, when I produced on my return, Kim told me were entirely useless as Kevin would be grown out of them in a week. I took my scolding. It had been tough on Kim.

She'd spent nearly two weeks in hospital without seeing her baby.

My memories of that week are hazy. I vaguely recall Declan Kidney and the Irish team management offering to stand me down, but I didn't take them up on that offer.

But, the days remain a blur. I had brought Kevin home from the Rotunda. My Mom and Kim's Dad looked after him mostly. I was playing and training. Kevin could not have been in a better double pair of hands.

But the guilt that my hands were not available to do more at that time remains, and I know that I should have been there for my wife. I should have remained by her bedside.

I should have been there for our boy.

I should have stayed and I should have said 'no' when Kim told me what she wanted me to do. It should have been my decision. I believe that now.

Now, and only now, do I understand it all.

WHETHER YOU ARE an amateur or a professional, a game of rugby is a game of rugby. Nothing more. You win or you lose, and life moves on.

Everyone moves on.

Outside of the bubble it is so easy to understand that, but a professional rugby player especially has this self-identity. Everyone you look to and ask will tell you that you are doing the right thing by putting the game first and foremost in your life, no matter what else is happening.

I could not wait to get home from Edinburgh after that game. I found Kevin in a Moses basket in my Mom's room. I found Kimberlee comfortable and slowly returning to full health in her hospital room.

I instantly knew that I should never have left them.

CHAPTER 26

WHEN KIM WAS well enough to travel we went back to the United States and spent some time with her family. She was still not one-hundred per cent that summer of 2011, but we got to have some time on the beach, and to chill together and take in the biggest year of our lives.

I had my first World Cup on the horizon.

I was excited, but I also knew I needed to relax with my family. It was difficult to balance that holiday. For all I knew, the 2011 tournament in New Zealand might have been my first and last World Cup. I was 31 years of age, and I was keen to come back from holiday and make a big impression.

Kim's family are from Manchester, Connecticut. Her grandparents have a big house by a lake that is amazing… Dick and Alice Kristoff, with German lineage. It was also a unique experience for us to be travelling with a baby for the first time. A friend of my Dad's, Joyce Anderson also had a cottage in Cape Cod, in Chatham, and we took that off her for another week.

Then, I was home!

Another pre-season, and a first World Cup

OUR WARM-UP GAMES were pretty much a disaster. We lost 10-6 to Scotland in Murrayfield, lost 19-12 to France in Bordeaux, lost to France again 26-22 in the Aviva, and still in the Aviva we lost to England 20-9. In the middle of all of that we managed to defeat Connacht 38-3 in Donnybrook.

It could be explained or painted any way ourselves and the management team chose to do so (and, of course, we did!), but it was not a good way to settle minds and bodies in advance of heading to New Zealand and taking on the rest of the World.

Our flight down there took 39 hours, 47 minutes and 23 seconds.

I know that for sure because that's what was on Donncha O'Callaghan's stopwatch by the time we walked through the entrance of the Crowne Plaza in Queenstown. He had started the watch when Denis Leamy picked him up at the Horse and Jockey pub in Tipperary… 18,000 kilometres and 11 time zones removed from our hotel. Though we were not permitted to crash straight away.

First of all, there was the traditional Maori welcome.

This was all new to me… and I didn't want to miss one single minute. Our party responded, as I guess rugby teams from Ireland should do, with Christy Moore's *Ride On*.

Queenstown was magical in every sense… and everything was on offer to us in order to help us unwind for what lay ahead. There was white water rafting, bungee jumping, skiing, snowboarding and jet-boating all on offer. There was a whole, long week ahead of us before we met the United States on September 11, the tenth anniversary of the attack on the Twin Towers.

Declan and his management team chose well in having us laugh and work together for the first week. The tournament was going to be long haul, if we managed to make it to the very end! We needed to lighten up at the very beginning, and after our awful warm-up games we also needed to relax and stop stressing about our performances. Easy enough to do when you are in a helicopter with Brian O'Driscoll, Shane Jennings, Donncha and Geordan Murphy and you arrive at Milford Sound and immediately awaken to Rudyard Kipling's description of it as the 'Eight Wonder of the World.'

WE HAD A two hours plane journey to New Plymouth, where Eddie O'Sullivan's Eagles awaited us. The rain was coming down horizontally as we walked down the steps and bolted to the terminal building. The rain continued most of the week, and by kick-off time in the Taranaki Stadium it was still not relenting. It was rattling off the windows in our hotel.

In the scrum we steamrolled them, as we knew we should do. On the final scoreline it was just 22-10, and we had no fourth try, no bonus point. Ireland had beaten Namibia 32-17 in the opening game of the tournament four years earlier, a tournament that quickly went south after that. Australia was next, and after that we had Russia, whom we beat 62-12, and then Italy whom we managed to see off 36-6, each of them more than respectable margins and befitting a team with intentions of taking on the tournament with a full head of steam.

We also got a bonus point from the Russians, but it was not all one-way traffic. They scored two decent tries. I got 30 minutes off the bench. I was back in from the beginning against the Italians. Their starting team had 745 caps between them. They were a grizzled force to be reckoned with, and they had 203 caps in their front row alone. Cian Healy, Rory Best and myself had a combined 88 caps in comparison. Plus, how would I even think of missing out on the delight of having Salvatore Perugini for company once again?

I also stayed out there on the pitch for the full 80 minutes. The walk off the field was not without incident as Perugini refused to shake Donncha O'Callaghan's hand, and Cian went one further and decided not to bother joining the line of players waiting to shake everyone's hands. It was that type of game, once again, with the Italians.

I knew they would come at us at the very first scrum.

We were ready and waiting for them, and they did not like that one little bit. We did some stats after the game, and we reckoned that out of their 10 scrums they only got decent ball from three of them. On the flip side, we did concede a couple of penalties, and we also lost the ball in one scrum when it ricocheted off someone's leg. In between all of that, there was constant niggle.

There was also a lot of talk out there and, foolishly, considering the fact that we would not be far behind them in getting to the airport for the journey home, I had kept telling them close to the finish to... 'Enjoy your flight home, boys!'

'YOU... NEXT WEEK.

NEXT WEEK... YOU SEE!'

Their front row were prophetic in their replies to me.

Cian did bloody well not to go completely off the rails long before the final whistle. The Italians had ramped up the provocation especially for him.

BUT THE TOURNAMENT, to begin with, was all about Australia. And our meeting with them in Eden Park on September 17.

That World Cup was also about Declan Kidney trying to make up his mind between his Leinster and Munster half-back pairings, and ultimately trying to work out a balance between the emerging genius of Johnny Sexton and his massive loyalty to Ronan O'Gara. That was a hard one. I had all the sympathy in the world for our coach trying to work that one out.

O'Gara had been there, and done everything. But Conor Murray was just starting out on his brilliant career and he would become a world class player soon enough, though in New Zealand in 2011 he was still largely an unknown quantity. Declan went with Johnny Sexton and Eoin Reddan for the first big test of the tournament against the Aussies.

With my Leinster hat on, and with the fresh memory of how Johnny and Redser did together in winning the Heineken Cup the previous spring, I was good with that selection. Redser was so strong in bossing his forwards and driving us on. He was especially good at that, and bringing up the tempo of the game.

But it wasn't Leinster v's Munster at any stage. We ended up winning the game because of the perfectly managed combination of Johnny and Rog, with the pair of them kicking two penalties, and Johnny also dropping a goal in our 15-6 win over the Aussies.

I don't believe Australia took us all that seriously.

If they had been with us the evening before when Declan worked one of his masterstrokes and asked Jerry Flannery to individually hand us our jerseys in our final team meeting they would have understood quite clearly what was coming down the tracks at them.

I'd known Fla for 12 years, since playing with him in UCC. And Fla and emotion went hand-in-hand, and with his World Cup over with a torn calf that had been troubling him for the previous 12 months, and that was possibly presenting itself as a career-ending injury, he was filled up with tears that he stubbornly refused to let loose. Declan called out our names, one by one.

Fla handed over our jerseys.

As he did so he looked each one of us in the eyes, and we knew what we had to do the next day. Bran O'Driscoll stood to say his few words afterwards, and told us there was no need to say a damn thing. We were ready.

Finally, we were ready for the 2011 World Cup.

I woke up around 10.30 am.

Breakfast on game day was porridge and ferociously strong coffee. Lunch at 1.0 pm and the pre-match meal at 4.0 pm meant a lot of eating, and carbs and more carbs. In between I took a two-hour nap and felt pretty good afterwards. Travelling to the ground in Auckland we had a police escort, something that always thrilled the little kid in me.

There's a ranking system of police escorts. In the top tier are the French and the Italians. They will drive down a jammed motorway opening up a path and literally kicking cars out of the way. Next up are our own lads, who'll take us through red lights and halt traffic, although not quite as aggressive as the Italians and French. Bottom of the rung are the police in the UK, who stop at every red light! They seem to be there as more of a ceremonial presence.

But I never failed to be enlivened by that sense of importance. For three-quarters of my adult life I had never even entertained the notion of a police escort, unless my life had turned upside down and someone was bringing me off somewhere in handcuffs.

LOOKING BACK ALL of these years later, I can see it was a game that we were destined to win, though we had no true sense of that in the hours that counted down to kick-off. First the Wallabies lost David Pocock, their expert at the breakdown, and then news came through that Stephen Moore went down with a bug.

We were ready.

There was a perfect pre-match downpour.

And there were 25,000 Irish fans in Eden Park.

We built our victory on the breakdown and the scrum. Cian and Besty were everywhere, carrying and tackling and clearing. With a wet ball there were more scrums than usual, and we were all getting stuck into them. Maybe we got too many decisions our way from Bryce Lawrence, the New Zealand referee, but there are days when you take them all. I'd been on the wrong side of enough such days in the past, thank you.

Cian, especially, was flying. It rubs off on the rest of us when we see one player right on top of things and, besides, props are like brothers. When you think about it, guys who find themselves in the front row all of their lives are likely to have similar personality types but Cian, if anything, was an anti-prop.

He liked his roller-blading and surfing and, for his size, he was one of the most nimble and mobile players you could find. He really liked doing his stupid shit… skateboarding in parks and grinding on railings. His agility for such a powerful man made him kind of freakish.

I was taken out of it after 77 minutes and while I was disappointed to exit at that stage, I did not want to be the man who was a little bit slow getting across and was found wanting as the Aussies scored a try.

At the breakdown we had forced three turnovers to their two and we had recycled far more ball through the game. Les Kiss' choke tackle also made a huge difference. Moore's absence helped, but Cian was giving Ben Alexander a torrid going over and I had Sekope Kepu well in hand as well. They were missing Moore, who as I found out since is a very good scrummager. In the third quarter we turned the screw and after a superb off-load from Stephen Ferris, Seanie O'Brien went on one of his gallops that led to Johnny Sexton putting us ahead. Declan then moved the pieces brilliantly around the chessboard.

Rog came in. Murray also came in, and Johnny moved to inside centre to take over from Gordon D'Arcy who was feeling a tightening hamstring. The noise in the stadium was building. Rog kicked penalties in the 62nd and 70th minutes to leave enough daylight between the two teams.

We had a few drinks that night. Nobody went baloobas. I ran into my old Quins teammates, Tani Fuga and Andy Gomarsall that night, which was a great reunion. The Russians and the Italians were still about the place in our group at that stage, and they needed dealing with. We were up bright and early the next morning at 8.0 am. Our flight was 10.0 am. I rolled out of bed feeling pretty rough. My body felt like it had been in a car crash and I had a nice raw patch on the back of my neck from the multitude of scrums the evening before.

We had a 45 minute flight to Taupo. We touched down at the tiny airport, and all we could smell was the sulphur. The town was next to Lake Taupo that formed in the cauldron-like hollow of a dormant supervolcano. The region is still heavily volcanic. Hot springs abound, but we were told the last volcano erupted 26,000 years earlier when it covered the entire North Island in a layer of ash up to 200 metres thick.

It was stunning.

The lake was rimmed with the snow-capped mountains that had once formed the rim of the giant volcano. I felt on top of the world. The Russians and the Italians were waiting for us, but we checked into the Hilton Hotel – one of so many grand hotels I always felt absolutely privileged to be bedding down in during my Ireland career – and everything seemed to be lining up just correctly for an Irish team, for once.

For me, there was no double room to be shared in Taupo either.

I was given the door key to an apartment in the hotel, and even though I had Tom Court and Sean Cronin for company I felt that I was being singled out to play an historic role in the story of Irish rugby.

A semi-final lay in wait for us all.

Surely?

WELLINGTON WAS RIGHT up our street, as we awaited our quarter-final meeting with Wales. There were lots and lots of coffee shops, which are always a second home to pro rugby players with time on their hands. And it was cosmopolitan, with choices of good eateries to choose from. Made for prop forwards, in other words.

On our 'down day' I took a trip out to the Weta Cave, which houses a lot of the props from the *Lord of the Rings* movies. The trilogy was filmed all over New Zealand. My inner geek was amazed to get up close to the many different costumes and models on display, and I was extra interested because

I knew that they were also filming *The Hobbit* around the corner. Though the enthusiasm filled up in me was not shared throughout our squad. Only Tommy Bowe, Geordan Murphy and Gordon D'Arcy set out with me for the afternoon.

That evening there was an increase in the number of movie buffs when Donnacha Ryan and myself provided popcorn in one of the team rooms, and had a projector and an in-built sound system to do fair justice to Daniel Day Lewis' *The Last of the Mohicans*. We had our captain's run the next day in the 'Cake Tin', which locals call the famous Westpac Stadium. The stadium forms a large oval around the pitch, that is also used for cricket and this combined with its silver-walled exterior does make it look like a tin that some giant from the *Rings'* movies might have found handy.

It was still raining when I awoke at 11.0 am on Saturday morning. I was meeting my parents who had arrived in the day before to witness their son, in the nick of time hopefully, on an historic day for Irish rugby.

AS I LAY on my bed resting, I could hear the singing and chanting from the Irish fans gathering in our hotel lobby. They sensed it, and we wanted it. *This is Wales...* I was thinking to myself... *we play these guys all the time!*

We can do this!

When the time came to walk down the stairs, through the lobby and get onto the team bus, I could also sense it. There were hairs standing on the back of my neck.

History.

It was there, at our feet and our fingertips. Though we got off to the worst of starts, conceding a try after just three minutes. As was the case when they had beaten us in our meeting in the inaugural World Cup, in Wellington in 1987, they had won the toss and had elected to play into the wind in the first half. We worked hard and pulled it back to 10-10 five minutes into the second half after Keith Earls went over and Rog kicked the extra points, and I honestly thought we were sure to advance from that point for our victory. But it was not to be.

Gatland had them geared for a high tempo from the very beginning, when a multi-phase move led to Shane Williams' opening try. They never dropped that tempo. They would make 143 tackles, to our 93. But they only had six minutes in our 22, while we were inside theirs for over 15 minutes. Those numbers told the story of the game that they won 22-10. We did a lot of things very well, but they played well… and they *undid* a lot of the things we were doing. Their performance was full of big hitting and hard, straight running.

I remember looking up at the big screen to see their Newport lock, Luke Charteris going off after 40 minutes with a tackle count of 15, which was a staggering figure. That's a good number to post after 80 minutes.

They won the bigger collisions.

And the breakdown.

Jamie Roberts and George North were immense for them. We had more ball, but they appeared to be stronger, fiercer, and they'd led 10-3 at half time despite having only forty per cent of the territory. We had fifty-seven per cent of the possession but they were chopping all of our big runners right down at the ankles. We watched our big runners falling, and we did not have a Plan B unfortunately. We should have had more points on the board.

Our scrum was solid enough. Adam Jones was entering a phase of his career that made him the best tighthead in the world perhaps and they got one penalty against us at a crucial enough stage. But we did okay in the scrum.

We did fine.

The lineout under Paul O'Connell's supervision did not let us down either. But we were less certain with the ball in hand.

We made 11 handling errors, while they had just four. That made a difference, and other little things helped them to remain on top of us mentally, like Rog missing a couple of touch kicks that went dead. The final scoreline did not reflect it, but there were fine margins in the game. Mike Phillips had them back in front in the 51st minute when he spotted the slimmest of gaps and darted through. Jonathan Davies clinched it for them with his try, with Earls losing the ball in a counter-attack and our defence slow in its reactions. Letting someone sneak down the blindside, missing a tackle in midfield… that was not us!

There were 14 minutes left on the clock.

It was a long time to face and get to grips with a defeat. They kept chopping us to the very end, and when Sean O'Brien was nearly in after a brilliant snipe and off-load by Eoin Reddan, Leigh Halfpenny did what they had been doing from the very start and tackled fearlessly, and low.

They had been able to stop us, nearly all of the time. For us, coming into the game with the best tackling stats in the whole damn tournament – one missed tackle for every 15 made – it was especially galling that we had allowed them in for two tries that we would have expected to stop early in their tracks.

OPENING MY EYES the next morning was a painful process.

A futile attempt had been made to drown our sorrows. Aches and pains were indecipherable. Some must have been from the game, others were surely from the alcohol. I knew we had ended up in a bar called Motel.

And, definitely, it had a selection of obscure but magnificent whiskies. And I was equally sure that I had met up once again with the actor, James Nesbitt who is from Ballymena, and was working on *The Hobbit*. At the beginning of the week he had taken us out to watch some of the movie being filmed, and he had texted a couple of us after the match to let us know where he was drinking.

He was more disappointed about our defeat than any of us. He wanted to talk rugby. I wanted to talk about anything but rugby. Even at three o'clock and four o'clock in the morning I knew in my head that we had failed to respond to the Welsh on the pitch, and I knew in my heart that we would never fully forgive ourselves. It was a match that had already morphed into one huge regret.

I honestly and truly did not want to talk rugby.

Bilbo Baggins and the cast of characters from Tolkien's *Hobbit*... Gandalf, Gollum and Sauron, and Thorin and his 13 dwarves, of which Nesbitt was one in the movie, were of more interest to me late into the night than recapping where we had gone wrong.

CHAPTER 27

THE VERY LAST place on earth Declan Kidney needed to bring an Irish team in the early summer of 2012 was back to New Zealand.

A judgment on the man who had ended our 61-year wait for a Grand Slam was already being formed by journalists and commentators, and too many unhappy people with a say in the immediate future of Irish rugby. Declan had led Ireland into four Six Nations Championships after 2009.

In those final two Six Nations the team was on a slide, however. In 2012 we won two, lost two and drew one of our games as we finished third in the table on a points difference of +27. Twelve months later we finished fifth, winning one and drawing one, and finishing below Italy on the table with a points difference of -9. We scored 13 tries in 2012. Five in 2013.

DECLAN, WITH THAT brilliant disposition he possessed, put a smile on what lay ahead of us all. I remember he likened going down there to meet the All Blacks like going bungee jumping.

Declan was always brave, especially so since the series was the first outing for new All Blacks coach, Steve Hansen. Also, this was a three Test series, and the third Test against the new world champions would land in what was officially the 51st week of our season. To top off the pressure on everyone, we were sitting in eighth place in the world rankings, which meant that we were clinging onto the very last of the second tier seedings for the 2015 World Cup in England.

Paulie O'Connell was ruled out of the tour with a knee injury, though Brian O'Driscoll was back after a difficult year with injuries. We were also without Stephen Ferris, Tommy Bowe and Luke Fitzgerald. I was also touch and go, as I had sustained a grade one tear to my hamstring before departing, courtesy of that collapsed scrum against the Ospreys. Our doc, Eanna Falvey worked on me every single day and his dry needling was complete… agony. The needle is used to keep poking at the tendon to try and break down any scar tissue or tightness, and to stop it becoming knotted. Half an hour into it, I was in a cold sweat every time.

But Declan stayed brave. I had no chance of making the first Test in Eden Park and Declan Fitzpatrick was chosen for his Ireland debut. Simon Zebo was the other new cap, and he was promoted alongside Fergus McFadden from the team that had started our 30-9 defeat to England in our final game of the Six Nations. Andrew Trimble, Gordon D'Arcy and Donncha O'Callaghan were also missing, but Pete O'Mahony was back in.

We'd been waiting 107 years to slay the All Blacks and it did not happen that evening in Auckland. Twenty-five defeats were at our backs. They scored five tries to our one from Fergus in their 42-10 victory to make it No.26.

It was tough to watch. I remember thumbing through the programme before the match and I noticed that the All Blacks had a habit of blooding an awful lot of their players against us, for some reason. I was wondering why?

I was also thinking at the end… *Bloody hell, we've got to play them again next week.*

And the week after!

A LOT OF people were looking at us after the second Test.

We came so close to a famous victory.

And, at the very end, with the teams level, I overran and knocked the ball backwards. We might have beaten them in Christchurch that evening, and we certainly should have walked off the pitch with a draw. Instead of losing 19-16.

We were considered 17-point underdogs for the first Test, but the bookies allowed that figure to drift out to +23 for the second Test. It was also the All Blacks first time back in Christchurch since the devastating earthquake the previous year that left 185 people dead. We took a tour of the city the day after arriving and it was fairly sobering. We could only imagine the emotion that would hit them as the home team in front of a Christchurch audience.

We all found it emotional.

For me too, it was a first time to view the Haka from up close. With me staring hard, I could see what the game meant to every single one of them. Every man in black was totally wrapped up in the significance of the match.

It was also cool to see them sticking their tongues out. As a kid I had always been mesmerised by the Haka, and as I waited and watched I felt like a kid all over again… telling myself… *HERE'S THE HAKA!*

WOW!

I genuinely loved it.

Though I also quickly understood, once it was over, what a distinct advantage the Haka also gives them over every other team. One minute I felt primed for the game. The next minute I was a little distracted by what I had just seen. As amazing as it is to view it, it is also unfair to allow them to do what is essentially a war dance to rev themselves up and leave the other team standing there and taking it all in like a bunch of dumb tourists.

I'd been thinking as they finished it off… *Okay, okay!*

It got the adrenaline pumping that little bit extra, I guess. But they were at a whole different level, with a whole lot of juice racing through their veins once they had finished.

Then, I waited for the first scrum!

My first scrum against the All Blacks… in New Zealand! Half of me felt like a lottery winner, and the other half of me felt a little terrified. I was waiting for Tony Woodcock. He would finish his career with 111 appearances for his country, making him the most capped New Zealand prop of all time, and one newspaper had labelled him the world's No.1 loosehead with… 'the best range of skills of any prop on the planet.'

Possibly I should have been one-hundred per cent terrified, but I wasn't. Within a minute of the kick-off I was ready. Woodcock was the same age as myself, pretty much the same size, and he had played all of his life with the Blues. Of course I respected him, but I also knew I needed to unleash everything I had in his direction and in the third Test, as they were hammering us, he fell over our ruck at my feet. Instinctively I dropped my knee into him.

He looked up at me and… time stood still.

Next thing he punched me in the mouth… and we both looked at one another, and again… time stood still for another half a second… as we grinned at one another… before the two of us ran away in opposite directions like two little kids who'd gotten away with something we should not have done.

But that first scrum, I saw it as a moment when you want to be a man! Seriously! New Zealand had garnered a hard scrummaging reputation. They had Woodcock, and they also had Hore and Franks in their front row. They were very canny, and streetsmart. I remember watching them a few years previously, where they had messed the French up and left them in a bad place. They had come in from a height on the piece I watched, and the French had buckled. They had no answer for it, and they could not think on their feet. The French were crying with frustration by the very end.

We did well though. Besty, Cian and myself ended up doing some damage to them, and we did not get as much back as I was expecting. In the last quarter of the game, we were the superior force all over the field.

With six minutes left on the clock and the teams level, we came at them hard once again. They were down to 14 men. Redser passed to me and… I left the ball behind.

Romain Poite, acting as a touch judge, signalled for a knock-on.

Inside their 22 we had applied three big shoves at the previous put-ins. We went for it again, though Nigel Owens allowed Piri Weepu a delayed release of the ball. We drove them back. Their flanker, Ben Cane broke from the scrum and got into Cian, and the scrum twisted and turned. We thought we should have been awarded a penalty, but Owens saw it differently. He pinged us for deliberately wheeling, which was controversial in our heads to say the least!

From the lineout they went through a dozen phases.

Seanie O'Brien deflected Dan Carter's first drop goal wide. Carter did not miss with his second attempt one minute into added time.

We had been 10-0 up midway through the first half after a Conor Murray try and Johnny's penalty. We had taken everything they threw at us after that and we were still standing at the end, unlike too many Irish teams before us.

It had been my first game since the Heineken Cup final victory over Ulster, and despite some ring rust I had achieved everything I ever dreamed of putting up to the All Blacks. I could not wait for more, and for the third Test in Hamilton's Waikato Stadium.

WE SHOULD NOT have lost 60-0.

Cane, Williams, Williams again, Smith, Cane again, Gear, Messam, Dagg and Thomson crossed for tries.

I had been out there for the full game the week before, but when I was called ashore in the 59th minute of that third Test they had already crossed for seven of their nine tries. It was week 51 of our season but, nevertheless, the embarrassment... the humiliation, it was total and overwhelming. Even though they were reaching the peak of their season and we were sore and absolutely weary, there was no excuse for such a capitulation. We were awful. We missed tackles. They could not stop running, and we could not stop missing tackles... that is my lasting memory of the match.

No doubt they were offended by the near-defeat of a week earlier. And the full fury of the All Blacks is a shocking thing to experience. It sobered me up. The kid in me on his first tour of New Zealand was, suddenly, all grown up.

The devastation, physically and mentally, was total.

We all wanted to get home as fast as possible.

Let me get to fuck out of here...

Get me out of here now!

IN THE SIX Nations preceding our tour of New Zealand we spent our time treading water. That was no help to Declan Kidney in trying to win back the fullest confidence of the Irish rugby public, or Irish rugby's bosses.

Even the surprise visit of Michael O'Leary to Carton House midway through the tournament failed to give the team wings. With some special guests, not everyone turns up in the team room, but O'Leary whose worth was estimated at €300million at that time won himself a full audience. There was a good audience for Ben Dunne a few months before, and Christy Moore before that! Everyone took a seat for Ryanair's boss of bosses, even our physios! He was impressive, totally down to earth and willing to go the full 12 rounds with Ronan O'Gara on their respective knowledge of horseflesh.

It was my second Six Nations.

None of us gained from the experience in all honesty. We started with a dispiriting defeat to Wales, our third in succession to Gatland's team, going down 23-21 in the Aviva though, in truth, while we led at the break we did not have what it took on the day to avenge our World Cup dismissal by them only a few months before. We were supposed to be on a revenge mission.

All the fire and fury came from them.

A week later our need to get up and running was frozen over when, just before kick-off, the Stade de France was deemed unplayable because of the cold weather. We beat Italy 42-10 in the Aviva, went back to France and drew with them (17-17, with Tommy Bowe crossing for two first half tries), got another four tries against the Scots in the Aviva (winning 32-14), and then we had England in Twickenham.

Rightly or wrongly, the Irish team was now being judged by how it performed against the likes of the English in their neck of the woods.

We played England on St Patrick's Day. I'd received my fair share of punishment through the tournament, and had a face to prove it after the French match. I'd been lucky not to lose an eye, as their lock Julien Bonnaire accidently landed on my face with his studs coming down from a lineout. He missed my eye socket by half an inch, and left me with three stitches and ridiculous looking bruising for the rest of the week. But against the English I was hit for six.

All of the novenas that my 'fan club' in the media had been saying for me went missing that afternoon. I damaged my neck in the first scrum in the first minute of the game.

England won the game 30-9, with a penalty try in the 58th minute clinching it for them. I had stayed out there until the 37th minute. Tom Court came in for me. In terms of job security it was great to have so many journalists writing after the game that I was 'irreplaceable' but it was also unfair on Tom on the day in question. Tom was a loosehead covering tighthead and he was left in an impossible position that day.

When that first scrum collapsed, I had been caught between Hartley and Corbisiero, and I felt something go crunch in my neck. That's the thing about the media… they might have called it a 'cricked' neck, but I felt an actual… CRUNCH.

I got up, and I could not look left. I had pins and needles down my arms, but I decided to stay out there. In training all through the week Tom had been going well at tighthead, but I did not want to leave the pitch. A couple of scrums later, I could hardly move my neck at all. The pain was beginning to mount. I guessed there was some serious damage done, and then I got another stinger… more pins and needles. I could not move. I could not hit. Near the end of the first half, another scrum went down and I stayed down for a bit. My neck was on fire. Eanna Falvey came racing over and eventually persuaded me to come off. I accepted that Tom's two shoulders were going to be better than my single shoulder.

I was a liability to the team.

But I also knew it was going to be tough on Tom. He had started out at tighthead early in his career, but then made the switch across to loosehead where he excelled. To do consistently well at tighthead you need to be playing there consistently. Very few players are comfortable both sides. A man could get seriously injured ending up on the wrong side of the scrum no matter how strong he is, because tight and loose are two entirely separate roles.

It was a serious safety issue in the game.

Inexperience is one problem. But on top of that, the opposition front row may have been given the hurry up before, and I knew in England's case that Graham Rowntree had been winding up their front row all week long. Corbisiero, in addition, was one of the best looseheads in the world before he got bad knee injuries. In his pomp, he was once the very best there is!

Corbisiero was always strong and explosive, dangerously so. He was not as impossibly strong as Andrew Sheridan, but he was a close enough second. On my very best days against Alex Corbisiero I always had to be one hundred and ten per cent on top of my game.

Anything less, and I too would have been in trouble.

IN THE SIX Nations following our tour of New Zealand the team never managed to lift itself up off the floor despite going to the Millennium Stadium in Cardiff for our opening fixture and handing a 30-22 defeat to the Welsh in a six-try thriller. We crossed their line three times, from Simon Zebo, Cian Healy and Brian O'Driscoll, before they returned fire. Johnny Sexton kicked six from six. It was the perfect start to the tournament.

But the Welsh won that Six Nations, and we avoided the wooden spoon due to a nine points smarter differential to the French. We drew with the French but in our final fixture, in a match in Rome that became a complete fiasco at the end due to injury after injury, we got turned over 22-15. Pressure on the coaching staff began to mount.

Calls for Declan to go, most of them respectful I'm glad to say, were coming from all sides. We could feel the wolves circling him, but we didn't really discuss it. We knew how things worked. Coaches come and coaches go, the great coaches and the entirely useless coaches.

His five years in charge had been momentous and undoubtedly left Ireland in a stronger place, despite the failure of his final season. Momentous because we won a Grand Slam, and momentous because Ireland opened its doors wider than ever before to players from all over the world.

For the first of the November internationals I had roomed with Richardt Strauss. Leinster's South African was about to make his Test debut against his homeland. Michael Bent, whose maternal grandmother hailed from Rathmines, also got a first cap in the game that we lost 16-12. But there was an essential difference about how Straussy and Benty got to wear an Irish jersey.

Benty, a tighthead who switched from Taranaki to Leinster on a two-year contract, spent his first night living in Ireland with the Irish team in our camp in Carton House. Once again, we were short on tightheads.

Straussy's case was very different.

He served his time here before getting his call-up to play for Ireland. Like CJ Stander further down the road, Straussy had been told in South Africa that he was not big enough for the international game. He came over here and he had a tough time settling. He wasn't valued by Cheika, and he worked even harder. People were slow to see his full worth. He was a pocket dynamo, and brilliant over the ball. And he was a strong scrummager, but he still had to put in the hardest yards with Blackrock College in the AIL. He became one of my best friends in the game, I admit, so I was delighted for him getting his first Ireland cap.

Back in South Africa, just like me, he's from farming stock. The guy is happiest when he is on that farm, heading out shooting and hunting. I've told him that when my young fella is old enough I'm going to send him down to South Africa so that Straussy can help him grow up, and Straussy can serve Kevin up his first testicle! If you go shooting down there and get a kill for the first time it's tradition to have some part of the animal served up to you, there and then... cut out, and eaten while it's still warm. If the kill is male you get a testicle, if the kill is female you get some liver.

The week before the game Straussy's biggest concern was learning off the words of the national anthem. It's not a trivial task, considering *Amhrán na bhFiann* is in a language he never learned, but Straussy was serious. Irish citizenship was important to him.

CJ has embraced us as a nation, and as his home at this point in his life also. As a kid it was never CJ's dream to play for Ireland, of course not! But he did want to play international rugby. He came here, served his time as well, and fought to earn his place and hold down that place against the fiercest opposition from within the Ireland squad. You can't ask for much more from a man than that. He can't change his spots. He can't 'time-machine' and go back and be born in Ireland, but he can fill that green jersey with his sweat and his blood, and Straussy and CJ and others after them have done that.

Would I be happy if a South African or a New Zealander was standing directly in the way of my dream of wearing a green jersey. I guess I would not be, not one bit. I might even feel a fairly resentful. And would I like to see a day when I'm sitting in the Aviva and watching an Irish team populated by eight or nine fellas who have been born outside of this country?

No, I would not. We've got to be smart about who we hand an Irish jersey to, but to begin with we can only judge the man. We've got to judge the man first, and then take on board what he might bring to the Ireland team. And in a two-horse race, an Irishman born here should get the nod over someone who wants to become an Irishman for a period of time in their lives.

A five-year period of living and working here before becoming eligible for an Ireland jersey would be better than a three-year residency rule. It would be fairer all round.

Straussy is back on his farm now, in Bloemfontein. It's where his heart is, but he remains South African and Irish, and he always will.

He served Ireland well.

Leinster and Ireland both gained from his time with us.

I'VE GOT TO know Michael Bent, and he is a great guy.

But at the time I wasn't a fan of how he was brought in. I thought about how hard I had had to work before ever getting to be in an Ireland camp. All the times I was named and cut from squads. And the long, tough wait for my first cap. Whereas Benty lands in and is in a green jersey.

It should be harder than that.

Declan should not have allowed that, no matter how short he looked on options in the front row. It was unfair on others, but it also was risky because there is a big difference between rugby in the northern hemisphere and the southern hemisphere. Declan, however, saw us playing a team from the southern hemisphere that day and thought Benty's inclusion made sense.

He still should have backed off the decision.

Wearing an Irish jersey is the apex. It's the ultimate. We all know someone who dreamed all their lives of wearing that jersey and fell just short after a lifetime of effort. If I was Jamie Hagan or some of the other lads in the queue behind him, I would have been absolutely raging.

I knew that Greg Feek had given Benty the thumbs up, so I knew he was going to be a decent operator. I had no idea, however, if he was going to come in and take my starting spot. In the previous 22 Test matches I had played in 20 of them, and started in 19, and it was going to take a fair effort from anyone to shift me. Benty came in for me after 71 minutes against the Springboks, and in that short amount of time he won a couple of penalties.

While I was out there I had given away a couple of penalties, against my Leinster teammate Heinke van der Merwe.

Like so many players I know, I never felt entirely confident of my position on the Ireland team. I never felt it was mine by right, and even when I hit 20 caps, and then 30 and 40 caps… I was always paranoid.

We are all waiting for the merry-go-round to stop.

In the end, Benty did nudge me out in Leinster. He deserved to do so. I was coming back from injury in my last season and there was no doubt, he offered Leo Cullen more than I was able to offer at that stage. He had also served his time with the club. He had proved himself as deserving and worthy as anyone else in Leinster. More than that, he became one of the club's most important players. He was a solid pro. He was never injured. He always did what was asked of him. His consistency was spot on, and he could play both at loose and tight.

Benty became one of us, and good for him if he was able to take my place on the team.

THE END AWAITS all of us who have played a pro sport.

And it never has a great big smile on its face. When your time is up, it's up… and you are asked to leave. It does not matter who you are, or what you have accomplished. Only a precious few in the history of Irish rugby got to choose the manner and timing of their exit from the great stage.

Declan Kidney's time with Ireland was up.

The clock had ticked down… like it does for nearly all coaches. Because the coach is no different than the player. He is there to do his job, and for him it is entirely a results-based business. Unlike the player who can plead a big performance within a disappointing defeat, the coach has nowhere to hide.

Declan Kidney's brilliant career with Munster and Ireland, in the opinion of those who have the final say, had come to its end.

CHAPTER 28

ONE MORNING BEFORE we played Wales in the 2013 Six Nations I ran, head first, into Jamie Heaslip's hip. Obviously I came off the worst for wear. An electric shock raced down my left arm.

I ignored it at first.

That afternoon I went for a normal upper body weights session, as usual warming up with 100 kilos on the bar. But I couldn't bench it. My left arm kept dropping. The physios told me I had pinched off my C4/C5 joint in hitting Jamie. The C4/C5 joint contains the nerves that run down your arm, and it left my tricep debilitated. The tricep is key to heavy lifting. It got worse and worse. A couple of days later I was struggling to bench 15 kilos.

There was the little matter of the Welsh front row to consider.

The docs put me on prednisolone, an anti-inflammatory steroid. I needed a Therapeutic Use Exemption (a TUE in the world of anti-doping) to try and stabilise the muscle.

But in the lineout as we prepared for the Welsh I was still lifting with only one arm and, truthfully… I was also panicky as hell.

I could not do one push-up.

I kept my worries to myself. I still did not believe that the No.3 jersey was mine for keeps for the whole season.

Scrummaging, I was okay, because I was still able to grip onto Rory Best. However, on the morning of the game I was genuinely shitting myself. I probably should not have been playing. Every day I'd been getting an electrical stimulation on the arm to wake the nerve back up. Progress was very slow.

But I could scrummage. I could get my man up in the lineout and... who cared if I wasn't able to do a push-up... *Who's going to look for a push-up from me in the middle of the game?*

Outside of that, my left arm remained perfectly useless.

We won the game. I got through it favouring my right arm most of the time, but nobody noticed.

My left arm never fully recovered the length of the 2013 Six Nations and I was not back to full strength with it until I began pre-season in the middle of the summer. It was seldom an issue, though in the final game I was carrying the ball in my left arm and one of the Italians came and took it off me as easily as if he had helped himself to a kid's ice cream.

That day with Jamie introduced me to whole new world of... stingers... and some inconvenience for the rest of my career. And, each time, total agony for 30 or 40 seconds! Regularly, I'd get crunched in training or in a game. I'd wait and I'd get up. And I'd try to avoid trouble for a minute or two, and then I was ready to go again.

I'd no interest in telling the docs or the physios anything much. I wanted to play in every game. How long had I waited to get my arse in the hot seat in the front row? Forever is the answer.

I was not volunteering my own ass for any medical help.

I WAS A one-armed Lions hopeful all through that Six Nations.

Because I was playing cagey I did not cover myself in glory. Nobody did in that Championship. And as Cian, Jamie, Seanie, Johnny, Drico, Rob, Tommy, Paulie and Conor posed dramatically in the famous red jerseys before heading down to Australia with Warren Gatland, I was packing for the United States and Joe Schmidt's first piece of business with the Ireland team.

IT WAS NO accident that Joe won back-to-back Six Nations Championships in his first two seasons. Same as it had been no long streak of good luck that he had stepped into Leinster and without delay totted up two Heineken Cups, one after the other. Joe Schmidt's ways work, and on the training field the youngest players and the oldest players can see them working.

As I said more than once already, Joe is unlike any other coach any of us had ever experienced before. He's not a magician... he's the exact opposite of a magician. We could all see exactly how we were going to work... *to win!*

Of course, we won those two Six Nations by small margins.

The first in 2014 found us just above England at the top of the table, both of us on eight points after the pair of us had won four games out of five. Except we scored 16 tries to their 14, and we had a points difference of +83, while they had a points differential of +73.

Joe Schmidt takes care of the tiny margins.

Better than anybody.

The second title in 2015 found us at the top alongside England and Wales, once again the three of us on eight points.

Wales scored 13 tries, England scored 18, and we only crossed for eight tries in that Championship. But Wales conceded 93 points and England conceded 100 points! Ireland had kept the opposition down to a paltry 53 points.

Wales were on a +53 points differential.

England on +57.

We were +63.

A tiny margin, but the smallest things count in Joe's great scheme of things.

THE NEW SCRUM laws had come in at the start of the 2013-14 season and I had to learn fast. And I did.

I had little choice, as I was facing Cian Healy mostly every day.

The... HIT... was gone.

Tightheads were at the mercy of looseheads for a few months to begin with, as we could no longer hit the loosehead down and chase through anymore. Cian was virtually impossible to deal with. The season before, my momentum could knock Cian down and he'd have to work from a low point, but suddenly, he was coming back at me from all sorts of ridiculous positions.

He was impossible to keep down.

I've got him now… he's screwed!

Always, he'd do something ridiculous and be right back where he wanted to be.

Goddamnit!

JOE STARTED OFF his first season on home soil against Samoa, and we got together as a team two nights before the game to look down at the whole world. We were all in the Guinness Storehouse for dinner, in the Sky Bar with its amazing views of Dublin old and new. As it was Halloween, fireworks were going off all over the place.

Samoa went as it should have, with five tries in a 40-9 victory, but then we got a bit of a hammering from the Aussies. We were beaten out the gate by them. It was four tries to nil, in a 32-15 win. Next up we had the All Blacks.

Joe remained calm. It had been my first time to play against James Slipper and with the new rules, and the Aussies hitting the ground running, we had some trouble. Though it wasn't like we were running backwards. But there was one scrum on the right touchline where they screwed us over and our scrum disintegrated. I knew everyone would remember that scrum.

And they did. And, of course, they judged every other scrum in the game on what they had witnessed in that one awful scrum. It was also a game where the entire team focused too much on Joe's systems and did not have enough passion at work. We did not balance the new systems with high enough levels of emotion. Too many of the lads were overwhelmed by what we were trying to do.

There was an eight-day turnaround, and we should have beaten the All Blacks. We had them. The most famous win in Irish rugby history was right there in front of us, and then Ryan Crotty crossed for a try one minute and 24 seconds into overtime to draw the teams level. Aaron Cruden's conversion from the touchline had to be taken twice. We had three tries on the board inside the first 17 minutes, from Conor Murray, Rory Best and Rob Kearney.

We led 22-7 at half time.

They won 24-22.

They won in the end, well... because they are the All Blacks. They know they can always win any game, and never stop believing. But Nigel Owens was also hard on us. He was incredibly harsh on Jack McGrath for the last penalty. And if Johnny Sexton had slotted one more of his kicks, we would have been there! Nine times out of 10 Johnny would have slotted it, but the All Blacks felt like a team given another life!

Many other referees wouldn't have given that penalty.

It was so like Owens, however. Sometimes he likes to make a big call! Calls that can leave everyone on the pitch scratching their heads! Personally I always liked the man and how he handled himself in games and worked with us, and I made sure to always tell him that I was giving him the long bind he liked in the scrum and make sure he was happy with me. But he also liked to make those calls.

For me, coming up against Wyatt Crockett of the Crusaders and Canterbury, I was full of fear. But it was a good fear!

It was probably one of the best performances of my rugby life. We went into the contest knowing that unless we upped our performance from the Aussie game we were going to be completely embarrassed. We also went in remembering the 60-0 scoreline from the season before. Yeah, fear was the huge driving factor at work in my head all through the game and I knew I could not switch off for even half a second.

As a team, we set out our stall as well. Our mantra every day leading into the game was... 'One man... One bullet.'

Joe knew there was nothing more important to us than our accuracy at the ruck. In Richie McCaw and Kieran Read they had two master poachers, and it was essential that we identified the threats early and made sure they were taken care of... 'One man'... One bullet.'

We knew we had to be pinpoint at every single breakdown. Nobody could waste themselves at a ruck, without taking a man with them.

'ONE MAN...

ONE... BULLET.'

It came down to the last 30 seconds.

We had the ball.

Two or three more rucks, and we had the victory that all of Ireland had been waiting patiently for, for over a century. And then Owens gave that penalty against Jack. A handful of phases later and they were over in the corner.

I was sitting on the bench at that stage.

I covered my face with my hands. Cruden's unorthodox little pre-kick routine caught us out the first time. Owens wanted the kick retaken.

My heart sank.

In the dressing room, nobody spoke a word. Nobody looked up. Every single man felt totally alone, as though he was attending his own funeral.

'SKILLS UNDER FATIGUE.'

That's what Joe called it.

The history of the Irish rugby team had been pockmarked by big beginnings... and bad endings. So many tough defeats were down to Ireland getting tired and making wrong decisions because of shattering levels of tiredness.

In our last week before embarking on the 2014 Six Nations Joe made sure he got a good look at how all of us performed when completely and absolutely fatigued.

Bolloxed, in other words!

And winning games while you are completely bolloxed is what marks the greatest teams out from every other hopeful team.

Joe had us doing 15 minutes of strongman fitness, followed by five minutes of skills and decision making.

This, he repeated twice.

If you want to really get to know one of your teammates then try dragging him a couple of hundred metres all over a rugby pitch.

The next day Joe wanted an intensive defensive session.

Five sets of four minutes of continuous defence.

Therefore, twenty minutes of damned good decision making while feeling dead out on your feet. It was one of the last pieces of the jigsaw as Joe Schmidt counted down to the first Six Nations game of his career.

Ten games later, and we were champions on the double.

CHAPTER 29

IN THE MIDDLE of the 2014 Six Nations we found ourselves down in Clonmel for a little R & R, and it was badly needed because although we had beaten Scotland and Wales on an aggregate score of 54-9 at the Aviva Stadium, and whipped the two of them 5-0 on a try count, we were needing some time out. We had England next.

Twickers!

And a Triple Crown?

Before any coronation, it was Clonmel.

We were all due down there by lunchtime. But the worst storms in 20 years were raging through the middle of the country, and driving down to Tipp it felt like the car was going to be wiped off the road at any second by the massive gusts of wind. We got there in one piece, but the electricity was kaput in the hotel.

They did have a generator. And as we tried to cosy up in the hotel and looked out at the rain rattling off the glass we assumed that Joe would cancel the afternoon session. We told ourselves that we would be doing something indoors.

Joe wanted us outdoors, however, and we were soon running out at Clonmel RFC in the filthiest conditions I, for one, had ever encountered. Passing the ball any further than three feet was impossible. The wind simply snatched it away and whipped it down to the other end of the pitch.

We did our close quarters handling drills.

Then some rucking, and tyre flipping.

The rucking was more like bog snorkeling because of the a nount of surface water on the pitch. Back in the dressing room, because of the power cut, there were no showers. Of course not! We wiped ourselves down as best we could.

R & R, right?

BY APPEARING AGAINST the Welsh, Cian and Besty and myself had become the most capped front row in the Championship's history, overtaking the previous record of 15 held by the famed Welsh and Pontypool trio of Bobby Windsor, Charlie Faulkner and Graham Price.

Their record had stood for 35 years, unbelievably.

We felt good for Twickenham where we were revisiting the scene of the 30-9 stuffing two years before. Ireland had been hit and miss at Twickers for too long, in truth. Our three wins out of our last five visits there had been by four, four and six points. However…!

We had not won by more than six points in the home of English rugby in 60 years, and out last five defeats in the place had been by 21, 23, 34, 32 and 22 points. This time around we lost by just three points, 13-10 having led 10-3. The Triple Crown was out the window. The Championship title looked in jeopardy.

Seven tries against Italy in a 46-7 victory set us up for a big finish in the Stade de France. In the last round of the Championship on March 15 England would put 52 points on the Italians in Rome, but they conceded 11 points.

Two tries from Johnny Sexton and one from Andrew Trimble saw us home safely in Paris. At 22-20 we had 10 points to spare over England on the final table standings.

The Championship title was ours.

My first, and when it was all over I had a very special memory to take away with me and keep forever. It wasn't from any of the matches. It actually came from the Shelbourne Hotel where we camp down for the night before all of our home games. The day before we played Italy Kim had called in with Kevin to see me.

I told her to leave him with me for a bit, so that she could get a break and wander through some of the shops on her own. I brought Kevin up to the team room in the hotel. He knew all of the lads.

He spotted Johnny, of course.

And he wanted to play with Johnny, naturally. And Johnny Sexton, one of the greatest No.10s in world rugby was happy to do so. Johnny grabbed a ball and they headed off to the large empty physio room and started kicking the ball around.

When I looked in, there was my three years old son receiving a one-on-one lesson from the great Johnny Sexton, with Kevin being taught how to step back and move to the side prior to taking the future and most vital penalty kicks he might take in his rugby career.

WHEN PEOPLE HAVE ever asked me about Johnny, and all of the trouble that has come his way on a rugby pitch, all of the punishment he has taken, all of those knocks on the head, those concussions, I always tell them that Johnny Sexton is one of the smartest men I have ever known.

Any time Johnny has been knocked over and is lying on the ground, people think... *Oh, he's gone again... HE'S GONE!*

It's absolutely true, Johnny is brave as any lion. But he also has people worrying unnecessarily about him at times. He receives ferocious amounts of punishment, and more than any man should be on the receiving end of, but Johnny's bravery should not be mistaken for foolishness.

He takes those big hits, because rival teams will always look to go down the 10 channel just to check out if Johnny can still take it? But do I think Johnny is going to allow himself suffer any permanent damage to his brain?

No. Of course not, he's no different than any of us. We have our head injury protocols and we all know where we stand after every bang to the head. We get tested at the start of the season to establish a baseline. Tests like remembering words, and patterns. There is a very real consciousness amongst every group of players that this is our life we are dealing with on the pitch... it's our brain!

Concussion is taken more seriously than it has ever been taken in the game. When I first started out nobody was too bothered worrying about hits to the head. Not any more.

We can get knee replacements... shoulder replacements, or anything we want for pretty much every part of our damaged bodies, but there are no new brains out there for sale or any man-made products that are a nice substitute.

Everyone, including Johnny, understands this.

WE ALL WANTED a Triple Crown the following season.

We wanted it all, our Championship title and the Crown, and why not? We'd toured Argentina in the summer of 2014 and come through a couple of Tests with decent winning performances. We didn't come through unscathed. Course not, we were in the Argentinians' back yard

I hadn't played for a month before the South Africans were in the Aviva in November but in a huge tackling performance we beat them 29-15. We made 143 tackles, with Paulie and Jack McGrath leading the way with 19 apiece. I put in nine of them. We beat Georgia 49-7. And we completed a first November clean-sweep in more than 10 years by seeing off Australia.

We were 17-0 at one stage, but then had to fight to the very end. It finished 26-23, and five minutes from the end and inside our own 22, we took everything they had in the scrum and won ourselves a relieving penalty. Jack and myself were left out there for the full 80 minutes. And that last scrum was right in front of our sticks.

It was me and James Slipper again.

We took them low.

And lower still, but staying legal just about.

We had them low and we had the full pressure on... and it was a wait to see which of us would blink first. The longer it went on the more we dropped in the front row.

And we dropped again.

Then, something gave! Getting up onto my feet I heard the whistle. I'd no idea which way it was going to go. Who ever knows for sure?

It was ours. And Michael Cheika had a big grumpy face on him when it was all over which was just a sufficient amount of cream on top of a magnificent team performance. We were absolutely ready and waiting to successfully defend our Six Nations title. In Rome our pack was in juggernaut mood and between the lineout and scrum we won three penalties against them in the first quarter. It was a thorough 26-3 win. Then, we more than competently took the French, 18-11.

We needed to be absolutely right for the French, whom Joe described as having 'the biggest human beings I have ever seen on a rugby pitch.' We all had to put our bodies on the line, and I also got to make one of the best tackles of my career when I managed to get a hold of Teddy Thomas. If his jersey had been slightly less stretchy he would have been gone, but I came around the corner and just managed to get a piece of that blue cloth.

In the scrum I was in against Racing's Eddy Ben Arous but before I left the field after 63 minutes I had Vincent Debaty from Clermont on my hands. He's a big awkward fella who does his best work at a medium height. I'd played against him often enough to know how I needed to work it with him, but Wayne Barnes was suddenly on my case. He gave two penalties against me after the scrum collapsed.

The first time he asked me to raise my body height.

'Okay,' I told him, while also telling myself... *fuck that!*

I'm not doing that...

I was down nice and low.

'Come up... COME UP!' I heard Barnesy ordering me.

You fucking joking...

Want me to stand up... and let him run me back?

'Yes... okay!' I told the ref again.

But I stayed right where I was, and the scrum went down. And Barnesy, true to his word, penalised me.

He was only looking at me, but I had no intention of going high where the French were strong. I was staying low... where they were not strong!

Why should I go high? Let them come down here... I'm not going up... nope!

BEATING ENGLAND ALLOWED not just a Triple Crown, but a mighty Grand Slam to feel so damned close.

We looked after them 19-10 once the pre-match snow and hailstones were finished. Since 2012, there was always a big focus on the scrums when we played England, and we got a nice penalty in the scrum after half time to push out our lead. We were 19-3 up after the hour and although they came back at us we held out comfortably and equalled the Irish record set in 2002-03 of 10 successive wins.

We had Wayne Barnes in control of things once again when we went to the Millennium Stadium to play the Welsh. He had penalised us a total of 11 times against the French.

Joe always asked us to take the control of the game out of the hands of the referee, and games like that French game, and then the Welsh game that we would lose 23-16, made him even more certain of the need to control our own destiny. What angered me as much as the loss was the inconsistency of the refereeing that day.

We were pinged three times in succession for being on the wrong side of rucks but, then, once that box was ticked and when the Welsh were doing the same thing in the second half, nothing! To be fair, the Welsh put in one of those epic defensive performances that they seem to summon against us, putting in over 250 tackles for the second biggest number of tackles ever in a Six Nations game.

We destroyed the Scots, 40-10 in Murrayfield in our last match and while we managed to hold onto our Championship by a slim enough points margin, there was more than a tinge of disappointment when the season came to a close. We'd lost just one game, but at a massive price.

More than ever before, Joe demanded lower and lower penalty counts against us after that, anything to keep the result out of the hands of the man in the middle.

Discipline, and smart decisions around the ruck became more important than ever to Joe after the 2014-15 season. Anything to keep the referee off our back, and make sure that games and whole seasons were not decided by one man who has a split second to make his judgment.

In reviews Joe spent more and more time highlighting penalties. If the call was wrong he was ok about it, but if it was a dumb penalty, or from laziness or lack of discipline, then you were in for it.

CHAPTER 30

I HAD SOLDIERED with Joe Schmidt longer than anybody.

That was something that was good to know when I saw the stat that I was the only man to start on a Joe team in his last 18 Test matches. And at the start of our 2015 World Cup warm-up I got to celebrate my association with Joe and also my 50th Ireland cap. Unlike 2011, we actually won some games in the lead-up to the tournament, and in the Millennium Stadium at the beginning of August we beat the Welsh 35-21. And I got to lead out the team for my half-century of caps, which was extra cool.

The statistics for the game heralded the fact that we did not have one blemish in our 15 set pieces, whereas Wales were turned over once in the scrum and lost three lineouts.

I fully realised that, because of my late start as an Ireland player, I was never going to hit the magical 100 mark. But I could live with that. Easily enough, as 50 seemed an outrageous number to me.

THE TOURNAMENT ITSELF was a let down for us and for Irish rugby supporters. We expected a semi-final. For once, we felt in our hearts that we were due a place in the top four nations in the world.

We dealt with Canada in the Millennium Stadium 50-7, and a week after we switched to Wembley and defeated Romania 44-10. In the Olympic Stadium in London we were too good for Italy, seeing off our old sparring partners 16-9. After that it was back to Cardiff where we met France. Our 24-9 victory was immense, and also very costly. We appeared to be on a roll.

However, there was another way of looking at it. While we were building up our momentum against weaker teams, before stepping up against Italy and France, our quarter-final opponents had their biggest test in their group at the very beginning. Argentina had met up with New Zealand in their opening game in Wembley two weeks earlier when they had fought hard but had gone down 26-16.

After that, the Argies had Georgia (54-9), Tonga (45-16) and Namibia (64-19) as they prepared for the last eight of the tournament. Our victory over France came at a terrible cost, as Paulie, Johnny, Pete O'Mahony and finally Seanie O'Brien were counted out of our quarter-final meeting with Argentina.

What team had ever seen such a cost?

During the win over France of course we had a level of belief that the lads coming in could see to it that we all got the job done. You don't think about the cost of injuries, not during the game itself!

Paulie was world class.

Johnny was the same.

Seanie... world class, and Pete was close enough. And Jared Payne, who was also gone. He was somebody we missed as well because of the manner in which he went about his job brilliantly, but quietly enough. Say somebody decided that Kaino, Carter, Retallick and Conrad Smith could not play for the All Blacks, and that McCaw would be outlawed from a game, what would their opponents be thinking? Every team would fancy themselves against New Zealand and, more than that, every team would smell some blood in the water.

In the dressing room at half time we knew we had to stay on top of France. Nobody wanted to meet New Zealand in the quarter-final (they would power through France 62-13) so we just concentrated on getting the job done in Cardiff that day.

WE HAD SHOWN remarkable character to dominate the French and finish them off. We lost Johnny at the end of the first quarter after he was tackled hard by Louis Picamoles and felt the full force of the No.8's shoulder, and Paulie before half time when he ended up been stretchered off after suffering a career-ending hamstring injury, but there was a raucous Irish support in the Millennium Stadium.

We had men stepping into the shoes of heroes.

Ian Madigan stood up at out-half. So too Iain Henderson in the pack, though too many people underestimated the loss of Pete O'Mahony who had done so much clearing out and poaching, tackling, and counter-rucking. O'Mahony, pretty much, was irreplaceable.

Our dressing room resembled a casualty ward after the game, though I was genuinely confident that Joe's systems would still see us through against Argentina. They had looked tough, as usual, but they had not looked in any way special in their group. Then we lost Tommy Bowe after 20 minutes of the quarter-final, and Luke Fitzgerald came in and got to work efficiently.

But, every whack on the chin had weakened the team.

The Argentinians had their act together. Their ruck ball badly exposed our defence early on and they were 17-0 in front quickly enough, though we fought, and battled hard. We came within one long-range penalty of levelling the game at 23-each, which was due in main to the feverish efforts of Fitzgerald, and Robbie Henshaw and Conor Murray.

But our scrum was under pressure.

And we were playing too much behind the gain line, and our decision making became flawed, and we executed the simple things poorly. The performance showed that while Joe Schmidt's systems were indeed expert systems, we also needed expert players in every position to see to it that the right thing was done every single time.

We had reached the interval 20-10.

But we lost the game 43-20, and we could have no complaints as we licked our wounds after our defeat. Midway through our fight-back I thought we had them, and I was thinking... *semi-final!*

WE HAVE THEM!

Get ahead of them... AND THEY'LL GO!

But we missed a penalty to go ahead and their self-belief was restored. By the finish they had upped their game. They were piling into the rucks. From the first scrum they had smoked us, and that had set a tone for the rest of the game. Ramiro Herrera, their tighthead, was a massive angler and he kept coming straight across us. We kept getting hit and, like a heavyweight fighter… there are only so many blows you can take on the chin.

After the game I felt sickened. To begin with, there was disbelief that we had lost. And then the nausea set in, and it remained resting in the pit of my stomach for several weeks. We had done everything right. Two times Six Nations Champs. Top of our group…

And then the feckin Argies!

JOE UNDERSTOOD WHAT had happened to us that day.

He knew he needed more options if we were ever in that position in the future. And his Ireland team might not be bullet-proof, but Joe Schmidt knows that the Irish team he has been building since the 2015 World Cup can take more punches to the chin than any Irish team that has come before it.

It is not a lesson, if you do not learn from it. Joe learns all the time, and he has brought more boys in and given them more caps. He had a depth to his squad that Ireland teams have never even dreamed of in the past. It has all been very deliberate on Joe's part since that massive disappointment of 2015 and he has been mixing and matching ever since, and taking every opportunity to see that he has a Plan B, a Plan C and beyond.

FOR ME? I was in mourning with how my second and last World Cup had ended.

At the same time, I now realise that I should have pinched myself and taken on board that I had completed a second World Cup. I still felt as insecure as ever about my position on the team. I wondered if I would play in the green shirt again.

I wondered if Joe had already made up his mind.

Selfishness is such an important and nourishing part of the psyche of the pro athlete and unless you put yourself centre and first, what else is there?

It was all about me, and more about me than Ireland, as I dealt with the intense loss of being kicked out of the 2015 World Cup. And why wouldn't it be? Who else was working my 35 year old body and desperately wanting to fight for one more game, and one more after that?

For the first time in 10 years, I had the Christmas week of 2015 completely off. The fury of a 140 kilos Toulon second row had seen to that, after I had foolishly tried to steal a ball at a ruck and my foot got planted in the ground. My hamstring went... POP! The road back if I wanted to go down it was arduous. I headed down.

For the first week I was unable to do anything at all.

The second week I was able to take four-times weekly Watt bike sessions, and also four upper limb sessions. At Leinster there was such a thing as an Alter-G treadmill that can adjust a player's bodyweight to meet his needs. There were also electro muscle stimulation units that are a distant relation to those belt they advertised in newspapers through the 1980s that promised an effortless six-pack. The EMS units actually worked a treat, and stimulated the muscles through small doses of electric current delivered via gel pads strategically placed on the larger muscle groups. Properly used, they prevent muscle loss during an enforced lay off, but at the higher settings it feels like your muscles are trying to rip themselves off due to the force of the contractions. For the first two weeks, I had four EMS sessions per week to minimise muscle wastage.

THIS TIME WAS also there to help me to get used to life after rugby, I guess. And I took Kevin, now four years old, down to see Leinster playing against Connacht. The weather in the RDS was foul, though Kevin and I sheltered behind the substitutes bench as best we could. As we cuddled up there, I felt like taking my hat off to all of the supporters who stood their ground, and cheered and moaned, in the absolutely Baltic conditions.

Kevin had the time of his life.

He got to see the game, and he got a match programme and some chips at half time. And after the game he got to walk into the dressing room and learn

DARK ARTS: AN AUTOBIOGRAPHY

some interesting new words to add to his expanding vocabulary.

I was a father who was temporarily situated in a life after rugby. But I wanted to be a pro rugby player for a littler while longer. One more game, two more games… I wasn't greedy when it came to the green jersey.

I finally came to listen to and see the Irish Six Nations squad being announced, and since it was the first such squad in five years that I would not be a part of, of course I felt sort of sorry for myself. I knew that lads always liked to miss a phone call from Joe. If Joe's number came up on your phone it was never going to be the best of news.

Joe called me. We had a brief enough chat.

He told me that I was not going to be considered for the first two games of the 2016 Six Nations. But, if I came back in decent form, he would keep the door open to me for the second half of the tournament. I could not have asked for more.

I had made 25 consecutive starts in the Six Nations.

Every single tournament was magical and a complete mystery to me. Every single one began with administration. Then the fun part… a fully packed wheelie bag with all of your kit for the campaign ahead, all of it carefully labelled with the initials of each player. There are also boxes of extra kit in the room, so that anyone can go and swap for a bigger or smaller size. Photographic requirements come next, with head shots of every player required for the print media and TV and websites.

Plus, the piece de resistance… introduced in latter years… every player got to walk towards a camera and stop and fold their arms, and give a 'I'm the King of the World' sort of stare.

Six Nations camp is busy, and the schedule that is emailed out to every player every evening keeps everyone on their toes from 8.0 am until the early evening. New arrivals have a whole new language to learn on top of all of this. Attacking plays… roles in those plays… and lineout codes that have to bc learned off by heart as quickly as possible. Training is a step up from club rugby.

In an Ireland camp, you are top of the world… or as close as you might ever get to be in that place in your rugby life.

CHAPTER 31

FOR MY FINAL year or two with Leinster I'd watched good friends walk out the door of the dressing room for the last time.

Gordon D'Arcy and Eoin Reddan... Shane Jennings.

Funny, one by one I was watching them exit. I was looking around the dressing room, thinking... where are they gone? It's funny and it's also strange. We're all part of that room for so long. Our lives rotate around that room. Then... flick of a switch one of them is gone. And a second, a third...

And then I left.

March, April, May... June 2017... and, just like that, I said goodbye and left friends behind me. Friends already gone, and friends behind.

Where am I?

Who am I? One flick and I was a... *former.*

Former Leinster prop, and former Irish prop, and future... *what?* I had my family, Kimberlee, and Kevin and Chloe, but they too would now have to join me on a mission to discover who on earth was this man, this husband and father in their house? And what was he going to do with himself?

It's not easy to find the friends who had left before you.

The friends behind, really, they have to be left alone. They still know who they are and they also know they are part of a group of professional rugby players. I'm no longer part of that same group. If half of that same group, even a handful of them, are in a café what business is it of mine to interrupt and talk to them about the past or the future.

As a group they're still in the present.

Individually, I find it easier, and I've probably talked to Cian Healy more than anyone else. I always talked to Cian. He didn't really listen to me at the start but we eventually got there, to a point where there's a brotherly dynamic going on. We had other things in common. We like food, and we love barbecuing, like all front rowers. All of us brothers in many ways, all of us aimed at 18% body fat or thereabouts (although I never quite made it, and Cian as usual was running with the backs in the body composition stakes) and not at all bothered about the skinnies in the room who are on 12%.

ONE SIX NATIONS myself and Jack McGrath decided we needed the distraction of brewing some beer. It looked simple enough. We'd looked it up.

We found a company in Dublin, over in Glasnevin, who were selling all of the supplies we needed. Jack and I bought two 25 litre buckets.

A night was organised, but only for the 18% boys.

We got the beer extracts. They were like food cans, and we tipped them in. First of all we sterilised it all, because if you get the wrong bacteria in there… well, let's just say you don't want it in your buckets.

It completely messes with the taste.

Jack and I were a success. We had a wheat beer and an IPA, but I realised I might have put a little too much sugar into the whole thing.

We had all the 18% lads over. In case anyone was hungry we ordered in about 50 pizzas. It did not help, not enough. We were pretty blind afterwards. The more sugar, the higher the alcohol content.

FRONT ROWERS HAVE always been of a similar mindset

There are things we have in common.

Like drinking. We all like drinking more than the skinnies, and we know we have the capacity to drink more than them.

We have more wriggle room on our side when it comes to body composition but, amongst us 18% boys, it is still competitive. While I never tried to compete with the rest of them when it came to the physique business, I would still have to push myself when it came to squatting and benching. Once you get over 200 kilos in a squat that is usually sufficient to calm the nerves of the watching professors of fitness, though I've seen Cian, and also Andrew Porter, squat 300 kilos. However, for me, it was always a law of diminishing returns.

If I tried to chase 300 in a squat I'd probably end up damaging myself trying to get there and, honestly, I wouldn't get there anyway.

The highest I ever got to was 230 kilos.

And that was at the end of eight weeks of intensive working in the gym with the professors. That strength is helpful, of course it is. You need a strong base. It is a large part of it, but you need the strength and also the technique, as I have been at pains to explain throughout this book. Strength alone will only get you so far. I saw that the length and breadth of England, in Ireland when I came back home to chase my dreams at 30 years of age, and across Europe with all of the men and beasts I had to compete against. Big was good. Strength was good too. Both only brought anyone so far.

The great tightheads have something else.

Strength, and also that something… that knowledge of what it is all about and, more importantly still, how to apply that knowledge when it truly matters, when there is every chance that you are going to get pasted by a superior force… unless…

UNLESS YOU KNOW… unless you know more than that force!

IT WAS KEVIN, my son, who dragged me back to the RDS for the first time after mt retirement. He desperately wanted to go.

I was unsure.

But we went, and we returned a second time, and the pair of us turned up for more games and, slowly, I calmed as I sat there in the RDS.

We are all human.

It was hard to watch in the beginning.

'OH SHIT...

'We could have done with Rossy out there!'

In the beginning that was what I wanted to hear, but quickly enough I asked myself why would anyone waste their time uttering such a ridiculous statement? When I was playing and guys retired, I took it for granted. It was about the next game, and the men I was packing down with.

I never wasted half a second thinking about who was gone. *Who am I to think I might ever be missed?*

Did I miss Brian O'Driscoll?

Well yes, a bit, at the start. After a while though, there were very few days I thought about my former teammate, the greatest player this country has ever produced, possibly will ever produce. BOD?

Who's BOD?

When you are gone, you are... GONE! Nobody has the time to think about the 'good old days' because all anyone in the dressing room is thinking about is making tomorrow one of those... 'good old days'. That's just how it is.

I read recently an article by Aidan McCullen (himself a former professional player) who said that the reason a lot of sports people struggle when they retire is that they need to be juiced up. That makes complete sense to me now as I put my suit on every morning and head out for another day's work. One day after another. Of course I want to have big days now that I am working shoulder to shoulder with everyone else. I want a day that is a prize day, and I aim to win those days.

But...

Days were not like this when I was a professional rugby player. Days were served up to me. You have a good session on the field and there is a serotonin hit. You go and have a big workout and there is a dopamine hit. You play a game and you do well, and there are bigger hits. Multiple hits, all making you feel like you are the king of the world for a short period of time.

All through the week the professional athlete is getting these hits, and psychologists recognise this... because we are all in one dressing room, we are all pulling towards a common goal, that perfect win... and that sort of week is so very different to the week you are going to have when you put on your suit in the privacy of your own bedroom. It's a world removed from suiting up for Leinster, or your country.

In an office environment you might have one guy who is sitting there marking time whereas, in Leinster, or at international level, nobody can do that. You sit back for one day as a professional rugby player and you will be overrun.

You will be wiped off the face of the earth before you know it.

I'M NOW ABOUT a year out of my old life. I retired, and I went straight into a 'real' job. I had a new shiny job to get used to and, next thing, I realised I had all of my weekends back. Brilliant.

I can eat what I like.

Pretty good.

Shit, I can go on holiday any time myself and Kim decide we'd like to go on holiday. And, when the holiday ends, I don't have to feel guilty for adding a few pounds. I have no one to be accountable to when I come back from holiday.

I reveled in that freedom for a little while. Couple of months I guess, and then the excitement of being Mike Ross Inc. wore off.

Right... what happens next?

There were no big days.

I had loved big days... and really BIG DAYS!

Rugby is like all professional sports. The highs can be massive, and the lows? The lows can be crippling. The lows are totally awful nearly all of the time... but!

There are lows that have an asterisk attached to them.

Good asterisk.

Bad asterisk.

Your team wins, but you have been tossed around in the scrum. Bad. Very, very bad indeed.

Your team loses, but you had a good day against the loosehead and you made him suffer, and everyone knows that you made him bend and moan, and your day is not so bad. Not as bad as everyone else's.

But the lows! They always lasted longer than the highs. Always. If you had a bad game then the smell of that game could easily hang around the place for days, until Wednesday, Thursday even.

Now, that is all becoming a distant memory.

Except, my memory is populated by games that stand out in isolation. Victories and defeats. Big victories... and big defeats. Also, for some inexplicable reason, the defeats come to the surface more than the victories, and they demand that I revisit them. And you find yourself replaying those defeats and forcing your brain to change the course of those same defeats.

For a few seconds only those defeats can be turned into victories.

Whereas, the actual victories, the brilliant and magical victories, they settle down in your brain more quietly, and pretty much mind their own business.

I NOW LOOK back on my last Six Nations and can savour every tiny portion of it. The good parts, and the not so good. The campaign started late, as Joe Schmidt had told me. Nathan White wore the No. 3 jersey in the 16-all draw with Wales and the 10-9 loss to France. Ireland's Championship title was up in the air and, meanwhile, all I cared about was getting one more game. That came against England in Twickenham where we would lose 21-10 and any hopes of a hat-trick of Championships were well and truly scuppered.

I got back in for that meeting with England in Twickenham, and another meeting for me with Joe Marler. It was my longest time out in my pro career. I was back and delighted with myself, but at the same time came the news that Paul O'Connell was forced to hang up his boots for good because of the injury he had received early on in our World Cup victory over France.

The curtain came down on his seismic career.

Meanwhile, I was desperately seeking to deal with the same damned curtain. Though I understood Paulie's loss more than most. Generally, there are two types of second row – the grunt second row who is usually behind the tighthead and provides ballast around the park, and the lighter and rangier second row who runs the lineout. The thing about Paul O'Connell was... he filled both roles.

Paulie was probably the best scrummaging lock I had ever worked with and on several engagements I was saved from ignominy by his incredible strength – it was like having a railway sleeper directly behind me. That was the greatness about Paulie! He made everyone around him look better.

Training had gone well for me before Twickers.

With Leinster, I had hit my first series of scrums in eight weeks and I was disgusted with how sore my neck and shoulders felt the following day. I had not seen much of the match against France as it was my son's fifth birthday party the same day. It was another early introduction to my life after rugby.

Because Kevin is rugby obsessed his mother and I had organised a rugby party for him, with the help of a company called Rugbytots, and he and a big bunch of his friends ran themselves silly before stopping and stuffing their faces with cake. Meanwhile, myself and the Dads at the party were huddled around one iPhone, trying to watch a stream of the Ireland game.

JOE STARTED ME against Italy and I got 54 minutes on the pitch in our 58-15 victory, and I also wore the jersey from the start against Scotland. I came off after 62 minutes in my last Six Nations game. We won 35-25.

But I knew that it was time for Joe Schmidt to look to the future.

And to look forward with Tadhg Furlong and younger men. I guess I was lucky to be part of one last Ireland tour when we went down to South Africa in the summer of 2016. When I think about it now, how glorious that whole experience truly was, from the very beginning when we had a mini-camp in Johnstown House in Enfield in County Meath and I got picked up by none other than Johnny Sexton.

What a highly decorated chauffeur.

Even if his choice of music was a bit questionable.

THOSE LAST MONTHS in the green jersey have stayed with me more than most others.

Beginning with the Welsh game in the Six Nations when I was not wearing the jersey at all and, because I was injured, had spent the critical hours before the game with Sony in a commercial event. I had left quickly.

I did not have a ticket for the game and I did not look for one I have to confess. I wanted to get home, and I wanted to sit down on the sofa with my son and watch Ireland play.

It was a weird experience.

Though I also loved it, because I knew what was coming. I felt physically and rudely disconnected from the team. But I also felt happy with my son, and being apart from my team.

So completely weird.

I WAS READY for my last Six Nations game.

If that was the case!

I looked into the crowd in the Aviva Stadium at one stage and it dawned on me that, soon enough, I would be amongst them.

Watching Ireland for good.

I was 36 years old.

I was not getting any younger, and all of the faces looking at me seemed to be getting faster and fresher, though Stuart Hogg had always been a speedster. The fastest pair of legs in the Six Nations belonged to the Scot.

Conor Murray hit one of his classic box kicks.

I chased up the line.

I could see Hogg, scanning, looking for someone. Then Hogg was looking at me.

I could see his eyes lock on mine

Shit.

Hogg was hunting.

I could see that in his eyes.

Hogg had always gone hunting for the likes of me more than others on a rugby pitch, whether he was playing for Glasgow or Scotland.

Rory Best was next to me and he pushed up just that small bit.

Ever so slightly.

Hogg was still looking at me.

Fuck off…

Don't come near me!

Rory... get to fuck back in here!

Hogg was still 20 yards away from me.

But, he was definitely hunting...

He was definitely... HUNTING ME.

I knew I was dependant on the line outside of me. I was going to need a hand out, but Besty had his hands full with Tommy Seymour outside of him, and he drifted off that little bit more, very slightly, and it wouldn't have mattered against anyone else, or for that matter, if he had someone slightly quicker on his inside!

Hogg's eyes widened.

He got the ball...

He was gone!